Voices from

D-DAY

Jonathan Bastable

David and Charles

For my father, Harry Bastable

A DAVID & CHARLES BOOK

David & Charles is a subsidiary of F+W (UK) Ltd.,
an F+W Publications Inc. company

First published in the UK in 2004
Reprinted 2004 (twice)
First paperback edition 2005

Text copyright © Jonathan Bastable 2004, 2005

Distributed in North America
by F+W Publications, Inc.
4700 East Galbraith Road
Cincinnati, Ohio 45236

ISBN 0 7153 1790 3 hardback
ISBN 0 7153 2204 4 paperback

Printed in Great Britain by Antony Rowe Ltd
for David & Charles
Brunel House   Newton Abbot   Devon

Commissioning Editor Ruth Binney
Researcher   Michael Paterson
Desk Editor   Lewis Birchon
Head of Design   Ali Myer
Production Controller Jennifer Campbell

Visit our website at www.davidandcharles.co.uk

David & Charles books are available from all good bookshops; alternatively you can contact our Orderline on (0)1626 334555 or write to us at FREEPOST EX2110, David & Charles *Direct*, Newton Abbot, TQ12 4ZZ (no stamp required UK mainland).

Contents

THE D-DAY LANDING GROUNDS

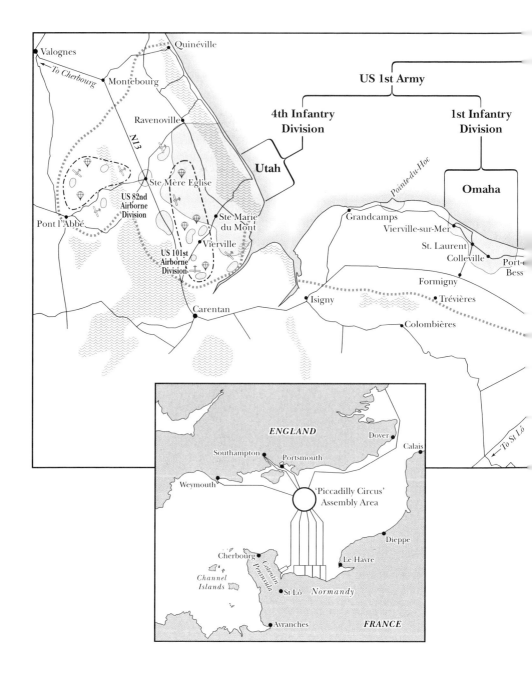

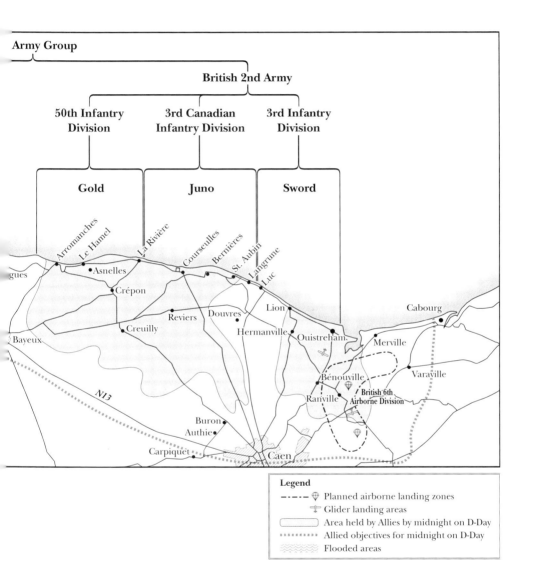

Army Group

British 2nd Army

50th Infantry Division | **3rd Canadian Infantry Division** | **3rd Infantry Division**

Gold | **Juno** | **Sword**

Arromanches
Le Hamel
La Rivière
Courseulles
Bernières
St. Aubin
Langrune
Luc
gues
•Asnelles
•Crépon
Reviers
Douvres
Lion
Creuilly
Hermanville
Ouistreham.
Cabourg
•Bayeux
Merville
N13
Bénouville
Varaville
Ranville
British 6th Airborne Division
Buron
Authie•
Carpiquet
Caen

Legend

–·–·– ⊕ Planned airborne landing zones

⛨ Glider landing areas

⬭ Area held by Allies by midnight on D-Day

··········· Allied objectives for midnight on D-Day

〰〰 Flooded areas

THE MEANING OF D-DAY

Sixty years after the event, people sometimes wonder what the 'D' in D-Day stands for. It has been said that it means 'Destiny Day', or (for the Nazi regime) 'Doomsday'. In fact the letter D signifies nothing at all. In the military parlance of World War II, a D-Day was the date on which any operation was due to begin. H-Hour was the precise time of day that it was to start. The term allowed strategists to talk about their plan before they knew exactly when it was going to be carried out. So D+1 meant the second day of the operation, whenever that might turn out to be; H+120 meant two hours after the off.

It is strange that this scrap of army jargon has come to denote one of the great feats of arms of the twentieth century. The word D-Day, once a lifeless military bureacratism, now has the same mythic resonance as Agincourt for the British or Bunker Hill for Americans. For the peoples of the many nations who took part – not just Britons and Americans and Canadians, but Frenchmen, Belgians, Poles, Norwegians, Dutchmen, Danes and some free Germans – D-Day says something meaningful about who they are as a nation, and about what they are capable of at their best.

The word D-Day rings with history, and so do the places where it happened. The powerful echoes of the events of 6 June 1944 can be felt on the Normandy beaches. Even now they have a stillness about them, a solemn air that makes you inclined to tread softly and keep your voice to a whisper. You go mindfully when you explore the landing grounds, as if you were in a church. And it is not hard to tell where this sense comes from: it is the sanctity of spilt blood. You can still sense it, though the tides have washed over the beaches forty thousand times since the day of battle.

Traces of the conflict are everywhere in Normandy. They are there in the crumbling gun emplacements which stand like concrete ziggurats all along the coast. They can be heard in the incongruous Anglo-Saxon names of streets and town squares: rue des Sherbrooke Fusiliers, place du Général Eisenhower. They are present in the sad geometry of serried headstones in military cemeteries. The violent events that occurred here have left an indelible mark on the peaceful landscape – and that is as it should be, for D-Day was the great turning-point of the war.

It was more than that, it was a pivotal day in human history. Every man who landed on the beaches was well aware of this. They had been told so by their commanders, but they already knew it in their hearts. As many of the first-hand accounts in this book testify, there were moments when the Allied soldiers were almost overcome with the vast and splendid righteousness of their undertaking. At the same time, they all insist in their letters home and in their reminiscences that their own role was insignificant, and that they were 'just doing their job.' This mixture of pride and humility is characteristic of the men of D-Day, and it is eternally to their credit.

It should be remembered that many of the men who stormed the beaches were teenagers who had never been in combat before. But on that morning they found it in themselves to charge headlong into mortal danger, to see their friends die before their eyes, to kill other men and to keep going forwards. It defies the imagination, but they did it. It is hardly surprising that those who came through the day were deeply affected by it. Some were left with painful scars, visible and invisible. But most came away with the knowledge, more precious than any campaign medal, that they had changed the world for the better.

The experience of D-Day could also transform a man's own view of the world and of his fellow men. One Normandy veteran touched on this when he was talking about attitudes in the British forces during the war. 'Everyone looked down on someone else,' he said. 'RAF looked down on infantry; we infantrymen looked down on the pioneer corps – little knowing that they were going to be the first men on the beaches. After D-Day I never looked down on anyone again.'

Jonathan Bastable

1
OPERATION OVERLORD

On 4 June 1940, a few weeks after becoming prime minister, Winston Churchill spoke to parliament and the people of Great Britain. He gave one of the best speeches of his life – perhaps one of the finest speeches ever made in the English language. At its climax he said:

> We shall fight them on the beaches; we shall fight on the landing grounds; we shall fight in the fields and in the streets; we shall fight in the hills; we shall never surrender.

The beaches and hills Churchill had in mind were the beaches and hills of southern England. The British army had just been ignominiously driven out of France at Dunkirk. The Nazi war machine was twenty-five miles away on the French coast, and so the prime minister was preparing his people for the worst. He was telling them that Britain was about to be invaded.

That invasion never came – and yet Churchill's words were prophetic. Four years to the day after he spoke them, a massive invasion force lay in wait in English harbours, ready to take the fight back to the Germans. But now the beaches were the beaches of Normandy. And the fight was not the latest phase in Germany's expansion, but the beginning of the end of Nazi power in Europe.

THE DISTANT SECOND FRONT
The battered troops of Dunkirk were barely out of their wet clothes when Churchill began thinking about sending them back as conquerors. But at that time there was no prospect at all of hitting back at Hitler. He controlled all mainland Europe. Britain – his only declared enemy – was weak and badly bruised. 'Britain fights alone,' said Churchill, and even he struggled to make it sound as if this was a good thing.

Events took some hopeful turns in the course of 1941. In March, US President Franklin D Roosevelt declared that it was in the best interests of the United States to support Britain in its lonely war. He undertook to provide Britain with every kind of aid – short of military muscle. In June, Hitler made his biggest mistake of the war. He attacked the Soviet Union, bringing down upon Germany the immense wrath and the countless legions of the Russian people. The Russian war became an all-consuming passion for Hitler, and for a while he turned his malevolent and baleful gaze to the east, away from Britain.

By October 1941, Churchill felt able to instruct Lord Louis Mountbatten to begin making plans for 'our great counter-invasion of Europe.' Churchill was certain that the outcome of the war depended on it:

> **Unless we can land overwhelming forces, and beat the Nazis in battle in France, Hitler will never be defeated.**

In December the inchoate invasion plans received a massive boost. After the Japanese attack on Pearl Harbor, Hitler needlessly declared war on the United States. Now the combined strength of Britain, America and the USSR were ranged against Nazi Germany.

But at the end of 1941 Germany was at the peak of its strength too. Hitler's armies were so close to Moscow that the artillery spotters could see the glinting gold domes of the Kremlin. Joseph Stalin, the Soviet leader, demanded that his new allies open a second front in the west as soon as possible to relieve the pressure on his forces. The British still thought that a new front in Europe could not be attempted for a long time to come, but the Americans agreed with Stalin, and were keen to strike a blow at Hitler soon. This disagreement caused a good deal of ill-feeling between the western Allies: the Americans thought the British were pessimistic and slow-footed about the invasion of Europe; the British thought the Americans were naïve and reckless. This difference in attitude persisted right through to D-Day and beyond.

DRY RUNS FOR D-DAY

For the time being, however, British opposition to an early invasion prevailed. All the same, the western Allies wanted to demonstrate to Hitler (and to Stalin) that they were still in the fight. So two major operations were planned for 1942: a bravado raid on the occupied port of Dieppe, and a landing by American troops in North Africa. They were both, in their separate ways, rehearsals for D-Day.

Operation Torch, the landings in Africa, took place in November. Torch taught the Americans some valuable lessons. It led to improvements in the design and deployment of landing craft; it gave many American troops their first taste of combat; and most important of all, it provided the first field command for a hitherto deskbound general, Dwight D Eisenhower.

The Dieppe raid was a different kind of learning experience. It was a bloody and utterly unmitigated failure. The plan was to land a sizeable force on the French coast near the port. This force was to destroy two large coastal guns, capture the port intact, wreak as much destruction as possible on the airport at St Aubin, then withdraw by sea on the first tide. It was to be short, sharp ambush – a hard punch on the nose for Hitler.

The troops chosen for the task were the Canadian 2nd Division. They had been in Britain since 1939 with absolutely nothing to do, and they were keen to show their mettle. They were to be supported by US Rangers and British commandos: like D-Day, this was a combined American-Canadian-British operation. The raid took place on the night of 18 August 1942. Six thousand men and more than a hundred Churchill tanks crossed the Channel in 237 ships. But they were spotted by German patrol boats on the way in, and the main force was cut to ribbons by machine-guns when the men got to the shore. Many of the tanks were shelled to bits before they could get off the boats and into action.

By the end of the day, the beach was piled high with Canadian dead. Around 3,500 men were killed or captured. The remnant of the attack force limped away as best it could. One British commando, as he waded off the beach to a departing boat, saw Canadian gunners blasting away from behind a barricade made with the corpses of comrades.

Colonel Lord Lovat, the commander of the British No 4 Commando at Dieppe, made it back to London after midnight. He went to the Guards Club, where a bed was made up for him. He lay awake trembling and reliving the day's carnage in his mind's eye.

> Tracer bullets probed the darkness, and leaden feet pounded desperately on slopes of slippery shingle, like shifting walnut shells . . .

The images that filled Lovat's sleepless head were like a vision of the horrors that were to come on Omaha Beach.

THE BIRTH OF OVERLORD

In January 1943 Churchill and Roosevelt met in Casablanca to discuss once more the prospects for a second front. They appointed Lieutenant-General Frederick Morgan to come up with a workable plan for invading France. He was designated the position of COSSAC – Chief of Staff to the Supreme Allied Commander – even though there was at that time no supreme commander. By June, the COSSAC team had chosen Normandy as the target area for the invasion. It had broad beaches where troops and armour could get ashore; it was within range of British fighter cover; and it was not a completely obvious choice – the Germans, who knew an invasion must come eventually, were expecting the strike to be in the Pas de Calais. This, the closest point to the English coast, was where they had concentrated most of their defences.

American troops were already massing in Britain. This feat of organization and diplomacy was managed by the arch administrator Eisenhower, by now well-known and well-liked by the British high command. In August 1943 Churchill met with Roosevelt again, and they set a date for the invasion of Europe: May 1944. They also assigned the undertaking a codename: Overlord. In December, Eisenhower was summoned to a meeting with Roosevelt in Tunis. He had no idea what the president wanted of him until he walked into the room and Roosevelt greeted him with the words, 'Well, Ike, you are going to command Overlord'. He was absolutely stunned.

Eisenhower went back to London with a new title, Supreme Allied Commander. He appointed a senior staff consisting mostly of British commanders, and set them to work on Overlord. For the position of commander of the land forces he chose (somewhat reluctantly) the British general, Bernard Law Montgomery.

General Montgomery was vain, prickly, fastidious and completely lacking in diplomatic skills. He was unspeakably rude to the Americans – up to and including his boss Eisenhower – because he thought they were all amateurs. But Montgomery was also a brilliant military strategist, an experienced fighter and a born leader of men. He also had experience of the German commander in charge of the defence of France, Field Marshall Erwin Rommel. They were old adversaries: Montgomery's Desert Rats had defeated Rommel's Afrika Korps in the desert war of 1942.

Montgomery's first job was to review and revise the COSSAC plan. He looked at it and saw instantly that it was too feeble and unambitious. With a few broad strokes he transformed it into a masterful blueprint for smashing through Rommel's Atlantic Wall. His main change was to make the whole invasion a much bigger affair. He enlarged the invasion zone so that it now comprised five beaches, not three, over a stretch of fifty miles. Three whole airborne divisions were to be used to secure the flanks, rather than COSSAC's two small brigades. Naval and air support were to be greatly augmented to provide cover for the attacking troops and to 'soften up' the defences in advance. The date of the invasion was put back another month to June, to allow for the procurement of more landing craft.

Montgomery realized that the beaches were the key to it all: if he could get past the static defences of the Atlantic Wall, the Germans would never be able to force them out. Rommel knew it too.

> **We'll have only one chance to stop the enemy,** said the wily German commander. **And that is when he is in the water. Everything we have must be on the coast. The first twenty-four hours of the invasion will be decisive. For the Allies as well as Germany, it will be the longest day.**

SECRETS AND LIES

The Dieppe raid had achieved almost nothing militarily, but two important strategic conclusions were drawn from it. Firstly, that in a full-scale invasion infantry troops need the support of heavy armour from the moment they arrive on the beaches; secondly, that it is suicidal to attack a well-defended port. So the Allies needed a way of getting tanks ashore without their becoming sitting-duck targets as they unloaded from ships; and they needed a substitute for a natural port, so that the troops could be supplied once they were ashore. Both these problems were solved by engineering skill combined with a dash of military genius.

The problem of the tanks was taken on by Major-General Percy Hobart. He was a renowned theorist in the use of tanks, but his irascible personality and his contempt for the military bureaucracy had made him enemies at the War Office. He was eased into retirement at the outbreak of war.

In 1940, while he was serving as a lowly corporal in the Home Guard, Hobart had received a telephone call at his home in Oxford. It was the prime minister, inviting him to lunch. There, Churchill listened to Hobart's ideas, and immediately arranged for him to be given back his rank along with a tank brigade to command and to experiment with. The

General Staff were horrified to see Hobart back in their midst, but Churchill would have none of it.

> I think very highly of this officer, and I am not at all impressed by the prejudices against him in certain quarters, he wrote to the Chief of the Imperial General Staff. Such prejudices attach frequently to persons of strong personality and original view. In this case, General Hobart's views have been only too tragically borne out. The neglect by the General Staff even to devise proper patterns of tanks before the war has robbed us of all the fruits of this invention. These fruits have been reaped by the enemy, with terrible consequences. We should, therefore, remember that this was an officer who had the root of the matter in him, and also vision. We are now at war, fighting for our lives, and we cannot afford to confine Army appointments to officers who have excited no hostile comment in their career. The catalogue of General Hobart's qualities and defects might almost exactly be attributed to most of the great commanders of British history. This is a time to try men of force and vision.

In 1943, Hobart took charge of the 79th (Experimental) Tank Brigade. He set to work designing tanks for the conditions that would be found on the invasion beaches. He adapted other people's ideas, took suggestions from subordinates and built prototypes. He saw that the tanks would be less easily targeted, as at Dieppe, if they made their way to the beach individually, under their own steam. This line of thought led to the development of the DD floating tank. It was a reconfigured Sherman tank with twin propellers at the back, and was called a Duplex Drive – hence DD. The propellers acted like an outboard motor to steer it through water. The buoyancy came from a canvas skirt fitted right around the tank and drawn up over the gun turret. This displaced enough water to keep it afloat, and had the added bonus of disguising the tank while it was in the water: it just looked like a rather strange dinghy. Once on land, the tank would drop its skirts with a flourish and begin blasting away.

This was the first and least outlandish of Hobart's innovations. He came up with a whole range of customized tanks designed to breach the Atlantic Wall with its myriad defences. Together they became known as Hobart's 'Funnies', though they were deadly serious and, when it came to it, highly effective weapons in the Allied armoury. There was the Bobbin tank, which had a thirty-four-metre spool of tough matting attached to the front. The matting was a kind of instant road: the tank would lay it like a long stair-carpet as it advanced over soft ground, and tanks or trucks could follow. There was the so-called Flying Dustbin, which could fire a forty-pound mortar the size of an oil drum at short range and so blow a man-size hole in thick concrete walls. Another of Hobart's tanks was known as the Crocodile. It should really have been called the Dragon, because instead of a gun it had a flamethrower which could send a long tongue of fire through the slits of pillboxes or into snipers' nests. There was a Churchill tank with a thirty-foot box-girder bridge fixed to the front like a long proboscis or the arm of a crane. The bridge could be laid across anti-tank ditches or shell holes. And then there was the Crab, or flail tank. This was the weirdest and most successful of the Funnies. It had a spinning drum at the front, and to this drum were attached balls-and-chains, like those used in jousting tournaments of old. The Crab would advance slowly through minefields, flogging the ground with the chains and so setting off all the mines in its path. Troops could then advance in its tracks.

The 79th Tank Division was not at first seen as a prestigious unit, either by those who smirked at Hobart and his contraptions, or by those detailed to serve in it. One of Hobart's tank drivers said:

> We were not at all delighted that instead of going into battle in the pride of a cruiser tank formation, we were to crawl into action in what appeared to be the menial task of scavengers and road sweepers, creeping along at a mile an hour.

But glamorous or not, the Funnies saved many lives on the British beaches on D-Day. The Americans took the DD tanks but said 'No thank you' to the rest of the menagerie – and certainly sustained higher casualties on the beaches as a result.

The solution to the second issue thrown up by Dieppe – the impossibility of capturing a port intact – was addressed on a larger scale than the tank problem, but with just as much ingenuity. With his usual prescience, Churchill had identified the need as early as May 1942. On the 30th he sent a memorandum entitled 'Piers for use on beaches' to Lord Mountbatten, chief of Combined Operations:

Hobart's flail tanks would crawl through minefields at one mile an hour. The chains on their spinning rotor arms thrashed the ground, churning up the soil, raising clouds of dust and detonating every buried mine. The chains had to be replaced every few hundred yards.

They must float up and down with the tide, wrote the prime minister. **The anchor problem must be mastered. Let me have the best solution worked out. Don't argue the matter. The difficulties will argue for themselves.**

The task of designing these piers was delegated to Bruce White, a civil engineer now working at the War Office with the rank of brigadier. He set to work on an artificial harbour which could be towed across the channel in pieces and quickly assembled once the beachhead was secure. If it worked it would be nothing less than a devastating secret weapon, and so it was imperative that the Germans did not get the merest hint of it.

I insisted that the project be given a codename, wrote Brigadier White. **The security chief turned to a young officer behind him and asked for the next code word appearing on the list. The**

officer consulted a large volume and announced the word 'Mulberry', which I accepted.

Absolute secrecy had to be maintained about the operation. In order to maintain it, this great engineering complex was divided into separate parts, particularly for the manufactured items. Orders for supply were placed with numerous firms – about 500 in all – spread throughout Britain. The manufactured items were brought together as near as possible to the date of the invasion. Nearly all personnel had to be kept in complete ignorance of the purpose of the components and their eventual use.

A testing site had to be found. A search of various sites resulted in the selection of a location in the Solway Firth where the rise and fall of the tide – about twenty-four feet – was similar to that off Normandy. At about this time, appeals were made to the public to send in any information, including photographs, postcards or holiday brochures of continental locations. When collated, this information was invaluable to the invasion forces and their planners. One such photograph, a seaside snapshot of a courting couple leaning against a cliff, enabled the engineers to assess the height of obstacles to be demolished, as well as other vital information.

Much effort was invested in making sure that the Germans did not get to know the details of the invasion – but the preparations could not be completely hidden. So all manner of trickery was brought to bear on keeping the enemy guessing.

There was a whole operation, codenamed Fortitude, devoted to persuading the Germans that the invasion would strike at the Pas de Calais. Plywood installations and inflatable rubber tanks were massed conspicuously around Dover, where they would surely be photographed by German reconnaissance and taken for the real thing. The night bombing of the railway network behind Calais continued mercilessly. Elaborate measures were taken to give the Germans the impression that an army was gathering in Kent. This imaginary host was given the name US 1st Army Group, and large amounts of fake radio traffic were generated to make it seem as if the phantom soldiers were busy. Knowing that a lie is much more effective when it contains an element of truth, the Allies gave command of the ethereal 1st Army to the very real General George Patton.

The Germans feared and admired Patton above all other American commanders. They would have been flabbergasted to learn that his job on D-Day was to be a decoy. And when it became clear after D-Day that he was still in England, that helped to convince the Germans that the Normandy landings were a feint, and that the real invasion was still to come.

So the Germans were completely in the dark – or most of them were. In March, Hitler's paranoid brain produced a flash of insight, a moment of genuine soldierly intuition.

> **Obviously an Anglo-American invasion in the West is going to come,** he wrote in his diary. **The most suitable landing areas and hence those that are in the most danger are the two west-coast peninsulas of Cherbourg and Brest. They offer very tempting possibilities for the creation of bridgeheads which could be enlarged thereafter by the massive use of air power. The enemy's invasion operation must not, under any circumstances, be allowed to survive longer than hours or, at most, days. Once defeated, the enemy will never again try to invade.**

The Führer lapsed back into brooding self-obsession before he found a moment to act on this dangerous thought.

THE AMERICAN INVASION OF BRITAIN

One and a half million American soldiers were shipped to Britain in the run-up to the invasion. This friendly onslaught made a huge impression on the British, and was quite a culture shock for the young GIs, especially the ones billeted with English families.

> **The army drove us down the street and they'd stop and say, 'All right, three of you out here,'** said Robert Wilkins, from Atchison, Kansas. **They'd march you into this house and say: 'These are your American troops; they are going to be staying with you.'** I can remember the place that I went to: their name was Glover. He was a retired piano dealer from New Zealand. Our boots were muddy, and everything about us, I suspect, was offensive – certainly to Mrs Glover. She made us remove our boots outside before she would even let us come in the house. We immediately thought that this was going to be a very difficult situation and

we certainly weren't happy with it at all. But after we became acquainted with Mr Glover, he would take us to his club and buy us drinks. The Glovers treated us like we were their own sons.

Private Willard Coonen was twenty years old and from Dundas, Wisconsin. He too detected the fatherly warmth behind the British reserve.

There were six or eight of us staying with an elderly couple in their large old brick home in Tiverton. The family was very cordial, and tried to make us feel welcome. They even offered us treats from the limited food rations that they had. I remember the elderly hosts knocking on our door the first evening, and offering us 'crumpets and tea.' This was my first taste of crumpets, and I believe they were made without any sugar. They were not too palatable for me. We were amused when, later on that first evening, he again knocked on our door and asked in the typical cockney accent: 'What time should I knock you laddies up in the morning?'

The US Army, on the other hand, adopted a rather less warm tone with its new arrivals. Harold Baumgarten received a somewhat foreboding address from his commanding officer:

Colonel Canham of the 116th Infantry of the 29th Division spoke to us at Crown Barracks and explained to us that we are going to be the first forces into the second front in Europe, and that two out of three of us aren't expected to come back, and if anybody's got butterflies in the belly, to ask for a transfer now, because it's going to be that kind of an operation.

With that the Americans got down to the serious business of training for the coming invasion. Many of them had arrived in Britain in the spring of 1944, so they had only a matter of weeks to get ready.

We trained on the famous Dartmoors, and we did tremendous forty-mile marches across England, said Baumgarten. We received combat infantry training where we did thirty push-ups every day, ran with a man on our back for seventy-five yards, and crawled under barbed wire. We also went on amphibious training missions. We boarded little assault boats of the British Navy, and trained in landing. Our maneuvers were made on the beaches of Slapton Sands, where there were pillboxes on the beach. We had a certain system of taking these pillboxes.

We went to special schools where each man was trained to be able to use his weapon – me, the Browning automatic rifle. We lived and slept and ate in boat teams. Each boat team consisted of thirty men trained to work as a team to assault enemy beaches and be able to establish a beachhead by neutralizing all obstacles and pillboxes. There was a lieutenant in command of each boat team, a man with a walkie-talkie radio set, two BAR teams (four men altogether), one flame thrower and his assistant, two bazooka teams (four men altogether), a wire-cutting team with four men, a demolition team with five men, a 60mm mortar team with four men, a sergeant and a second in command, and five riflemen armed with M-1 rifles and rifle grenades.

On amphibious training we used real ammunition at all times, and actually went out on ships and boats and hit beaches near Slapton Sands. These rehearsals were very realistic.

The Americans were, in a sense, honoured guests. The invasion could not happen without their manpower and military muscle, and the British authorities were very glad to have them around. So the high command took a very close interest in their training, and visits from the top brass were frequent.

We were one of the first units to get a Presidential Unit Citation, said Michael Kaufmann of the 9th Infantry Division. Mr Churchill, and Generals Eisenhower and Bradley came down to Winchester where our battalion was lined up in the courtyard of the British 60th Infantry Regiment, the King's Royal Rifles. We were lined up for the purpose of Mr Churchill and General Eisenhower putting the presidential unit citation on our battalion flag. I recall very vividly that we were in formation and the order came down to call your battalion to attention. Mr Churchill got out of the car with President Eisenhower, whispered something to an aide, and the order came back: 'Give your battalion parade rest.'

We executed and Mr Churchill took off for which we all knew was the men's latrine, and in a few moments, he came out buttoning his fly and the order came back: 'Call your battalion to attention.' And the ceremony went on.

Another incident involving Eisenhower. We were on a shooting range, and Ike was watching one of the soldiers shooting at the targets. He couldn't hit it worth a damn. Suddenly, a rabbit took off about two or three hundred yards away, and this guy brought his rifle over and killed it deader than the devil. Eisenhower said, 'How come you can hit that rabbit, but you can't hit the target?' The guy said, 'Well, I'm from West Virginia, and I'm used to shooting rabbits.'

The training was mostly hard slog and fraught with danger, so it was no surprise that occasionally the visitors sought a way to let off steam. London was the jackpot destination for every GI with a weekend pass.

After settling down for several weeks many of us received passes to leave camp for a few days to see what London was like, said JC Friedman, a tankman with the 29th Infantry Division. At night there were blackouts. I could hear planes overhead and see tracer bullets shooting through the sky. In addition, buzz bombs whistled through the night and air raid sirens blasted away. My thought was how could these people survive under such conditions. Yet in pubs, men and women were drinking and singing and dancing as if nothing were happening.

The Americans were more than happy to join in the revelry.

The first night we were out on pass we really tied one on, said Joseph Camera, a veteran of General Patton's Africa campaign. Being very jolly and combat-free for a while, someone wanted to make a toast. So we asked the proprietor of this pub: 'How much are these glasses worth?' He told us. Then after we drank to our toast, we flung the glasses into the fireplace and paid their value to the proprietor. Then someone felt he had to do something more exciting, so he asked the proprietor what was the value for his storefront window. The proprietor told him. We collected the money amongst us, and paid the proprietor. Then this person picked up a chair and threw it through the storefront window. We thought this was hilarious, but the proprietor called the police. When they came, he was yelling 'One of your chaps did this.' When the bobby questioned us, very calmly, we told him we had paid for the damages. He then let us go. The proprietor then said, 'No more hard liquor for you Yanks.'

Captain Anthony Duke of the US Navy had a rather less boisterous experience when he went up to London – but it was no less memorable for that.

I went to see an uncle of mine, Tony Biddle. He had been the ambassador to a whole bunch of countries occupied by the Germans: France, Norway, Belgium, Poland and so forth. When I called him up he said, 'Well, let's meet for lunch in London.' We did. During lunch he said, 'I've got a friend who wants to meet you and you will really enjoy meeting him.' So we got in a taxi afterwards and went over to his office on Grosvenor Square. He knocked on a door right next to his office and he ushered me in, and who did that friend of his turn out to be but General Eisenhower.

I was awestruck. I stood in front of his deck and he said to me, 'We've been waiting for you, Captain Duke.' Then he rang a bell and called for someone and said, 'Now that Duke is here, we are going to get on with the invasion plans.' And I can tell you that I was very embarrassed but I was very thrilled at the same time. It was a moment in my life that I'll never forget.

The trips out grew fewer in the first days of spring, as the invasion plans reached their final stages. All the soldiers' time was taken up with exercise after exercise, drills and then more drills. At the end of April 1944, a full-scale rehearsal took place for 'U Force', the troops destined for Utah Beach. It was codenamed TIGER.

Thousands of American troops gathered at the training area of Slapton Sands, ready to storm the beaches of Devon. They loaded up their LSTs (Landing Ship, Tank) and their LCAs (Landing Craft, Assault), just as they were intending to do on D-Day. It was a large undertaking, but by this stage it was in many ways just part of the routine. And yet it turned into one of the most tragic episodes of the war.

On April 25, we loaded army troops and equipment at Brixham Harbor, said Eugene Eckstam, a medical officer with U Force. There were 125 navy men as ship's company, plus our 42-man medical group; and we took on about 300 army men with their trucks and Jeeps.

We rode at anchor for about two days while other ships loaded. The tank deck and the main deck were completely filled with vehicles and army personnel. They slept anywhere and received their C-rations on deck, parading around in a large circle about the main deck.

After we cleared the Brixham Harbor and were out a few miles, I heard that the British destroyer escort which was to have been following us had a collision in port and we would be proceeding with only a trawler as escort. I retired early to get a good night's sleep before the practice invasion the next morning.

I was awakened at about 01.30 by the General Quarters alarm. After dressing, as always, with helmet, foul weather gear and gas mask, I reported to the wardroom, which was the First Aid Station for the ship. I found that there were reports of some shooting, but I heard none. I remember talking about the possibility that some gunner on the next ship or so was shooting at shadows. Someone said some of the bullets came sort of close to us, and whoever it was should be more careful.

Since all was quiet for about twenty minutes, I decided I would go topside to see what was going on. The passageway to the hatch on the starboard side led past the captain's quarters. As I was passing there was a BOOM!!!, followed rapidly by the sound of crunching metal, then darkness and silence.

The rehearsing American fleet had happened upon a flotilla of nine German E-boats. The German ships seized the opportunity and launched torpedoes before slipping away in the darkness.

A torpedo had struck the side of the ship in the auxiliary engine room, which was about thirty feet forward of where I was standing, continued Eckstam. Since the auxiliary engines were out, there was no electricity for light, for the water pumps to fight fire, or for the motors to lower the small boats.

I knew where every battle lantern was located. One was by my right hand as I stood up, just across the passageway from the captain's door. The force of the explosion had popped the first-aid cabinet partly off the wall and the supplies were all over the wardroom. Casualties came in. There were only a few. But as more reports came in, we realized the mid part of the ship was an inferno and no one could pass from one end of the ship to the other, either on the main deck or below decks.

I decided to check out the aft part of the ship, to be sure that there were no casualties needing care, and to secure the ship. Securing the ship means closing all the hatches between compartments to preserve buoyancy and so delay or prevent sinking. Since the officers were otherwise busy and since I knew what to do, I did it.

One of the most difficult decisions I have ever made, one that still gives me nightmares, was to close the hatches leading to the tank deck. I tried to call and go in, but it was like looking and trying to walk into a huge, roaring blast furnace. The trucks were burning, gasoline was burning and small arms ammunition was exploding. Worst of all were the agonizing screams for help from the army men trapped in there. I can still hear them. But knowing that there was absolutely no way anyone could help them, and knowing that the smoke inhalation would end their misery soon, I closed the hatches.

After checking all the compartments possible, I returned to the wardroom. One or two other injured had been cared for. Many of the soldiers were jumping or diving into the water. I didn't relish sudden entry into cold water at about forty-two degrees, so I checked the small boats, but the explosion had lifted the boats and set them down hard, bending the bars. They were jammed.

A life raft seemed the next alternative, but the metal pins that released the rafts were rusted in place and only a few rafts were able to be used. Also, the ropes that were so nicely folded and wrapped at intervals around the raft had shrunk so tightly, they could not be strung out.

I inflated my life belt and proceeded down the cargo net. The water was very cold, so I entered slowly. I swam quickly away from the ship to avoid the suction in case it did sink. About 300 yards from the LST, now burning with flames shooting high in the sky and lighting up the whole area, I found a life raft. On the raft was one of our very responsible corpsmen. He had taken a man with a broken leg with him after lowering him with a rope into the water. And he kept off all others that were clamoring to get on the raft. To allow too many on would capsize it.

At first I was hanging on to other guys and was in about the fifth or sixth ring of men hanging on to ropes attached to the raft. As the ones in front of me lost consciousness, I had to let them drift off. There was nothing to fasten them with so we could stay together. Eventually I could reach between two guys and I twisted my hand around a rope that circled the raft, so I would not drift away. I was getting very sleepy and was no longer cold, and I knew I would be unconscious soon.

The next thing I remember I was climbing up a ladder on the side of a ship.We were torpedoed at about 02.05, and we were picked up at about 06.00. Somewhere in between I was hauled out of the water.

About 700 men were killed. This was far more than were to die on Utah Beach itself, come D-Day. The human loss was nearly compounded by a security breach, something that could have put the entire invasion plan in jeopardy. Some of the officers on the two ships that were hit were carrying briefing documents that specified the location of the landings. When daylight came, rescue boats searched the water and the shoreline for the drowned bodies of these men. The planners held their breath until all the corpses with their sodden papers were recovered and accounted for. This was total war, and the preservation of the great Overlord secret was more precious than life – more precious even than 700 lives.

THE FINISHING TOUCHES

Three weeks after Slapton, Montgomery unveiled the finished invasion plan to a select audience which included Winston Churchill, King George VI and high-ranking officers of all the Allied armies. The presentation took place in St Paul's School, London, where Monty had studied as a boy and where he had now made his headquarters.

The invasion was to begin on the American beaches, codenamed Utah and Omaha, in the west of the landing grounds. The first wave would go in at daybreak in order to give the invaders a full sixteen hours of daylight for their work. It was also important the tide should be turning from ebb to flow as the invasion got under way, so that beach obstacles installed by Rommel would not be hidden under water. The run of the tide – from west to east – meant that the invasion would have to begin one hour later on the British beaches, which were codenamed Gold, Juno and Sword. The airborne commanders wanted a full moon for their night attack. Their men were to descend by glider and parachute in the hours before the dawn of D-Day. The first day in June that met all these conditions was the 5th. The 6th was also a good day – but after that the combination of circumstances would not be right for weeks. D-Day was provisionally scheduled for 5 June; H-Hour, 6.30 in the morning.

Monty was full of optimism and vigour as he expounded upon the plan. He told the assembled VIPs that 175,000 men would land in the first twenty-four hours, along with 1,500 tanks, 10,000 motor vehicles and 3,000 big guns. If all went as he envisaged, the Allies would be several miles inland by evening; all the beachheads would have linked up with each other, and with the paratroopers at the extremities. Everyone left the briefing with the conviction that the Allies could not lose.

But in the course of May there was a series of security scares. The first was bizarre. British security operatives noticed that a number of highly sensitive code words were appearing as crossword answers in the London *Daily Telegraph*. On 2 May, the solution to 17 Across was UTAH; on 22 May, 3 Down was OMAHA; on 30 May, 11 Across was MULBERRY; and on 1 June, 15 Down was NEPTUNE, the codeword for the naval operation to ferry the invasion force to Normandy. On 2 June – the most worrying of all – the paper printed the solution to the previous week's puzzle: the answer to 11 Across was OVERLORD.

This was the last straw. That morning, two MI5 agents paid a visit to Leonard Dawe, a physics teacher who compiled the *Telegraph* crossword in his spare time. They sat him down, told him what he had done and asked him where he got the words from. He said that they were all common enough words. But why was he using military codewords in his puzzle? 'How am I supposed to know,' asked Dawe, 'what word is a codeword and what word isn't?' It was a reasonable enough question. Baffled but reassured, the MI5 men shrugged their shoulders and left the puzzling Mr Dawe in peace.

A far more serious breach occurred in those last days. In separate incidents, an American general and a British colonel made terribly indiscreet references to the coming invasion. The American told some officers at a cocktail party that the invasion was definitely going to happen before 15 June. The British officer dropped a heavy hint to some civilian acquaintances that his unit was headed for Normandy. Both men were reported, then instantly demoted and removed from their commands.

More damaging still was a lapse that occurred on Sunday 4 June, the eve of D-Day. An Associated Press teletype operator in New York had been practising on a spare machine. She typed her dummy message in the abbreviated, staccato style by which breaking news was transmitted at the time. This is what she chose to write:

URGENT PRESS ASSOCIATED NYK FLASH EISENHOWER'S
HQ ANNOUNCED ALLIED LANDINGS IN FRANCE

She did not know that the machine was live – the message went out to the world. It was corrected within a minute, but by then it was too late. Groups of people gathered in Times Square, New York, to contemplate news of an invasion that was still a top-secret non-event. The Germans picked up the message too – but simply discounted it on the grounds that if the invasion had started, then they would surely know about it.

At Allied HQ in Portsmouth, where nerves were already taut, the teletype caused deep consternation. But they were grappling with a bigger problem, something that right at the last was putting the whole invasion in doubt: the English weather. The worst storm in thirty years was raging across the south of England and in the Channel, and it did not look like it was going to let up. But if the invasion was to go ahead on the 5th as scheduled, then the order had to be given now, on Sunday 4 June.

Lieutenant Commander Larry Hogben was one of the Admiralty meteorologists providing regular weather forecasts to Eisenhower.

All we had to go on was hundreds of observation reports from posts all over Greenland, Iceland, America and the Azores, said Hogben. **There were two Americans and they claimed we could**

forecast the weather five days ahead. That was proved nonsense. We could forecast one-and-a-half to two days ahead, and that was enough for Eisenhower.

As naval officers we knew that a convoy would have been scattered. There were 3,000 ships which had to assemble at the Piccadilly Circus point in the middle of the Channel for the landing to go ahead; this would have been impossible in a storm. Also, most of the men were sailing in landing craft. They were no more than barges, and would not have been able to withstand a storm. There would have been a huge loss of life.

In the dead of Saturday night, Eisenhower held a conference to discuss the chances of unleashing the invasion on Monday 5th, as planned. Among those present were General Montgomery, now itching to get on with the job; Admiral Bertram Ramsay, the Allied Naval Commander; and Air Chief Marshall Arthur Tedder, Eisenhower's deputy. These representatives of the three services – land, sea and air – listened to the weather forecast with mounting gloom. Then they all sat round a table to talk it over. This is Eisenhower's own account of the meeting:

The final conference for determining the feasibility of attacking on June 5 was scheduled for 4am on June 4. However, some of the attacking contingents had already been ordered to sea, because if the entire force was to land on June 5, then some elements stationed in northern parts of the United Kingdom could not wait for final decision on the morning of June 4.

When the commanders assembled, the report we received was discouraging. Low clouds, high winds and formidable wave action were predicted to make landing a most hazardous affair. The meteorologists said that air support would be impossible, naval gunfire inefficient and even the handling of small boats would be rendered difficult. Admiral Ramsay thought that the mechanics of landing could be handled, but agreed with the estimate of the difficulty in adjusting gunfire. General Montgomery, properly concerned with the great disadvantages of delay, believed that we should go. Tedder disagreed.

Weighing all factors, I decided that the attack would have to be postponed. This decision necessitated the immediate dispatch of orders to the vessels and troops already at sea and created some doubt as to whether they could be ready twenty-four hours later in case the next day should prove favourable for the assault. Actually the manoeuvre of the ships in the Irish Sea proved most difficult by reason of the storm. That they succeeded in gaining ports, refuelling, and readying themselves to resume the movement a day later represented the utmost in seamanship and in brilliant command and staff work.

The commanders met again on Sunday evening, but there was no improvement in the situation. If D-Day had to be postponed again, then the entire gargantuan mechanism of the invasion would have to be thrown into reverse. All the ships would have to be docked and unloaded, thousands of men disembarked and sent back to camp, plans rescheduled and remade. No-one knew if this backward step was even possible. And given the security blunders of the last days, the planners were concerned that the secret could not be kept for much longer. All these thoughts were on Eisenhower's mind when the commanders gathered.

> The conference on the evening of 4 June presented little, if any, added brightness to the picture of the morning, wrote Eisenhower. And tension mounted even higher because the inescapable consequences of postponement were almost too bitter to contemplate.

Now everything was down to the supreme commander, and him alone. Eisenhower was about to make a decision that would affect the course of the war, that for better or worse would change history. For some time he looked down at the table. Then he raised his head and said: 'I am quite positive we must give the order. I don't like it, but there it is. I don't see how we can do anything else.' In this reluctant, half-hearted way, D-Day was fixed for 6 June. On Eisenhower's word orders were flashed out to the fleet to prepare to set sail.

Even at this point Eisenhower left himself room to change his mind. He asked the commanders and the weather men to meet for one last time in the small hours of Monday morning. If the unforgiving storm was still raging, then the fleet would be recalled and the invasion postponed for two weeks at least.

At 3.30 our little camp was shaking and shuddering under a wind of almost hurricane proportions, wrote Eisenhower, and the accompanying rain seemed to be travelling in horizontal streaks. The mile-long trip through muddy roads to the naval headquarters was anything but a cheerful one, since it seemed impossible that in such conditions there was any reason for even discussing the situation.

When the conference started, the first report given us by Group Captain Stagg and the meteorological staff was that the bad conditions predicted the day before for the coast of France were actually prevailing there and that if we had persisted in the attempt to land on June 5 a major disaster would almost surely have resulted.

This they probably told us to inspire more confidence in their next astonishing declaration, which was that by the following morning a period of relatively good weather, heretofore completely unexpected, would ensue, lasting probably thirty-six hours. The long-term prediction was not good but they did give us assurance that this short period of good weather would intervene between the exhaustion of the storm we were then experiencing and the beginning of the next spell of bad weather.

The prospect was not bright because of the possibility that we might land the first several waves successfully and then find later build-up impracticable, and so have to leave the isolated original attacking forces easy prey to German counteraction.

It would have cheered Eisenhower at this moment to know that Rommel had also taken a look at the impossible weather, and decided that now would be a safe moment to take a couple of days' leave. The Field Marshal had already left for Germany, clutching a pair of grey shoes which were a present for his wife: it was her birthday on 6 June.

But Eisenhower confirmed his decision without this pleasing piece of intelligence. He paced silently up and down the room, came to a stop and calmly pronounced:

OK. Let's go.

2
ON THE EVE

In the last days of May, as the invasion machinery ground into motion, Churchill's thoughts had turned to his own plans for the big day. He asked Admiral Ramsay to arrange for him to go to sea with the fleet, so that he could see the naval bombardment for himself. 'I thought it would not be wrong of me to watch this historic battle from one of our own cruiser squadrons,' he wrote in his memoirs.

Ramsay was not so sure. He organized a berth for Churchill on the HMS *Belfast*, but he let Eisenhower know of Churchill's plans. The general immediately voiced his doubts, saying that he had enough worries for the day without Churchill putting himself in physical danger. But Churchill replied that 'while we accepted him as Supreme Commander of the British forces involved, we did not in any way admit his right to regulate the complements of the ships in the Royal Navy.'

The matter seemed settled, until a new complication arose. Churchill went for lunch at Buckingham Palace in the week preceeding D-Day. When the King heard what Churchill had in mind he eagerly insisted that he would like to come along too. Churchill thought it a fine idea, and set about finding a place for the King of England in the armada. But meanwhile His Majesty thought better of it. He sent a letter to Churchill the next day.

> My dear Winston, wrote the King. I have been thinking a great deal of our conversation yesterday, and I have come to the conclusion that it would not be right for either you or I to be where we planned to be on D-Day. I don't think I need emphasise what it would mean to me personally, and to the whole Allied cause, if at this juncture a chance bomb should remove you from the scene; equally a change of Sovereign at this moment would be a serious matter for the country and Empire. We should both, I know, love to be there, but I would ask you to reconsider your

plan. The anxiety of these coming days would be very greatly increased for me if I thought that, in addition to everything else, there was a risk, however remote, of my losing your help and guidance.

But Churchill was not persuaded. He felt he was entitled to lighten the burden of responsibility with what he called 'the refreshment of adventure'. He had once remarked, remembering his time fighting the Boers, that nothing makes a man feel so alive as being shot at. He dearly wanted to be under fire once more.

Eisenhower had accepted that it was no concern of his if a British citizen – albeit the Prime Minister – decided to enlist in the Royal Navy. Now the King's aides turned the tables on Churchill with an equally legalistic argument, telling him that 'no Minister of the Crown could leave the country without the Sovereign's permission.' Churchill trumped this by saying that he would not technically be out of the country as he would be on one of His Majesty's ships. As Churchill grew increasingly petulant, the King was forced to write another personal letter.

My dear Winston – I want to make one more appeal to you not to go to sea on D-Day. Please consider my own position. I am a younger man than you, I am a sailor, and as King I am the head of all these Services. There is nothing I would like better than to go to sea, but I have agreed to stay at home; is it fair that you should then do exactly what I should have liked to do myself? You said yesterday afternoon that it would be a fine thing for the King to lead his troops into battle, as in old days; if the King cannot do this, it does not seem to me right that his Prime Minister should take his place.

Then there is your own position. You will see very little, you will run a considerable risk, you will be inaccessible at a critical time when vital decisions may have to be taken, and however unobtrusive you may be your mere presence on board is bound to be a very heavy additional responsibility to the Admiral and Captain. I ask you most earnestly to consider the whole question again, and not let your personal wishes, which I very well understand, lead you to depart from your own high standard of duty to the State.

At this, Churchill relented – but not without a little eloquent grumbling.

> **Sir,** he wrote back to the King. **I cannot really feel that your letter takes sufficient account of the fact that there is absolutely no comparison in the British Constitution between a Sovereign and a subject. If Your Majesty had gone, as you desire, on board one of your ships in this bombarding action it would have required the Cabinet's approval beforehand, and I am very much inclined to think, as I told you, that the Cabinet would have advised most strongly against Your Majesty going.**
>
> **On the other hand, as Prime Minister and Minister of Defence I ought to be allowed to go where I consider it necessary to the discharge of my duty, and I do not admit that the Cabinet have any right to put restrictions on my freedom of movement. I rely on my own judgment, invoked in many serious matters, as to what are the proper limits of risk which a person who discharges my duties is entitled to run. I must most earnestly ask Your Majesty that no principle shall be laid down which inhibits my freedom of movement when I judge it necessary to acquaint myself with conditions in the various theatres of war.**
>
> **Since Your Majesty does me the honour to be so much concerned about my personal safety on this occasion, I must defer to Your Majesty's wishes, and indeed commands. It is a great comfort to me to know that they arise from Your Majesty's desire to continue me in your service. Though I regret I cannot go, I am deeply grateful to Your Majesty for the motives which have guided Your Majesty in respect of Your Majesty's humble and devoted servant and subject.**

And so the matter was settled. Churchill knew that he would spend D-Day, now only days away, far from the sound and fury of battle.

THE EXPECTANT ARMY

In May, formal training for the invasion came to an end. A kind of quietude – not unlike the Phoney War of 1939 and 1940 – descended on the vast numbers of soldiers strung out for miles through the byways and country roads of Hampshire, Sussex, Kent, Devon and Dorset.

Bill Colyer was a private in the Hampshire Regiment. He found that this lull was a good time to get out of camp and make friends with his American neighbours.

> One night we went to the PX, which is what they called their NAAFI. I was mad about jazz, and I was looking at a pile of 78s when a Yankee sergeant came up to me and said: 'You look interested, help yourself.' Well I picked three records: Jack Teagarden, the Casa Loma Orchestra, and Jack Hylton. I took them in with me on D-Day, and kept them safe all the way through France and Germany. I ended up in the Sinai Desert when the war finished. That's where I first listened to my 78s.

For EW Broadhead, an LCT (Landing Craft, Tank) crewman, the days and weeks before the invasion were like a holiday – the calm before the storm.

> Life on the whole was pleasant, it was summer time at its best. The days were spent with a little training, mostly practice on our assault bikes. Our evenings found us in Southampton, where the servicemen outnumbered the civilians by seven to one. The walk from Southampton back to camp was a pleasant one, and often I and my mates would stroll back talking of home, parents, wives and sweethearts, and of the day that must surely dawn soon, the day when we sailed for a destination that only a few men knew. We discussed our ideas of where it would be, but the burning question was: When?
> Around May 10th, a drastic move took place, the camps were sealed, our training was over. The days that followed were strange to be sure: barbed wire skirted the camp area, armed guards too. We received no mail, but were still allowed to write home, subject to strict censorship. There was little or nothing to do, except for the army cinema shows which were daily in most cases. The boys spent many hours playing cards or Housie-Housie in the NAAFI. Some of us read books, any old thing to kill time, for we knew the day must be near at hand.

The sealed camps stretched for miles along the roadsides. They were called 'sausages' because of the shape they made on maps of the embarkation plan. From the inside they bore more of a resemblance to prisoner-of-war camps – and the oppressive confinement that they engendered was to lead to tension in the coming weeks.

The fields beside the long encampments were full of artillery and ammunition dumps, and the roads were clogged with trucks and tanks, all bound for the ports of the south coast. Every last clip of bullets had been assigned to a man, every man and machine to a unit, every unit to a regiment that had a pre-ordained place on a ship. Every ship waited at anchor in port for its cargo of men and weaponry, and every ship's captain knew his place within the fleet. The logistics of it all were staggering. One American planner remarked that 'something comparable to the city of Birmingham hasn't merely got to be shifted, it's got to be kept moving when it's on the other side.'

The Allied planners had arranged all of this in six months, using pencil and paper, initiative and delegation. What is more, they had kept the great secret of Overlord from the Germans and (for a little while longer) from the men who were to carry out the plan. It was a kind of hidden triumph, one of the great accomplishments of the war.

But for the fighting men it was an awful bore, and the tedium made them do strange things. US Army captain Richard Fahey, who as an officer and a medical man should have known better, could not help getting involved in schoolboyish pranks.

> We were convoyed by trucks to the Southampton staging area and put inside a large enclosure of barbed wire fencing. There were instructions that anyone trying to leave or climbing the fences would be shot dead on the spot, no questions asked. I found myself in a Quonset hut with about twenty strangers, officers from the Canadian, English, Polish and Indian forces. I remember a couple of Signal Corps men making a bet that they could escape from camp and come back with a case of beer. They did, to the amazement and satisfaction of everyone.
>
> I recall another episode in that hut. One of the Signal Corps men showed me a hand grenade that he had in his possession. I slyly asked him how the thing worked and when he explained to me that the pin had to be removed to release the lever, I challenged him to remove the pin. He called my bluff and removed the pin but in doing so, the pin was bent and he could not place it back into the lever. Within seconds the Quonset hut

was cleared of all its military members except him and me. While I struggled to straighten the pin and get it back into its place, he held the lever of the hand grenade for dear life. When all the others came back into the hut, they were a growling bunch, but they were able to laugh about it after a short while, because they were also a great bunch of men.

Major David Thomas also wore his Hippocratic oath lightly in the last days before the off.

As part of our preparation for the D-Day invasion, we gave each medic a canteen of alcohol, which we thought we would use for sterilization purposes when we got to Normandy. I doubt that a drop of it ever got out of England. That's a fact.

All the American troops were issued new uniforms for the invasion. Like boys on their first day at big school, they chafed and chivvied at the uncomfortable new gear.

They had this big open mess area where they had all the guns, said Raymond Bednar of the US Navy. Every officer got a .45 and a carbine, every enlisted man got a carbine. Then we were outfitted from head to toe. New helmets, new helmet liners, underwear, shirts, all army equipment, new boots, foul weather gear, parkas, blankets, mess kits, and most of all we got this gas impregnated clothing. That was the last. When we got that we started to wonder, 'Hell, where are we going now?' We were quite upset when we had to carry that everywhere.

Paratroopers had new gear of their own, and they weren't happy about it either.

We received our jumpsuits and put those suckers on, said Edward Jeziorski. I want to tell all they were the lousiest, the coldest, the clammiest, the stiffest, the stinkiest articles of clothing that were ever dreamed up to be worn by individuals. Surely the guy that was responsible for this screw-up received a Distinguished Service Medal from the devil himself. These things in no little part accounted for a lot of short tempers of the guys and being honed to the sharp edge that we were, more than one black eye appeared on troopers who were quite close to each other. It didn't take much of a difference of opinion to bring out the sporting instinct. We were an extremely close outfit though. These things were forgotten as fast as they occurred.

Lieutenant Richard Conley of the 1st Infantry Division used his time in confinement to get familiar with his equipment, and to pick the brains of his combat-hardened comrades.

We were in a marshalling area, sealed off from the rest of the country behind barbed wire. We held daily equipment inspections in detail, we conducted weapons cleaning, we were issued special clothing which was impregnated against chemical warfare attack, and we were issued assault vests which had many pockets which we over-filled with ammunition, grenades, some extra clothing, and rations. We would carry rations for three days when we hit the beach. We conducted gas mask drills, and we talked. My platoon and I, we talked. Some of the men were combat veterans. Some had gone overseas with the division in 1942 and made the landing in North Africa, fought through that campaign, made the assault landing on Sicily and completed that campaign. Most of us, however, including myself, had no combat experience, but were more than willing to draw on the experience of those who had seen combat.

Joseph Camera, a combat medic, was one of those who had fought in Italy. The prospect of another beach assault, and the company of unblooded GIs, brought back memories of Sicily.

Then, the Germans sent in their waves of dive bombers, strafing and bombing continually, and we had over 40 air raids in eight days taking its toll. After Salerno, we were relieved. As the replacements were coming in, I asked one, 'What was first on the hit parade?' He answered, 'You'll Never Know.' I wanted to punch him out for that remark till one of his friends said 'No, that's the name of the song!'

Towards D-Day we were quarantined in staging areas, awaiting embarkment. Some of the fellows were singing *Over There*, and when they got to the line '. . . *and we won't be back* . . .' they would stop singing. Seriously, this wasn't very funny to me.

RITES AND RITUALS

The caged men spontaneously invented all manner of superstitions, hoping in some pagan way to buy protection for themselves in the coming battle. One British soldier, Gunner H Barca of the 7th Field Regiment, Royal Artillery, on being issued some French francs as 'invasion money' noticed that the last three numbers on one of the notes, 331, were the same as the number of the boat on which he had been training. As a result of this tiny circumstance, 'I was at once offered a shilling, two shillings and even half-a-crown for it. But I refused all offers and decided to keep it. They said it might bring us all luck on our Landing Craft Transport 331.'

Lots of Americans adopted bizarre and terrifying haircuts in the week before the invasion. Paratroopers sported wide Mohicans like broomheads down the centre of their scalps; others shaved letters or designs into their GI crew cuts – expecting, like ancient Britons in their woad or Apaches in their warpaint, that the mere sight of them would send the enemy running.

> The fellows in my squad wanted to grow goatees and moustaches and I told them to go ahead, said Sergeant Roy Arnn. They said we all had to or none, so I agreed. Captain Howard told me to have everyone shave their beards off. I told him that I had checked beards with the gas masks on and they did not interfere. He said to shave them off anyway, and I refused. He said that he would court-martial me, and I told him to go ahead as none of us might be alive tomorrow anyway.

Private Lindley Higgins, meanwhile, was subjected to a strange and rather unnerving ritual. An order came from his commanding officer on grounds of security:

> We were asked to take all of our personal possessions and build an enormous fire – this in spite of blackout conditions – and throw everything we owned which could identify us into the fire. (Apparently the Germans didn't have similar directives for them,

There was a fashion among US servicemen for bizarre D-Day haircuts – but none so outlandish as the ones worn by these sailors. Some American paratroopers even went into battle wearing Mohicans and with streaks of warpaint on their faces.

because when they were captured, they often had more photographs than one would imagine.) In any event, having burned all our letters, photos and other identifying means, we were sent to a marshalling area in Plymouth. Oddly enough, we were permitted to go out to pubs in the vicinity and drink.

The seriousness of the situation was most closely brought home to us by the fact that there was a marked improvement in the food that we ate during our stay in the marshalling area. We were receiving steaks on a regular basis, and other food we weren't quite used to. Another interesting aspect in the marshalling area were the number of poker games involving French money, American money, British money, and even some Dutch guilders, some Luxembourg francs and some Belgian francs. It required a skilful mathematician to keep up with the rates of exchange and the like.

Money was swilling around the American camps like bilge water in a leaky boat, and this gave Private Ray Voight a rather cynical idea.

> I thought we were going to end up in Paris or some large town, so I borrowed quite a bit of money from fellows I knew in the outfit. My idea was, if I got hit or killed, I wouldn't have to worry about it, and if I didn't, I'd have the money. And if they got killed, I wouldn't have to worry about paying them back. This was a good thought on my part, really. Good thinking, because I think I was broke before we got on the ship.

In some of the British camps, meanwhile, the warlike mood of the men was struggling to find an outlet. A certain Sergeant Mackenzie of the Royal Engineers noted in his diary the rather surprising level of aggression and violence directed, for want of a better enemy, at army property.

> All leave and short passes cancelled, curse it. Nearly all the vehicles are waterproofed now, and what sights they do look. All pipes and paste.
> We have no work to do, and not much recreation either, but can't blame the authorities this time as they are doing their best. Most of the time is spent 'yocking', or discussing our chances, sometimes with confidence, sometimes with blood-curdling pessimism.
> Second night in confinement. The boys are on the rampage: one can't bottle one's emotions up after three or four years of nomadic existence. Windows are being smashed, every crash of glass is loudly cheered. They are now making their way to the officers' quarters, and a shower of bricks and cans, or whatever is handiest, goes crashing through the windows.
> The officers discreetly file out the back door, apparently none of them wish to be 'senior rank around'. Personally I keep well out of the way as I don't wish to get in the way of a flying missile. Their destructive appetite is apparently quenched, and at midnight all is quiet.
> Morning shows what has become a common sight, only this mess wasn't caused through bombing. The following night it is the NAAFI's turn for a bashing. Chairs and glasses through the

windows. Stupid thing to do. A lance corporal who tries to restore order gets arrested for inciting, which only proves that discretion is the better part of valour.

Major ARC Mott had a rather more restful and civilized time of it in his sealed camp, undisturbed by other ranks. His quiet wait ended on a peculiar festive note on 4 June.

> Beer was available at the canteen and Dick Baines, Tony Boyd his second-in-command, Cecil and I had a pleasant party during which our D to D+30 whisky rations became casualties.
>
> Next day we were driven to Southampton docks, instead of having to march the last half-mile. As we drank tea and ate chocolate and biscuits, the *Crossbow* docked and we quickly embarked. In addition to my clothing I carried: steel helmet, Mae West, binoculars, compass, Sten gun with 180 rounds, two bakelite grenades and two high-explosive grenades, map case, entrenching tool and a small pack containing 24-hour ration, washing and shaving kit, socks, PT shoes, mess tin, emergency ration, flask with medicinal whisky, gas cape. Also we had two containers of three 2-inch mortar bombs to drop at the top of the tide. Other ranks were liable to include bangalore torpedoes, ladders or tapes, and special assault kit.
>
> We stayed on board, not knowing when the great day was to be. On Sunday 4th I got a hint from the padre who was fixing Sunday services. The service was excellent, with only assault troops and the LCA crews there, popular hymns and a sermon saying that there is no such person as an atheist in a slit trench.
>
> The rumour about D-Day was correct, but we were disappointed to learn that due to the weather it had been put back twenty-four hours. Nevertheless we ate our pre-D-Day dinner of turkey and Christmas pudding.

MARCHING AS TO WAR

In the last days of May and the first days of June the great convocation of men and armament began to stir like a waking dragon. Tents were struck, engines revved, and men in their thousands formed up and marched south from their bivouacs. Their columns made unbroken lines winding deep into the countryside, and the tramp of their boots sounded through the nights. Half of England lay in bed and listened to them as they marched towards Portsmouth and Plymouth and Portslade and Newquay.

> The trucks loaded with battle-clad men and tons of boat repair and hydrographic gear rumbled noisily out of the strangely quiet and vacant camp, said W Garwood Bacon, a US naval engineer. The feeling of 'this is it' was evident on the grim faces of the veterans of previous invasions, and on all the inexperienced men. We could all sense that this is not just another dry run, but would be the test of the training.
>
> As we careened crazily down the narrow country lanes of Devonshire towards our unknown destination, some of us started to sing some old songs to break the tension. Since most of our battalion consisted of young men nineteen or twenty years old, it wasn't long before our entire company of trucks and jeeps were yelling away lusty on such refrains as *Marching Along Together*. It was a relief to get rid of the pent up energy caused by the weeks of waiting.

British civilians stood like mourners at a funeral and watched the men of three nations marching off to the front. Many of them will have recalled similar scenes from thirty years before, when the fathers of these soldiers trooped down the same roads on their way to fight the German enemy in France. One young girl, Jean Getley, the daughter of a greengrocer, gazed on it all in uncomprehending awe.

> We had many soldiers bivouacking in the country a few miles from our home, and a couple of days before the landings they all left. I don't know why, or how they were transported, but they came down our road in single file in each of the gutters.
>
> That morning my mother had received a consignment of delicious Canadian apples – the first we had had for years. She didn't know how to share them out among her customers. As we went to the shop door to wave the soldiers farewell, my mother seized on an idea. My Auntie Nelly and my little sister filled a large butcher's basket with apples. We happily gave the whole lot away, and all the soldiers went away munching lovely shiny

apples. I am sure my mother and aunt realised where these soldiers were bound, but we didn't.

Gifts were bestowed as well as received by the soldiers. Betty Boorah was a young mother living in Portsmouth, and so she knew the invasion was near: 'Cages for prisoners had been built on the common and there was the ceaseless roar from boats along the sea front.' She came out to watch the soldiers embark.

> There was a constant stream of army vehicles, tanks, lorries, bailey-bridge carriers, guns. The troops were waving and calling out. As one lorry drew abreast of me, one of the soldiers threw a football to my eldest son. He was only small and couldn't catch it properly, and another boy picked it up. On it were written names and a message: 'We have no further use for this and I hope it will give you a lot of pleasure.' I tried to buy the ball off the boy but he wouldn't part with it. I would have treasured it always.

Thelma Brooks had an even more poignant meeting with a departing soldier, a marvellous one-in-a-million-chance encounter.

> I was a bride of exactly four months, when I received a phone call one afternoon in my office, to tell me that my husband would not be coming home that evening. The soldier who rang said, 'I believe you know why,' and of course I did. I knew something big was brewing. I was quite devastated that the moment had actually arrived, and I couldn't answer him. I thought, 'if only I could see him one more time, I'd be all right'.
>
> The next morning I was walking to work and I could see this convoy slowly making its way along Egham bypass from Aldershot. It had been doing this *all night long*. Suddenly a truck stopped, and of course everything behind it. And there was my husband waving and shouting, and all his friends with him. The two roads, mine and the bypass, converged at that point. The moment that I appeared, his truck reached the same spot! It was a wonderful, superb moment, and I felt it was a good omen. We kissed goodbye, and I felt so much better.

THE BRIEFING

Most of the ordinary soldiers had little idea, as they headed for port, on what hostile coast the ships would set them down. The mass of fighting men were briefed only when they were already at sea, after the ships had been sealed, so that no word could leak out to friendly civilians with gifts of apples, or to lonely new brides in a last-gasp embrace. But many of the officers knew. The process of briefing the men on their mission started at the top, and the information was passed down the ranks in a secretive and highly orchestrated game of Chinese whispers. 'We were briefed at Beaulieu Abbey on 25th May . . .' said Major ARC Mott, who found he was to go in on Gold Beach.

> . . . Officers were told the real place-names; other ranks were given codenames, such as Odessa and Albany. I was not sure where the Cotentin peninsula was, so was not much wiser than the others. The maps were of several scales, some of them showing known minefields among the shore defences. There were photographs, including people's pre-war snapshots, such as bathing belles with part of Arromanches behind them.
>
> The landing was to be at quarter-tide, differing from previous landings made at full-tide. This was because of underwater obstacles, designed to wreak havoc on assault craft, placed between high- and low-water marks. Before we arrived, sappers were to land and deal with these under cover of the bombardment and DD tanks.
>
> The battalion's plan was for A Company to land at Le Hamel and seize the strongpoint before its inhabitants had time to recover from the preliminary bombardment, then to mop up the rest of the village. My task was to land and get through the beach defences, then push on to Asnelles-sur-mer where there was a defensive post and an anti-tank gun. C was to pass behind A and clear Le Hamel West, another strong-point, while D would land behind us and deal with the radar station on the cliffs by Arromanches, and what was left of a coastal battery. The battalion would finish up in this area, including clearing Arromanches and Tracy, about a mile away. We were told about the preliminary bombardment, and that we should find the smoke and dust blotting out all recognisable features before we

landed, so I was responsible for guiding the first wave to the right spot. I studied air photographs of the beaches and picked out a large log at just the right point.

Monty's forecast was that we could not lose: we might draw, but would probably win. We were also told of the Mulberry harbour coming to Arromanches, and PLUTO, the pipe-line under the ocean to bring our oil. We embarked in our LSI, the *Empire Crossbow*, a flimsy ship which we were told might last for thirty seconds if she sustained a direct hit.

We had been inspected by the King and General Montgomery at Long Melford, and General Eisenhower saw us shortly before D-Day. I well remember a parade of many arms, formed in three sides of a square, being told to come round him. We tried to do this unscheduled movement in a military fashion, and ended up far from anything in a drill book, some at the slope, some not. Ike watched and said, 'Can't you stand easy? I thought I was going to talk to a bunch of guys, not stand up in front of a firing squads.' Then he looked forward to a 'monumental party on the Rhine' when the war was over, and this was just the right note.

Officers were told exactly where they were to go once they got to France, right down to very field in which they were to meet up with the rest of their unit. The French end of the operation was all so minutely planned, so punctilious and precise, that it seemed almost churlish of the Germans to want to disrupt it.

The day before we were due to move we were given our briefing, though we were not told where we were actually going, said Austin Baker of the 4th/7th Royal Dragoon Guards. We knew more or less what the beach looked like, and we knew that we had to make for an orchard near a little village a short distance inland, where the fitters and the first vehicles of A1 Echelon transport were to rendezvous. It was arranged that we should come under the command of Captain Collins, the Technical Adjutant, or if he didn't get there safely Captain Verdin, the A1 commander, or Captain Dyson.

We were expecting to move at about midnight on June 2nd. We packed up our kit and stowed it away on the ARV, then we sat on our beds and waited for our serial number to be called over the loudspeaker system. At about midnight an announcement came over to the effect that our serial would be delayed for at least two hours. We had a little sleep, and at two o'clock we heard that there would be another two hours' delay. We had already had one late supper, but we went along to the mess room and scrounged another to pass the time. We finally moved off, behind RHQ's [Regimental Headquarters] tanks, soon after dawn on June 3rd.

We rolled through Southampton and down to the docks. We were loaded onto an LCT with surprisingly little delay. The LCT was absolutely jammed with vehicles and guns and men. In addition to the ARV there was Major Barker's tank (Major B was second in command of the Regiment), the Intelligence Officer's tank, one A Squadron tank, Captain Collins' scout car, a bulldozer, a Jeep and three carriers towing 6-pounder anti-tank guns belonging to the Green Howards.

We stayed at anchor in the Solent all day. We were due to sail the following noon, but before that time came we were told that the whole operation had been postponed for twenty-four hours because of bad weather out in the Channel. I didn't know whether to be relieved or sorry. We on the ARV were better off for sleeping than anybody else, because the inside of the vehicle was very roomy and we were able to sleep in it. Most of the other people on board slept on the deck. We eventually sailed off down the Solent at midday on June 5th.

The American briefings followed the same pattern. Some men were apprised of their task in remarkably optimistic and upbeat terms, others were drawn the gloomiest possible picture. Robert Adams of the US Navy got one of the happy briefings.

Our boat division, along with key officers and non-coms of the 1st Division, were taken to a school. Here, laid out on several long tables, were topographic landscapes, maps of the Omaha Beach area. This particular topographic layout showed the valleys and the rivers and the towns, hopefully as they would actually appear to us as we approached the beach. At that time, we were given detailed information about the support effort that we would have. We were told of how many battle wagons, cruisers and destroyers. We were told how we would bomb the German positions prior to the landing. We were told that thousands of ships were to be involved. Most important to us in the boats, we were told, in our group, that we would be the sixth wave, a wave that most of us guys felt was going to be a comfortable deal.

Sergeant Alan Anderson was on the receiving end of a rather pessimistic forecast, but made the best of it.

We were all called into a tent and some colonel got up and made an impassioned and a patriotic speech about what a privilege it was for us to have this opportunity to be in this eventful invasion which would change the history of the world, and then at the end of his speech he made the remarkable announcement that he couldn't go with us. My buddy, Arkie Markum, poked me and said, 'Well, he can have my place if he really wants to go.'

Another interesting thing that he said was that the army was prepared to accept one hundred per cent casualties for the first twenty-four hours. It was interesting that we all turned around and looked at each other and said: 'Well, it's tough that you have to go.' It's really strange that the human mind doesn't seem to be able to comprehend that you could very well be in a suicide mission.

Private Harold Baumgarten of the 116th Infantry Regiment came away from the briefing having drawn his own conclusions about the nature of the mission, and his own chances of coming through it.

We would hit Omaha Beach at Dog Green strip, near the seaside town of Vierville-sur-mer. The 16th Infantry Regiment of the 1st Infantry Division would be on our left and the 5th Ranger outfit on our right. The British and Canadians were on the left side of the 1st Division, so we were to land on the west flank of Omaha Beach. We saw photos of the Germans preparing the defenses. They were taken in May 1944 by our P-39 planes over the beach.

Having my college education and a good background in American history and wartime battles, I realized that it was not

Stakes were set in beaches to impede assault craft, and in fields to stop gliders landing. They were known as 'Rommel's asparagus'. In this reconnaissance photo, taken by a low-flying Allied fighter, German soldiers can be seen running for cover as the plane swoops in.

going to be easy, and I did not expect to come back alive. I wrote as such to my sister in New York City to get the mail before my parents, and to break the news gently to them when she received the telegram that I was no longer alive.

Captain Richard Fahey was impressed by the rubber mock-ups of the beaches. These had been manufactured under the utmost secrecy in toy factories around Britain. But he had precious little opportunity to admire the workmanship.

We were told that there were so many to be 'briefed', we each would be given only ten minutes to memorize everything that might be so important to us as individuals during the invasion. Well, I was impressed by all those welcoming gun emplacements and minefields, but I'll be darned if I ever could memorize all that I saw in that ten minutes. What were they thinking of?

The Easy Red section of Omaha beach, where I was assigned my landing, consisted of a sandy beach stretching from the seashore back about two hundred feet, at which point it angled up a steep slope about fifty feet to a plateau. The plateau was continuous along the beach for probably several miles with sections of valley-like entrances to the beach, here and there, where people came and went from the sandy beach. We were told that we were to run along the sandy beach and go inland when we reached one of these valleys between the plateaus.

We knew that the sand on the beach was ladened with personnel mines and ratchet mines to blow up our trucks, but I did not know that the plateau had long tunnels in them parallel to the entire beach. The Germans inside the tunnels were able to shoot out their peep holes at point-blank range at the invaders coming on to the beach. They also had gun emplacements at the mouths of the tunnels overlooking the valley passageway between the series of plateaus. The Germans in the tunnels no doubt had the means of wiring communications of the location of ships and crafts off the shore to their soldiers who were located at a more rearward position behind the plateaus, and who were shooting the bazooka shells that were continuously raining down on the beach invaders.

On June 4 1944, we were told the invasion would be tomorrow. I would once more be with the soldiers that I trained with and had grown so close to. I was pleased to know that. I had a deep affection for these soldiers, just might as well say so.

It was announced on the loud speakers in camp that 'there will be no going back, even though the bodies be packed six-foot high on the beach.' Most of the men did not care or have a fear. This thing had dragged out too long and all of them were anxious to have it over with. Like so many of my companions I had the idea that nothing was going to happen to me anyway and that I would be coming back home. We never lost any sleep worrying.

At this point, D-Day was still scheduled for Monday 5th, and many of the seaborne troops were aboard ship and waiting before the weekend. The American airborne paratroopers waited at their bases, but were no less bored. Like the infantry now bobbing gently at anchor, they passed the time by watching the darkening skies and by checking their equipment over and over again.

We were sealed in tighter than a cork at that airfield, said Trooper Edward Jeziorski. We did a lot of briefing and practising there, rolling our para-packs so that they would fit under the bellies of the C-47s into their receptacles. The packs contained the stuff that we would need, light machine guns, mortars and ammo.

My recollections of June 1, 2 and 3 are a jumble of maps, overlays, terrain scale models, mockups of our DZs, the surrounding territory, and the areas we were actually to secure and establish positions upon our landing. An admonishment to me was that, 'Remember, by golly, here's where you go, here's where you set the machine gun up, and by God you just don't reveal your presence at all till you are ordered to put the thing to use.' Of course that was far from being what actually took place.

On the third of June we rigged up our para-packs under our ships and my C-47. We were surprised as dickens to see the big wide stripe painted on the wings and also on the fuselage. You thought they would be up there like sitting ducks for every ground gunner to try his luck on.

After a good breakfast on the fourth of June, we were notified that we would be going in that night. We were told to take it easy and do the things we needed for ourselves. I don't know one of us who didn't attend a religious service by Father Verret. We each made our own peace in our own way. Some of us looked over our main chutes and reserves, to see that they had not been disturbed or run over or messed with in any way. Some of us piddled around and sharpened our knives and our bayonets. Others of us wrote letters to the ones that meant the most to us back home.

When the invasion was postponed for a day, paratroopers found there was nothing for it but to go through the same obsessive checks all over again on Monday 5 June. It was the only way to keep the torturesome tick-tock of the clock out of their heads.

June 5th, breakfast was kind of tough, I don't recall eating too much of it, continued Edward Jeziorski. I thought about home a lot. Kinda hard to shut those thoughts out. I wrote some more letters to Mom and Pop and to my brothers and sisters and also to the girl that would be waiting for me.

I talked to Father Verret very briefly, and he asked me if I was scared and I told him that I didn't think so. I was wondering what might be waiting for us, but I didn't think that I was afraid. Father Verret took me by the hand and we both knelt down and said a little prayer.

At around eight o'clock someone yelled that the Berlin Bitch was coming on the radio. We all gathered around and sat up as she spoke. 'Good evening, 82nd Airborne Division. Tomorrow morning the blood from your guts will grease the bogey wheels on our tanks.' This I remember very clearly.

Barrie Pitt, a British infantryman, was in a barracks in Hampshire on the eve of the invasion, and had a pretty dull evening in prospect. But against all expectations it turned out to be a memorable, uplifting and deeply emotional night.

Over the last few days we had been inspected by Monty, who issued us with pep talks, by Ike, who chatted to us like a friendly and well-disposed uncle, and by His Majesty, who beamed while Her Majesty smiled gloriously at us. We weren't allowed to write home, though we could go to the pubs and watch the Canadians try to get drunk on the very mediocre beer. There were very few girls to flirt with or quarrel over, for they had all apparently been moved out.

Tonight, however, there was to be an Ensa show in the garrison theatre, and because there was nothing else to do and nowhere to go, it was full. Not that expectations were high. There was the usual lot of plain, hard-working girls kicking their legs up into the air and singing out of tune; the usual unfunny men working on the quite reasonable assumption that a load of soldiers would laugh at any bloody thing; and a chap whose name I can't now recall, with a splendid baritone voice which kept even the jazz fiends quiet.

Then the interval came and we sat on, as there was no bar, and no point in moving. And then the curtains opened again, music struck up, and from the wings came a soaring, light golden voice. And to the wonder of the entire audience and the astonishment of those who recognised her, on to the stage walked Evelyn Laye – what appeared to be eight feet of slim, fair beauty with laughing eyes, wondrous grace and a heart-stopping smile.

She must have filled that stage for over an hour, but to us, it seemed like minutes before the unforgettable end. She told us jokes – not off-colour like the ones before, but very funny; she sang songs like *Jeannie with the Light Brown Hair*, *The Lambeth Walk* and, for us to join in, *Stardust*. And having dived down into the auditorium and picked out the fattest and ugliest sergeant in the regiment, she then dragged him up on to the stage and with him sang: 'I pushed the damper in, and I pulled the damper out, and the smoke went up the chimney all the same.'

We laughed and sang and cheered until finally she said, 'All right, to finish, what shall it be – *Chiribirbin* or *One Night of Love*?' and collapsed in helpless laughter when the entire audience roared '*One Night of Love*!' She wiped tears of laughter from her eyes and said 'Yes, well . . .' The music struck up and she sang again, that glorious, golden voice soaring up into the clouds, taking our hearts with it despite the banality of the words – and when eventually the last chords died away and her voice became just a sigh, a deep silence then filled the theatre.

I am told that there is no greater tribute that can be paid to an artiste than a moment of complete silence at the end of a performance. And this silence went on for a long time, at first in wonder and appreciation, but then our eyes left the slim figure on the stage and lifted to the ceiling. We were pretty used to overhead roar at night by now, but this was different. There was a hammering urgency about it that had been absent before. It came down directly to us, and we guessed that they were flying lower – and it went on and on.

There was, eventually, a pause in the thunder, and we could turn our attention back to the stage. She still stood there, as transfixed by the sound overhead as we had been. There were tears running down her face, but not now of laughter. She looked out across the lights and spread her hands in a gesture that none who saw her can have forgotten.

'Good luck, my dears,' she whispered. And the curtains slowly closed.

SAILING TO FRANCE

I remember the scene off Spithead on the evening of 5 June 1944, the most stirring experience of my life.

ADC Smith was an intelligence officer in the Special Service Brigade. He was now sailing for France aboard an LCI in the company of some excited French commandos.

We had embarked during the afternoon in a grotesque gala atmosphere, more like a regatta than a page of history, with gay music from the ships' loudhailers. There were more than the usual quota of jocular farewells bandied between friends and the quiet flippancies of understatement with which the Englishman seems to cloak his emotions at such moments, and of which I was as guilty as any others, more so perhaps because I was so acutely conscious of it. I am reported to have remarked with elaborate cynicism and studied resignation that 'I was a man of peace and what had I done to deserve getting myself entangled in this affair?'

About five o'clock embarkation was complete and the flotilla of LCIs sailed out into the Solent to anchor there. It was a perfect summer's evening. The Isle of Wight lay green and friendly and tantalizingly peaceful behind the tapestry of warships. The water was thick with them, large and small. A sense of expectancy was in the air, so strong that it seemed to embrace the whole expedition.

We sailed again about nine in the evening, almost the first to leave the anchorage, and nineteen little ships in line ahead set out to war. All those years of planning and preparation were ended. The vast machinery of invasion had started to move, inevitably and relentlessly. It was exhilarating, glorious and heartbreaking. As we sailed out so proudly and impudently between the assembled shipping, the crews and troops began to cheer, faintly across the water it came, until gradually it was taken up by ship after ship and the whole vast gathering rang with it. I am told even the Admiral threw his hat in the air.

I never loved England so dearly as at that moment of leaving it.

In the moment of departure there were lots of people entertaining very fond feelings for the safe, dry soil of England. One of them went to the captain of his LCT, Anthony Duke, with a story to tell.

We had a young sailor, seaman 2nd class, named Gene Sizemore from Tennessee, said Captain Duke. He came up to my quarters just after the ship had been sealed. He said to me, 'I'm only 15, captain, and I don't want to go on this trip.'

'Well, Sizemore, you are going anyway.'

'Well, Captain, I am scared, I want to get off, NOW.'

'Well, no way,' I said. 'We are sealed, and that's that.' I told him I felt sorry for him because he was scared. Well, so were all of us. But Sizemore was a young kid. I said, why don't you report to me from now on at least once every watch. And that way, I'll be able to see how you're doing and you'll be able to see how I am doing. Well, that's what he did for the next several days. By D+2, he called off that reporting. He grew up on the 530 and became a damn good solid member of the crew.

Major ARC Mott, like many of the English soldiers, was moved by the sight of the fleet and by a parting glimpse of the pale cliffs of the Isle of Wight.

The build-up of the armada had been incredible. We had been anchored in the Solent for six days and there seemed to be no room for more ships when we sailed there from Southampton, but day after day more ships had come and taken up their station. I went up to the cable deck at about 8pm to see us sailing and to see the last of England and the Isle of Wight – perhaps for ever. Everywhere we could see ships, landing craft ploughing along, landing ships overtaking them, landing ships towing (presumably) bits of Mulberry harbour at about 1 mph. Out to starboard, from Weymouth, came a US force, and we knew of the other British and American forces. We steamed close to

Hurst Castle and the big guns near the Needles, wondering how many people on land suspected that this was it – or did they think this was just another exercise?

On Monday 5th the weather was a bit worse, overcast and with a gale. At about 9am the message came – 'Tomorrow is D-Day' – and everyone's spirits soared. The troops were really keen on their job and it was great to have people like that to take into action.

Dick Baines and I went in a LCA to the *Empire Arquebus* to see the CO for a last-minute tie-up. In the evening I assembled B Company and let them into the picture of where we were really going. I had seen G Force's orders in SNOT's [Senior Naval Officer, Troops] office and in it were the outlines of the places where other landings, including airborne, were to be. There were messages from Monty and Ike to read out.

Captain Richard Fahey of the US Army got a first intimation of the size of the invasion force as he made his way into Southampton. 'I have never before and never since seen so many vehicles: Jeeps, trucks, gun carriers, in long rows, probably twenty or thirty abreast and aligned up to be put on those waiting ships and boats.' Once aboard ship and sealed off from the rest of the world, he was afforded a very secret and privileged view of the lumbering armada.

I was invited up into the forecastle of the ship that I was aboard, and one of the naval officers asked me if I would like to view the ship's radar screen. 'Of course, I would!' I was amazed to look into the dial and have him point out to me all the vessels in the English Channel that were located within a mile of the ship which we were on. Then he turned a knob on the radar and showed me all the vessels in the surrounding water within a few miles of the ship. I was amazed again.

He then asked me if I would like to see the shores of France, some twenty-two miles away. I said, 'Of course I would!' He turned the knob and I was able to see the coast of France and little boats of the enemy, riding along the coastal waters of France. I am sure these enemies in their boats did not know that they were under surveillance.

They smiled for the cameras, but some men spent days aboard wet, crowded landing ships while waiting for the order to sail. Most soldiers were miserable and sickened by the time they reached France. All speak of the inescapable stench of vomit on the ships.

The holiday atmosphere endured for a few hours, perhaps until English shores were out of sight and the seas grew uncomfortably rough. Lieutenant-Colonel Jones found that his berth was fairly snug and that there was even a wartime treat in store.

On Saturday 3 June, the battalion embarked on the LSI *Empire Broadsword*. There were several of these LSIs of American pre-fabricated build in use, roomy ships, with the assault craft (each of which held a platoon) slung on davits like ship's lifeboats. One luxury amongst the rations supplied aboard was real white bread, which we hadn't seen for years. Although it was far from fresh, we cut it into chunks and ate it as it was, like cake.

Major RMS Maude embarked on Sunday and began a letter to his mother during this happy interlude. His tone is so cheerful and boyish one might think that he was describing his first night on scout camp. His mother was no doubt glad to hear that he was enjoying 'terrific food – like peace time,' but may have been less cheered by his jokes about sinking ships.

My dear Mum,

You certainly won't get this letter until after the event, as it were, but I hope it won't be delayed too long. I thought you might be interested to know what we are doing, and how we are all feeling now.

I am writing this on board the ship in which we go across. At the moment, of course, we are at anchor off the coast of England, surrounded by a great many other ships and craft.

We embarked yesterday afternoon. We had lunch in camp and then got into buses and drove – very slowly – down to the harbour. The men were all very cheerful, cracking jokes and cheering every girl we passed on the way. You would never have dreamed, except from the amount of equipment we were carrying, that we were not going on another exercise. I must say I didn't feel any different myself.

I have known for over a year of course that we would eventually go off on this, or something similar, and I used to dread the last preparations and the final parting from friends and England. But in actual fact I haven't minded at all, now that it is really happening. We all feel very confident and optimistic about the result of the landings, and we all think it is going to be a walkover – at first anyway. Also it simply doesn't occur to anyone as a possibility that anything unpleasant can possibly happen – to other people, yes, but not to oneself – so naturally nobody worries about it.

And also we are all intensely interested to see how this thing which we have been planning so long and training for so long does work out in practice. I want to see the effect the terrific preliminary bombardment has, and what France is like after four years of occupation, and what the Germans are like, and all sorts of things like that. So it is something I am really looking forward to, and the unpleasant things that are bound to happen don't seem to me as possibilities at the moment, and don't disturb me at all.

The atmosphere on board ship is so far quite normal. I have a lot of friends and we have an amusing time pulling each other's legs, and of course we feed like kings. There are six of us in my cabin – Llewellyn, who is very nice and good-looking, and David Smith, another Sapper Major who I like very much and three other gunners, only one of whom I know at all well.

Others in the ship are Charles Boycott, who was at Bradfield with me, and Dick Goodwin and Geoffrey Riley and lots of other pleasant officers, mostly from the battalion in our brigade. We don't know yet when D-Day is, but we think it is likely to be Tuesday, or possibly Wednesday – provided of course the weather is OK. At the moment it is much too windy and rough. Curiously enough, the first unsuitable day for about a month; it always does that. On every exercise it has been the same – perfect weather until we embark, and then a gale or storm gets up.

5th June

Tomorrow is the day, as you will know when you get this – provided the ship carrying it isn't sunk! This is the afternoon, and we heard definitely at midday that we are landing tomorrow morning. It is a curious way to go into battle. A few days ago we were leading an almost normal life in England, and even now things are pretty much the same as on all the exercises we have done – and tomorrow the fighting begins.

I still feel very cheerful and well, and not particularly frightened – no doubt I shall be tomorrow morning, but it will all be so exciting that I hope it won't otherwise be too bad.

Anyway, please don't worry, I am sure to be all right and no news is good news. I have been washing all my clothes in Puritan soap. Rather fun! I must stop now and get my maps sorted. I hope you get this, but you can never tell these days. So annoying the way these ships will get sunk! All my love to you, and don't worry. Your loving Rodney.

One can almost feel the slow stiffening of Major Maude's upper lip as he comes to the end of his letter. He was surely aware of the possibility that these might be the last words his mother might ever have from him. The thought of impending death combined with the fast-spreading epidemic of seasickness rendered everyone a little sombre. And the longer the soldiers were at sea – and many of them had been sealed aboard ship for days – the more unpleasant it became.

We went below decks and laid on our bunks fully clothed, said EW Broadhead, a British servicemen on LCT 501. **Outside the wind was howling. I dozed off, only to be awakened by a horribly sickly feeling inside. 501 was rolling in every imaginable direction, the seasickness pills had failed, if ever anything did fail. There was only one thing to do, to lie still, and even that was dreadful.**

Time passed on, I felt more ill than ever before. About 5am I made a supreme effort and crawled on deck. The Yankee sailors were manning every gun aboard, all dressed up in sheepskin clothing, and all wearing a revolver as only a Yank dare wear it, Hopalong Cassidy style. The lovely fresh air on deck was worth a million pounds. Overhead Spitfires and Hurricanes, the immense power of the RAF, roared through the skies heading for France.

I was on deck less than half an hour. Looking at the sea only served to send me back to my bunk.

THE CROSSING

All the ships were massively overcrowded. Few of the men were as lucky as Broadhead; most had no bunks or sleeping quarters. They dossed down like hobos wherever they could, and tried to while away the last hours in fitful sleep or fretful conversation.

I managed to scrounge a blanket or two and settle myself down mostly under a DUKW so nobody would walk on me in the night, said Arden Benthien of the US 112th Engineer Combat Battalion. **I probably slept some during the night of the 5th, but perhaps not a lot, because I remember being up very early. We had a lot of troops on board. There was a *Life* photographer on board with a Rollei camera, complaining bitterly because they weren't going to**

let him go ashore. He had to watch the big show from afar. We
told him he was nuts.

At this moment a third of a million men were moving through the
darkness of the Channel like a seaborne Birnam Wood. Every individual
soldier and sailor knew that this night, 5 June 1944, might be the last
night of his life. Sergeant Alan Anderson shared his concerns with one of
his comrades.

I remember trying to think what this really meant to me, and all I
could think about was the fact that I was twenty-five years old,
and still single and a college graduate, and whether this was to be
all of my life and really what for.

I was thinking about the meanings of democracy, and that sort
of thing, but it doesn't have any meaning to a man in a situation
such as that. The only thing that meant anything to me was: as
long as I was there and my two brothers were not, then maybe we
could get this mess over with before any more of the family had
to be dragged into this situation.

I had a conversation with Private Mouser, in which I relayed to
him my fears of my competence as a sergeant leading men into
battle for the first time – whether I was actually equal to the task.
I remember very vividly his response to me:

'Well, sergeant, the only way this war is ever going to end –
we're going to have to cross the Channel and we're going to have
to end it. It's obvious this is the only route, and the quicker we
get at it, I suppose the better everyone will be off. I want you to
know that of all the men that I have trained with here in this
organization, I would rather go with you into combat than
anyone I know.'

I treasure that remark and it helped me at a time of great
doubt.

Anthony Duke, the young captain of LCT 530, was ravaged by waves
of self-doubt and pangs of pity for himself and his comrades. Like all
brave but untested soldiers his greatest dread – far more troubling
than the prospect of dying – was the fear of acquitting himself less
than honourably.

I know the thoughts that kept coming through my head: when we get back, get back from what? Would there be a lot of bloodshed? Would I get hit? Would we be torpedoed? Or dive-bombed? In my youth I'd seen a lot of movies about people facing warfare, and flashes of how they'd reacted kept coming into my mind.

The main thing I did was to try and get as close as I could to the men of my own crew and talk to them: about home, about doing a good job when the chips were down.

The chaplains worked hard that night, listening to men who needed to share their fears – of dying, of leaving behind their wives, their children, their grieving mothers.

I am sure no one had slept or could go to sleep, said Wilfred Bennett, a Canadian rifleman bound for Juno Beach. Reverend Horton, our padre, came by at midnight and passed out air mail forms for those who wished to write a letter home. Now, how could one write at a time such as this? Emotions were running high that night, and were truly mixed. Well, some wrote letters, some did not. I did. Most of that night, my thoughts were of my mother and my sister. I knew they were all alone that night in Manitou, Manitoba, a small village 100 miles southwest of Winnipeg. I told them in my letter as soon as we got Jerry on the run, I would write them a longer letter. I told them I was putting my trust in my Savior Jesus Christ, and prayed he would be near them always and keep them in his care. I closed that letter with much love and many tears.

A special mass was held on many ships for the Roman Catholics. For some of the soldiers on board ship, the unusual nature of the proceedings served only to underline the awful seriousness of their circumstances. 'Father Edward Waters gave us General Absolution,' said Louis Quirk. 'This eliminated confession so we could receive Holy Communion. This is only done in dire situations.' Captain Richard Fahey drew the same conclusion, but at the same time felt a twinge of ecumenical sympathy for his non-Catholic comrades-in-arms.

The chaplain aboard ship announced that he would like for all the Catholic soldiers on the ship to gather on the deck so he could give them what is known as General Absolution without personally hearing their confessions – presuming of course, that these men would privately confess their sin with due contrition to some priest at more convenient date. I went on deck and accepted the General Absolution, knowing full well that it was just what I needed. But I was concerned all the while about what was going to happen to all those Protestants, Jews and atheists that did not have this privilege extended to them. It's going to be so lonely up there. I am not so sure I want to miss my friends, all those good guys that were with me.

He need not have worried about the Jewish contingent. There were many Jewish Americans in the invasion force, and they were making peace with God in their own way.

I was one of the Jewish officers on board ship, said Aaron Caplan. There was probably one or two others. We had no Jewish chaplain with us. Father Mike Donovan, the Catholic Division Chaplain, asked if I would perform the service for our Jewish boys on board ship and this was carried out.

While the Christian soldiers prayed to be delivered from evil, and the Jewish fighting men covered their eyes and whispered the ancient Hebrew words of the Shema Yisrael (Hear O Israel, the Lord our God, the Lord is One), the agnostics hedged their bets as usual.

I wasn't doing very well in the poker game so, not wishing to miss touching all the bases, I thought I'd better go and listen to the chaplain, said David Thomas, a US Army doctor. As I was sitting down in the last row and on the only seat left in the house, Chaplain Elder says 'Now, the Lord is not particularly interested in those who only turn to him in times of need.' I thought 'Gee, he must have seen me come in.' So I got up and left again. I still didn't do very well in the poker game, which didn't do my morale any good for what was coming up for us.

KIDDING MR HITLER

As the fleet steamed in Indian file through Germany's offshore minefield, the airborne troops were making their way to the drop zones at the extremities of tomorrow's battle front, and bombers were heading inland. Ralph Steinway, a US Army sergeant en route to Omaha Beach, was in mid-Channel, and saw them 'flying in a formation that looked like a checkerboard: each plane seemed to have its own piece of sky.'

Most of the bombers had specific invasion targets, but some were on workaday missions to obliterate German lines of communication and to batter troop concentrations. The Allied planners did not want to suggest to the Germans that this was anything but an ordinary night in the struggle to destroy Nazism.

Much thought had been given to ways of confusing the Germans, trying to make them believe that something other than the full-scale invasion of Europe was about to unfold on the beaches of Normandy. Bombing of the Pas de Calais continued on the night of the 5th, reinforcing the already strongly held German belief that the invasion, when it came, would arrive by the shortest route across the channel.

In a slightly facetious but highly effective sleight of hand, the Allies dropped stuffed dummies by parachute behind German lines. The dummies looked convincing enough as they floated down. They were adorned with firecrackers which went off when they hit the ground and made German garrisons believe they were under attack from real paratroopers. Many a German was pinned down for vital minutes by an inanimate scarecrow decorated with a handful of fireworks. The confusion continued even after one of the little popping manikins was captured and presented to German commanders: it made them believe that reports of British and American paratroopers actually referred to the straw dummies.

A still more ingenious deception was played out at sea. Aeroplanes flying tightly choreographed patterns dropped strips of aluminium foil or 'chaff', codenamed Window. These strips were cut to a length that exactly corresponded to the frequency of German radar. The effect of releasing the chaff into the wind at the right moment and in the right pattern was to create the illusion of large numbers of ships on the German operators' screens. Two 'ghost fleets' were conjured out of the air – one ostensibly heading for Le Havre, and the other for Boulogne.

Flight Lieutenant RA Hine was one of the men involved in this consummate piece of trickery.

I was a navigator in No 218 Squadron (3 Group) then stationed at Woolfox Lodge. Our Mark 3 Stirlings were the first to have been fitted with G-H, a highly accurate bombing device for which the transmitters were carried in each aircraft. We had already trained extensively and used G-H for successful attacks on marshalling yards in France in the softening up process.

However, for D-Day a very special use for the accurate flying allowed by G-H was planned, nothing less than an air-mounted false invasion of the Pas de Calais. For this the boffins had designed a special type of 'Window', which had to be thrown out from each aircraft with great precision in time and position.

To obtain the greatest accuracy, the crew was doubled up for navigators, bomb-aimers and pilots, so easing the strain of the intense concentration needed by these crew members. The job of one navigator was to keep the aircraft exactly on predetermined run-in courses, consisting of wide, parallel orbits. Since the position lines were arcs of a circle, this meant constant small corrections to keep the aircraft within a few yards of its proper position. The other navigator had a separate G-H tube and determined the stop and start positions of the orbits. These co-ordinates had to be reset on each orbit moving nearer to the French coast each time. One bomb aimer had a stop watch to time the precise intervals for the Window dropping and he tapped the other bomb aimer on the shoulder to signal the points. I believe we had seven aircraft which would give the impression on the radar screens of the waiting Germans that 14 lines of ships were approaching at a speed of 7 knots. We understood that one or two radar stations had been purposely 'missed' in the air attacks preceding D-Day so that our phantom fleet would be spotted by the enemy.

If the wind was too high (I believe it was over thirty miles per hour) the Window was likely to be scattered, with disastrous results. In the event, we took off in our usual aircraft with my pilot Flight Lieutenant King as captain. It all went like clockwork but the fatigue at the end of the operation was enormous. We flew home on a course that took us over the real armada bound for Normandy, a never-to-be-forgotten sight.

The next morning the teleprinters carried a message from

Bomber Command C-in-C congratulating us on the success of the operation. The message said that intercepted signals from the German side showed that great confusion had been caused and for a considerable time they did not order in their back-up troops because they were uncertain where the invasion was really going to be. We felt that if we had helped to cause this uncertainty, even for an hour or two, it must have been of critical value to our troops going in to the beaches.

THE GAME'S AFOOT

Some men managed to sleep during the crossing, but all were awake in the small hours of the morning. Now they began their final preparations. First came breakfast, then the long process of dressing for battle.

> **We were awakened at 2:30am and we had chow: wieners, beans, coffee and doughnuts,** said Harry Bare of the US 116th Infantry. By 4:00am the ship had stopped, and all the men climbed up on deck. It seemed strange, but the men seemed a lot different, more cheerful than they were before. There was a lot of handshaking, 'See you in Berlin,' and 'Watch out for those French girls,' and kidding like that.
>
> Our equipment consisted of impregnated OD uniform, treated to prevent gas, our assault jackets containing four fragmentary grenades, one smoke grenade, and one phosphorous grenade. Each of us had one quarter pound of TNT, and sixty rounds of M-1 ammo plus three bandoliers around our necks.

Anthony Duke, the thoughtful LST captain, was carrying men of the British Eighth Army – the Desert Rats. These were his impressions on 5 June as his ship took its place in the vast echelon.

> God, I'll never forget the feeling that welled up in me as I viewed the ships headed more or less in the same direction, coming on in endless columns from all over England and converging at that point south of the Isle of Wight. It was a funnel-like mass, headed for France – huge, overwhelming numbers. A feeling of power there on the water. Power that was going to be unleashed. The enormity and complexity of the operation was almost too

great to absorb. And yet there we were, moving along, almost creeping through the sea towards the enemy. It was a sort of quiet throughout the ship, a quiet that was eerie in a way.

Gradually, all the innumerable columns of ships and their destroyer escorts and the minesweepers up on the vanguard, the battleships and cruisers came looming behind us, well behind us, on the horizon. We could only see the big ships every once in a while. Finally, they dropped way behind us and we couldn't see them at all. The ships around us were of every size and description. And there were the Liberty ships and all the other freighters in columns, and this whole wave of ships in columns began to flow towards France. How, in God's name, could it be a secret, could THIS be a secret from the enemy. I found myself looking skyward frequently, fully expecting to see enemy planes diving to attack the oncoming gathering of this endless fleet that stretched as far as I could see on all sides. You got a feeling of living in a dream, and you had to keep looking around to see if what you thought you were seeing was for real.

Ships, ships, ships, everywhere, everywhere you looked.

Everyone who ventured on deck could see this same wonderfully martial sight, and every man who did was moved by it. Elsewhere in the grand armada, Major CK King of the British East Yorkshire Regiment succumbed to the sheer Shakespearean grandeur of the moment, and read a chunk of *Henry V* to his company over the tannoy as the LCA went in. His chosen passage: 'And you, good yeoman, whose limbs were made in England, show us here the mettle of your pasture. The game's afoot: Follow your spirit, and upon this charge cry "God for Harry, England, and Saint George!"'

Captain Duke was inspired to address the troops on his ship in his own words. Before he did so, the British colonel on board offered a word of advice on the subject of addressing English soldiers, particularly these English soldiers.

I'd planned to give them quite a speech, said Captain Duke. I think that Colonel Givens had the insight to recognize that. He'd been in North Africa fighting against General Rommel. He came up to me and he put his hand on my shoulder, and he said, 'Careful young fellow. Most of my men have seen the worst of desert warfare and a good many of them were in France and evacuated through Dunkirk. So I'd advise you to go easy, go quick, and don't get dramatic or emotional.'

I took his lead, and I made a very simple announcement. But believe me, my own emotions were thumping, straining inside of me as I spoke. I realized later that I would have made a real ass out of myself if I'd let go with exactly how I did feel. He saved me from considerable embarrassment. I'll never forget Colonel Givens.

It was a kind and fatherly act, but no more than Duke had himself done for the terrified boy sailor who had come to him the previous day. The time for words was almost over now anyway – almost, but not quite. In the last hours before the assault began, every man involved in Overlord was read a short address from General Eisenhower. This is what the Supreme Commander said to his troops on the eve of one of the greatest and most important battles in the history of warfare.

Soldiers, Sailors and Airmen of the Allied Expeditionary Force!
You are about to embark upon the Great Crusade, toward which we have striven these many months. The eyes of liberty-loving people everywhere march with you. In company with our brave Allies and brothers in arms on other Fronts, you will bring about the destruction of the German war machine, the elimination of Nazi tyranny over the oppressed peoples of Europe, and security for ourselves in a free world.
Your task will not be an easy one. Your enemy is well trained, well equipped and battle hardened. He will fight savagely.
But this is the year 1944! Much has happened since the Nazi triumphs of 1940–41. The United Nations have inflicted upon the Germans great defeats, in open battle, man to man. Our air offensive has seriously reduced their strength in the air and their capacity to wage war on the ground. Our Home Fronts have given us an overwhelming superiority in weapons and munitions of war, and placed at our disposal great reserves of trained fighting men. The tide has turned! The free men of the world are marching together to Victory!
I have full confidence in your courage and devotion to duty and

skill in battle. We will accept nothing less than full Victory! Good luck! And let us beseech the blessing of Almighty God upon this great and noble undertaking.

As his message was being read to the men on the high seas, Eisenhower himself was at his desk in Southwick House, his headquarters in Portsmouth. In the rain-filled afternoon he had composed a communique for the press – one he desperately hoped that he would not have to release. He did not dictate it. He wrote it in his own hand and, in the great strain of the moment, dated it 5 July. It reads as follows:

> Our landings in the Cherbourg-Havre area have failed to gain a satisfactory foothold and I have withdrawn the troops. My decision to attack at this time and place was based upon the best information available. The troops, the air force and the navy did all that bravery and devotion to duty could do.
> If any blame or fault attaches to the attempt it is mine alone.

3
TAKING UTAH

Colonel Howard 'Jumpy' Johnson, it was agreed by everyone who knew him, was one tough cookie. Once the word came down that the invasion was on, the commander of the US 501st PIR (Parachute Infantry Regiment) went to give his men a few words of encouragement. Parker Alford remembered the speech vividly:

> He came roaring into the hangar in his Jeep. He had pearl-handled .45s on each hip and knives in his belt, and many hand grenades on his person. He gave us a short pep-talk, grabbed a dagger from his boot and said: 'Before I see the dawn of another day I want to stick this knife into the meanest, dirtiest, filthiest, Nazi in all of Europe.'

The young paratroopers bellowed and clapped their approval. The colonel made a theatrical exit in his jeep, and the men were given the order to board their aeroplanes. All of them were carrying so much gear that they could barely get up the steps. Like old ladies climbing on to buses, these superfit young men wheezed and puffed their way on board, eased along by the helping hands of the ground crew and the man behind.

They had all done many jumps in training – 'I had never landed in an airplane until after my thirteenth jump,' said Robert Flory of the 506th PIR – but none of them had ever parachuted with so much gear. The extra weight they were carrying meant that the troopers were more in danger than usual of breaking an ankle on landing. Here is what Robert Flory took with him on to the waiting C-47 Dakota:

> First of all, our jumpsuits. The pants had one large pocket on each side, plus the regular two front and two back pockets. The jacket, which reached below our hips, had two side pockets and two breast pockets. The jumpsuit was olive drab, and our jump

General Eisenhower reviewed the men of the 101st Airborne just before they emplaned. He spoke with men and shook their hands. In his car on the way back he said to his driver: 'It's very hard to look a soldier in the eye when you fear that you are sending him to his death.'

boots were Cordovan brown leather and laced half-way up our calves. A plastic helmet liner and steel helmet with chin straps. Our parachutes were called the T-5 assembly. The main chute was camouflage nylon, twenty-eight feet in diameter. The reserve chute was white nylon, twenty-two feet in diameter. The harness consisted of two leg straps which came between our legs and fastened on each hip. The chest strap fastened on the center of our chest. The reserve chute fastened to the chest strap. The T-5 assembly weighed about sixty pounds.

My equipment consisted of the following: an M-1 rifle with a nine-inch bayonet, two bandoliers of M-1 ammo, four hand grenades, a first aid kit, a jump knife and holster attached to my right calf, a thirty-foot jump rope in case I landed in a tree, a musette bag containing three K-rations and three B-rations, a carton of Camel cigarettes, a gas mask, a canteen, and a small

Bible sent to me by my sister. And believe it or not, two extra pairs of socks and a change of underwear.

At the last minute the American airborne troops were also issued with little tin clickers that they called crickets. They were told that the crickets were intended to be used to identify friends in the darkness: one click of the cricket was to be answered by two. No clicks, and you shoot.

THE AIRBORNE ALOFT

The confident mood instilled by Jumpy Johnson dissipated somewhat as the paratroopers of the 101st Division (called the 'Screaming Eagles') and the 82nd Division (known as the 'All-American') heaved themselves into their planes. Roger Airgood, a C-47 pilot, watched his passengers climb aboard. 'We had worked with the airborne before and they were cocky, unruly characters. But this time they were very serious.' Parker Alford, who only a few minutes before had so appreciated the colonel's warm-up routine, was now feeling the creeping cold of fear: 'The moon was bright and the feeling was lonely. I looked around the airplane and saw some kid across the aisle who grinned. I tried to grin back, but my face was frozen.'

The officers were feeling the tension too. Robert Flory witnessed a well-respected lieutenant give in to a flash of temper before take-off:

Before suiting up, we had camouflaged our faces by smearing charcoal or chocolate on our cheeks, noses, and foreheads. I remember Lieutenant Minton striking one of his men who had not darkened his face. That man had to go to the exhaust of one of the plane's engines and collect carbon to cover his face.

Shortly after 11 o'clock the planes started taking off. I'll never forget the roar of hundreds of planes taking off and circling to get into formation. When we entered the plane, we were issued Dramamine pills to ward off air sickness. I threw mine away and was glad later that I had. Many of the men became drowsy or uncoordinated because of them.

It was a cool, damp night, with clouds that skimmed the moon frequently. I got up once to go to look out the door. I got the immediate impression that every C-47 in the American Air Corps was on the way to Normandy. As far as I could see in any direction, there were troop transports. I found out later that 490 planes carried 6,600 paratroopers of the 101st Airborne Division.

It was not easy for the pilots to remain in tight formation as they made their way to the south coast of England and out over the blank and featureless sea.

> The plan for getting the troops to the drop zones in Normandy was the most complex and ambitious mission we had ever faced, said Roger Airgood. There were several changes in altitude and direction over the course. There were no checkpoints to aid in maintaining the desired course. The pathfinders who were supposed to be on the DZ did not reach the area and no signals were emitted.
>
> Our serial of six waves of nine planes each was led by Lieutenant Colonel Kreyssler of the 79th Troop Carrier Squadron followed by the 80th TCS and 85th TCS. Everything was working fine until we got to the last light-boat, at which time we were to turn off the amber down light and reduce the formation lights to half power. The pilot flying on Kreyssler's left wing turned off the formation lights so low they were not visible. At that time we could see nothing of Kreyssler's wingman from the left seat, so I flew from the right seat since I could see the exhaust stack glow and the phantom outline of the plane. We maintained our position flying as tight a formation as possible. When entering an unexpected cloud bank we continued on without any appreciable difference in visibility.
>
> We maintained the course and when coming out of the cloud bank we could see tracers coming up from many angles. The lines of tracers arched over us as we flew under them. There was a tremendous racket such as experienced when flying through hail. I had very few glimpses of the ground since I had to keep the outline of the plane in sight.

The flak was troubling many of the more inexperienced pilots. They began to duck and weave to avoid it rather than hold their course and fly straight through it. They were supposed to slow down as they approached the drop zones, so that the paratroopers would not be too roughly buffeted as they left the plane, and so that they had a reasonable chance of landing close together. But some pilots were so spooked that they actually speeded up. The paratroopers were well aware of how fast they were going, and grew alarmed when the red light came on – signifying that there were four minutes to jump time – and the aircraft were still hurtling through the skies at top speed.

Airgood could not slow to jump speed until the leader of his wing did so, and he was as worried as his passengers:

> When Kreyssler did slow down it was too sudden. Wingmen had to cut power and hold the nose up to keep from over-running the lead planes, which in turn was followed by a blast of power to keep the plane from stalling out. The result was that when we got the green light, we were flying at about 105 mph and pulling a lot of power. The paratroopers went out in a terrific prop blast, which was the last thing we wanted to happen.

In hundreds of planes above Normandy, men were tugging each other to their feet and hooking up to the static line, waiting for the signal to go. 'The light turned green and we started to pile out the door into the darkness,' said Trooper Edward Barnes. 'There is no sweeter feeling than that rude jerking, letting you know your chute has opened.' Gerard Dillon, as platoon commander, was first off his plane and he was taking no chances about where he was going to land.

> I told the men to forget the green light and not to push me out of the plane until I jumped, because I was going to be looking to see where we were going. It was about 1.15am when the light came on. I was looking down and could see a river underneath me, just ahead of the plane. We did not jump for about five seconds, but as soon as we passed the river, I went out of the plane. My whole platoon jumped when I did. We landed on high ground, about one mile northwest of Sainte Mère Eglise. The whole platoon assembled without the loss of a single man.

At this point the attention of the Germans was still directed mostly at the endless waves of aeroplanes above them, rather than the paratroopers amassing on the ground. Hundreds of C-47s were dropping their human cargo, then turning great circles in the sky and heading back for the relative safety of the coast. Charles Bortzfield was a pilot with the 100th Troop Carrier Squadron. His night began on an airfield in Somerset, and ended in a hospital bed on the south coast.

About 23.00 hours our engines were started. Over a hundred planes were lined up halfway down the runway and around the perimeter of the field on the taxiways. Hundreds of propellers spun furiously as they awaited the go signal. The signal came and two abreast the C-47s roared down the runway, then another two, then another.

Finally it was our turn. I was in my position between the pilot and co-pilot. Lieutenant Worl pushed the throttles full forward. We were rolling, tail up, we were airborne. The air was a little rough at this point from all the prop wash from the planes up front ahead of us. We dipped a wing once in a while, mushed a little bit, but finally we levelled out into smooth flight. We were a formation of nine planes wide, three V-groups across. Later on we would form up with other groups. I guess our formation was a hundred miles long, maybe a thousand airplanes or more. We were on our way to France.

I went back into the passenger compartment where the lieutenant in charge of the paratroopers could confer with me briefly on what he expected of me. He wanted to know how far we had to go and where he was at all times. It wasn't easy to converse back there because the jump door was off and the roar of the engine and the wind noise was very loud. I went back and forth between the pilots and paratrooper lieutenant a number of times as we were streaking across the English Channel.

As we approached the French coast, I had to take up my position right across from the jump door and next to the paratrooper lieutenant. At this time, I had to take off my helmet and put on my headsets for the intercom radio. I would be in communication with the co-pilot. If the signals light system would be shot out, I would have to yell to the paratrooper when to jump.

We flew into France. I could see the tracers of ground fire floating up towards us. Search lights were probing the skies trying to give the German gunners targets to shoot at. At about

01.00 hours on June 6 we reached our drop zone with our load of fighting men. All of the sudden, I was down on one knee. I was holding on to a stringer with my left hand, and I had the mike in my right hand. The red light came on for the paratroopers. The paratrooper lieutenant ordered his men to hook up to the static line, a steel cable on the top of the airplane.

The green light came on, and the paratroopers jumped out into the dark night. One yelled to me as he passed by 'Are you hit?' I said, 'I think so.' 'Me too,' he replied, and out the door he went.

They were all gone now. It was my job to pull in the static lines, but I felt too weak to do so, so I got out of my flak suit and hobbled forward to the navigator's compartment. I sat down across from Sergeant Small, our radio operator. He looked at me and said I was hit. I told him I couldn't pull in the static lines and he would have to go back and try to pull them in. He went back, but he didn't have enough strength to pull them in by himself, so I yelled to Lieutenant Stewart, our co-pilot, if he would go back and the two of them pulled the static lines in.

Sergeant Small came back, cut away my jacket on my left arm, and cut off my right pant leg and applied sulfa powder to my wounds. We were back over the English Channel now headed back to England. Lieutenant Worl came to look me over and wanted to give me a shot of morphine. I declined the offer because I was afraid we still might have to abandon our aircraft. I could smell 100 octane gasoline inside the cabin, and this is not a normal condition, and if we had to use a parachute, I didn't want to be doped up. The left engine on the plane was very rough, was not running right at all, so I guess it took some flak also.

Sergeant Small got us clearance to land at the first air base we could find, because we were afraid we couldn't get back to our home base safely. We started our approach to the base. The pilots lowered the landing gear, and yelled back to me that they had no brakes, because the hydraulic pressure was gone. I asked them if they had a green light to land, and they said yes, so I said, 'Land it,' hoping that we had a long runway and could roll to a stop. Anyway, we were lucky and landed safely.

An ambulance came and took me to a first aid station. From there, I was sent to a hospital. I was taken to an operating room where they patched up a broken right leg and four holes in my left arm and hand. I was a real celebrity at this hospital, because at this moment I was their only patient. All their patients were evacuated and they were waiting for D-Day casualties. The doctors really interrogated me, because I was their first troop carrier patient, and now they knew the invasion was on.

I was probably back in the ward by 6am when the boys were hitting the beaches. I was told later my plane never flew again – they used it for spare parts.

SCREAMING EAGLES GO IN

For most paratroopers the jump into France did not go smoothly. Pilots were confused as to their exact locations. Many of them were miles from the intended drop zones when the green light went on. The high-speed leap scattered sticks of troopers so far and wide that they could not find even the man who had jumped before or after. For many paratroopers even the short and gentle descent to the ground turned into a terrifying journey.

I couldn't see much of the ground, it was more or less of a blur, said Frank Brumbaugh, a radar operator. But I watched all these tracers and shell bursts and everything in the air around me, and I watched one stream of tracers – obviously a machine gun – which looked like it was going to come directly at me. Intellectually, I knew that I could not be seen in the air under this camouflage chute. But that stream of tracers came directly up at me. I lost three shroud lines that were clipped by bullets from my parachute, and it obviously had punctured some holes in it.

In an obviously futile gesture (but normal, I guess) I spread my legs widely and grabbed with both hands at my groin, as if to protect myself. Those machine gun bullets traced up the inside of one leg, missed my groin, traced down the inside of the other leg, splitting my pants on the insides of both legs, dropping two cartons of Pall Mall cigarettes to the soil of France.

As paratrooper Ray Aebischer waited for the green light he could hear bullets 'coming up from the ground, drumming like hail through the wings and sides of our plane.' He was carrying the heaviest load, and he stood at the open door of the plane. It was swerving and jinking like a tailback on an upfield run and travelling much too fast. Aebischer's platoon leader was directly in front of him.

Seconds before the green light came on, the platoon leader took a bullet across his upper lip. Never faltering, he went out the door, and the rest of us followed. I never saw him again.

As I exited the door, the chute deployed. The jolt from the opening shock was more intense than usual. At the same second the chute opened, my leg pack broke loose from the straps around my leg. All of my equipment, except one trench knife, and a canteen of water attached to my cartridge belt, went plummeting to the ground, never to be seen again. I was on the ground a few seconds later, landing with a thud on some concrete in a church yard. I remember removing my parachute, grabbing my trench knife, and slowly moving toward the church door, thinking that if I could get inside I would have some security and some time to collect my thoughts.

The church bells were constantly ringing, drowning out any hopes of communicating with other members of my unit. Not seeing any movement in the moonlight by anybody, friend or enemy, I felt very much alone. Trying the church door, I found it locked. Not wanting to attract attention or to be a living target for some German soldier, I crawled around the church to the rear, then along a high wall which surrounded the church grounds. A machine gun was firing down the street. As another wave of friendly aircraft flew over, the machine gun was directed toward the planes. This appeared to be a good time to make a run for it, crossing the street and into an orchard.

As the planes flew off in the distance, the machine gun began firing down the street again. One man whose chute had gotten caught high in the trees in the church yard, was hanging there lifeless. He had either been shot while descending or upon being trapped in the tree, high above the ground. Another man who landed in the street never did get up. My only thought all along was how to defend myself against an enemy soldier without any weapon but this one knife. I kept a firm grip on it, realizing that I would have to be quick to survive.

Robert Flory, like Aebischer and dozens of other paratroopers, was alone from the second he stepped into the black nothing of the night sky.

> I honestly don't remember the opening shock. I remember the sky was being criss-crossed with tracer bullets and flak. The noise was terrible. I looked down and immediately went into a state of shock. I was over water. My first thought was that that SOB pilot had dropped us over the English Channel. I looked to my right and saw a herd of dairy cows grazing. About that time I landed in water up to my chest. I was in a salt marsh. It seemed like an eternity before I could get out of my harness and wade to dry land. All this time, the gunfire was deafening and the planes kept going over. I saw one plane take a direct hit and explode in mid-air. Every man in that plane died a quick and merciful death.

Flory was lucky to land on his feet; many paratroopers who came down on their backs drowned in just two or three feet of floodwater because they could not haul themselves up into a sitting position.

It was no bad thing for a paratrooper to be alone for a minute or two – at least he could undo the cumbersome buckle on the parachute, and get his gun at the ready. Edward Jeziorski of the 541st PIR was unfortunate enough to find company as soon as he touched France. 'I slammed into the ground and I was immediately pinned down by machine-gun fire. There was no way to raise up. Every time I tried to turn, the machine gun would open up.' Jeziorski had landed in a spot where he was silhouetted against the burning wreckage of a C-47. The German gunner could see every desperate twitch of his body. Like Gulliver in Lilliput, he was held flat to the ground by threads he could not see; every time he tried to move, more strings of gunfire arched over his body.

> I finally was able to bring my right leg up close enough to where I could get my jump knife out of my boot. I cut the harness loose. I cut the belly band off and I also cut the emergency off. I couldn't get any of the darn hardware loose, I couldn't get the bugger unhooked. In the mean time, this guy is still shooting. Every time I make a move, he's letting a burst or two go. When I finally cut loose, I rolled over in a little depression. I had my hand on my rifle and I was able to squeeze off a couple of rounds. I'm sure I

didn't hit him but, by golly, it got his attention.

A little bit after that, there was a good deal of thrashing going on the other side of the hedgerow, where I was. The sound was coming on; something or somebody was coming on through the underbrush. I still had my rifle real tight and I just lay prone and pointed it at the sound. When the sound got very close I said 'Flash'; counter-sign 'Thunder' came back. It was my assistant gunner, Grover Boyce. There were two of us together, now. It seemed like a better world all of a sudden. In the next half hour we were joined by Tony Guzzon and a first aid man, Andy Mander.

Around 4am we located a parapack and believe me, we were fortunate. One of the packs we opened had a machine gun. We got it out and a couple of boxes of ammo. We really felt pretty good having that thing in our hands.

Everywhere paratroopers were wandering around in the dark, looking for the rest of their platoon, or indeed for anyone who was on their side. They were spread over a vast area of countryside, most of which consisted of identical hedgerows or featureless floodplains. Often they had no idea where they were.

Some chanced upon another trooper, and so had the comfort of numbers. One of these ad hoc units consisted almost entirely of top brass. Parker Alford attached himself to a group of thirty paratroopers which included General Maxwell Taylor, commander of the 101st, as well as one full colonel and three lieutenant colonels, four lieutenants, and several non-commissioned officers. General Taylor cast an eye over his mixed bag of underlings and remarked dryly: 'Never in the field of human conflict have so few been commanded by so many.'

Harold Canyon of the 82nd had a difficult time getting out of the plane, and when he did finally arrive on the ground he came immediately under fire – first from the Germans, then from one of his own men. His experience was typical of the confusion of the moonlit battle. This is how he spent the night:

I was number six man in the stick. A stick is one string of men that jump on one command. Normally, a C-47 maximum stick would be sixteen men. Going towards France, there were twenty-two in our stick.

I remember how helpless I felt at the time while sitting in the airplane. There was absolutely nothing you could do to improve your situation in the event that you were fired upon. Absolutely nothing you could do. You were completely helpless.

It took considerable effort to get up. I hooked up, and then we started out the door, and just as I approached the door, the top of the airplane opened up. It had been hit by some type of explosive shell. As I turned into the doorway, the plane started a right wing dip, as it was going into its death spiral. It took everything I had to get over the threshold and out as the threshold was coming up. I managed to roll out. It seems to me the threshold was just a little bit more than chest high as I rolled over and got out. I was the last man out of the plane.

When I felt the opening shock of the chute, more by habit than anything, I looked up to check the chute and I remember seeing clusters of tracers going through it. I then reached for my trench knife, but having taped it to the sheath, I couldn't get it loose. I hit the ground with one leg up trying to get the trench knife out and, fortunately, didn't break anything.

I landed on the ground, and lay there momentarily, fully expecting a German to run up and stick me with a bayonet. But nothing happened, which quite surprised me. I had landed in front of a German bunker, which was about thirty yards away, but someone who had hit the ground before me dropped a gammon grenade on it and put it out of order.

I immediately grabbed my trench knife, and with all my strength, I tore it loose from the tape that was holding it and started cutting all the straps that were binding me. I grabbed my carbine in one hand, trench knife in the other, and I ran for the hedgerow, dove over it and lay against the bank for a short while.

I saw two Germans approaching on the other side of the hedgerow. We had orders not to load our weapons until we were organized, so my carbine was not loaded. As the Germans approached, I fully intended to let them go on by, but just in case, I unscrewed the cap on my gammon grenade. When they got just opposite me, they noticed me and ducked. I sat there and waited as one of them started slowly rising. I saw the top of his head, and when I saw his shoulders, I then threw the gammon grenade, and he at that time fired. I had not seen the rifle, but the bullet passed through the crotch of my outside pair of pants. The muzzle blast knocked me out and when I came to, my face was in the bank, in the dirt, my mouth was open, blood and spit was trickling out. I could hear, but I couldn't move. I thought I was dead, and that this was the way people died.

I heard moaning on the other side of the hedgerow, so I knew that my grenade had had some effect. While on the airplane, I had some English coins in my pocket, so I took out all the English coins and I lined them around the outside of the C2 under the cloth skirt of the gammon grenade, making a fragmentation grenade. Those two Germans would have been buried with British coins imbedded in them.

After a while, it got quiet on the other side of the hedgerow. I don't know how long I was out to begin with, and I don't know how long it took before I could move. I heard and saw someone approaching on my side of the hedgerow, and it turned out to be a couple of paratroopers, and I told them that my ears were ringing, and I couldn't hear. Anyway, we talked for a while and noticed someone else approaching us. They ducked down behind me. I knelt down and waited the approach of this other person, and when he got within range, I shouted, 'Flash!' He came back with 'Thunder!' and I thought that everything was OK.

But the next thing I saw was a ball of fire, and a bullet hit my helmet between the eyes and glanced off. Fortunately, I have a small head that fits quite deeply in the helmet. I rolled to my left and started swearing, and the next bullet caught me in the hip pocket, and went through a couple of layers of two paper maps I had folded in my left hip pocket, ODs. He then quit firing when he heard my swearing. Swearing turned out to be one of the best passwords. No one can swear in American like an American, or in English like an Englishman.

We talked for a minute, and then we saw some movement off to one side, somewhat in the same direction this person had come. So we laid down and waited. The next time I looked up, I was all alone again. The guy had moved on, and it was about that time that I decided it was kind of useless to move around in the dark, as it was too difficult to identify anyone.

I noticed a kind of a brush-filled gully some short distance away, so I ran for that and dove into it. I was laying on my back in the dry brush, my trench knife was under me, my carbine was off to my left, unloaded when I heard two Germans approaching. You could tell Germans by the amount of leather they wore. You could hear it creak as they walked.

They stood over me and looked down at me. There wasn't anything I could do, just play dead. I waited. I had to go to the bathroom very badly, and I went. It's quite possible the Germans mistook what they saw for blood. After a while, I opened my eyes and saw they had gone, so I crawled deeper down to the bottom of the gully and lay there and later went to sleep. While laying there, I heard a glider coming in through the trees. It seemed like it would never stop. It must have had something heavy in it, because it just kept crashing through the trees.

I went to sleep, and then when it was daylight, I woke up and heard someone approaching. Just as the person got within about five or six feet from me, I challenged him with 'Flash', and he took one more step, and when he took that one more step, I saw his paratrooper boot through an opening in the foliage, and I looked up and saw his face and recognized him and he had a very perplexed look on his face – he was trying to remember what he was supposed to say, but couldn't remember. And I hollered out, 'That's OK, Malcolm. I recognize you.' He and I embraced each other and jumped up and down. We were so happy to see somebody. He and I then started to move in the direction in which we thought our objective was.

We met three other troopers and the five of us approached a hedgerow. As we looked over the hedgerow, there was a German truck with two Germans sitting in it. One of the guys threw a gammon grenade and hit the windshield. It exploded, the Germans tumbled out, one on each side of the truck, and began running up the road. We were firing at them, but in the excitement we forgot to aim. They kept running and we kept firing, and they reached a turn in the road and continued on out of our range.

Then someone threw an incendiary grenade at the truck and set it on fire, and it burned with black smoke spiralling up into the air. One of the boys stated that there was a German battalion approaching down this road that the two Germans had run up, so the five of us decided that we would ambush this German battalion, and we crossed over into the hedgerow, and lined up along this road. We spread out far enough to what we thought was far enough to cover a battalion of Germans. All we had were carbines. There were five of us with five carbines, and I think we were all out of gammon grenades. I still had my two fragmentation grenades. We waited and waited and suddenly, German machine gun opened up behind us. We were taken completely by surprise. We vacated the area in a hurry. One of the boys got hit in the leg, and we were helping him out of the area. We never got to ambush our German battalion. I think it was them who ambushed us.

We continued on looking for other troopers. We reached a point where we couldn't carry the wounded guy any further, and it seemed kind of hopeless anyway, as we didn't know where we were going really, and we didn't know whether we were improving our position or not. So, we figured he would be just as well off if we hid him in the brush, and if possible, we could get back to him later, whenever we found our unit.

About a hundred yards further on we joined a group of about thirty men. There was a sniper firing on us, and it hit one of the boys in the belly, and he was laying there. There was nothing we could do for him, and we remembered the story at that time, that if he lived an hour, he would live. Well, one of the other guys decided to dispatch the sniper. He went over the bank toward the sniper, hit the dirt, and when he did, the sniper killed him.

Someone then told us that there were a group of our boys stranded on an island and that the Germans had them pretty well surrounded, so we decided to go join them. We went for quite a while before we saw them, and they saw us. But there was quite an open space in between. We stayed where we were and waited for them to come to us. They had to cross this opening, and the Germans had a machine gun, zeroed in on the opening. As they ran across the opening, the machine gunner fired at them. I borrowed a pair of field glasses from someone and looked over and located the machine gun, and then I went away from the troops so I wouldn't draw fire toward where everyone was congregated. I started shooting at the machine gun, and he started shooting at me, and while we were so occupied, the boys on the island were able to come across and join us. My carbine got so hot I couldn't even see the sights anymore, it was smoking, but the machine gun quit firing altogether.

We were roughly about a hundred strong now, just about company strength. Our senior officer there was my battalion commander, Lieutenant Colonel Shanly. We began hiking toward our objective, which was a bridge across the river, somewhere near Sainte Mère Eglise. The Germans shelled us for a while, but they would fire all their guns at once, and when you heard them coming in, you hit the ground, and after they quit exploding, you could move away from the area.

We kept marching that night. We moved, and then we would rest, and then we would move some more. Another guy and I fell asleep, and when we woke up it was daylight. We were surprised, because we were still alive. We went in the direction we were hiking, and it turned out that our unit was only a hundred yards away, that they had set up a defensive position on the banks of this river. We joined them there.

Frank Brumbaugh, the radar operator who had had his cigarettes shot away in eye-watering fashion on the way down, was now looking out for some form of compensation. His opportunity came after he had set up his radar beacon, and was scouting around in the darkness.

I went around the periphery of this small field, and I heard German voices on the other side. I sneaked up through the brush and stuff on top of the hedgerow, and I saw two German officers talking to each other, apparently totally unaware that we were in this field right next to them. Well, I couldn't shoot. We were ordered not to shoot unless it was totally in self-defense, but just to be as quiet and as secret as possible. And of course, the main thing was to keep the beacon in operation as long as possible.

But when I saw those two German officers, in my mind's eye I saw two beautiful Lugers, a souvenir that I wanted very badly. Since I couldn't make any noise I tossed a white phosphorus grenade down at their feet through the hedgerow. This makes a small pop when it goes off, very little noise, And of course it can't be put out.

It burned the two officers to death. I got back out of the way and waited until the thing was finished burning. When the fire died down I went back to collect my Lugers, not thinking what damage the white phosphorus grenade would have done to them.

Well, of course, both Germans were burned to death and hardly recognizable as humans. Unfortunately, the ammunition had exploded in the clips of the Lugers. It had blown them apart and they were totally worthless. So that was not the best idea that I'd ever had, but at least it got rid of those Germans, my first two Germans.

Frank Brumbaugh got his souvenirs of Overlord later in the day: two pristine Lugers taken from the dead bodies of some machine-gunners. Though this was Brumbaugh's first time in combat, he found that he had quite a talent for killing Germans.

We accounted for quite a number. We had orders to take no prisoners for the first nine days. The reason for this was that the paratroops, when they land behind enemy lines, are all by themselves, even if they are in a group. They can't afford to set up a POW compound, use personnel to guard prisoners, or anything like that. It's just totally impossible.

So even though some of the Germans surrendered, or thought they were surrendering, of course, they were disarmed and killed. In fact, we used bodies for roadblocks. We'd stack them up like cordwood in some of the road junction – German corpses.

For the next two or three days we gathered up other small groups of paratroops, all mixed up together. There were no officers with us, but fortunately we were trained to live on and fight either alone or with one or more of our paratroops buddies. So, this was no big deal. In fact, it was kind of fun not to have some officer telling you what to do.

Instinctively, these fearsome young American fighters adopted the tactics and the attitudes of the hoary Russian partisans who were terrorizing other Germans three thousand miles to the east. The All-American and the Screaming Eagles became impromptu guerrillas, taking on the enemy any way they could and wherever they happened to bump into them. Robert Flory, for example, had only been able to find one other man from his stick. They picked up another stray paratrooper and together this threesome went off in search of a fight.

> We had no idea where we were and which way to go. After checking our compass, we decided to crawl towards a hedgerow approximately a hundred yards west. As we crawled up to the hedgerow, we could see a sunken road on the other side. Then we heard voices – German voices. It was a patrol of about fifteen or twenty soldiers approaching from the south. Can you believe that the German patrol was marching in formation? After whispered conversation, we decided that each of us would throw a grenade at the same time and then take off north at top speed.
>
> As they drew abreast of us, we each pulled a pin and threw our grenades. The three grenades exploded at the same time, and then we took off. After running for about 150 yards, we came under machine-gun fire and had to go to ground. We could hear the screams and moans back down the road, but didn't go back to finish off the survivors.
>
> For the next hour, we crawled up and down hedgerows, looking for some of our buddies. Machine-gun and rifle fire was all around us. You could tell the difference between German and American machine gun, because the German machine guns fire at a much more rapid rate. We finally located two more troopers and were shocked to find out they were from the 82nd Airborne which was supposed to land ten to fifteen miles west of us. Then we realized there were American paratroopers scattered over many, many square miles.

Some troopers were entirely alone, and could do nothing but hide in the hedgerows until daylight; at least then they would be able to see who they were shooting at, and who was shooting at them. Edward Barnes found himself so far from his designated objective that his location was not on the map of the invasion zone.

But everywhere the Americans were coming together, nervously clicking their crickets at creeping shapes in the darkness, finding friends, or at least friendly strangers, and moving in small bands towards the sound of gunfire. Men attached themselves to any officer who crossed their path, and took on that officer's objectives as their own.

THE FIRST FREE TOWN IN FRANCE

One of the main objectives of the night was the little town of Sainte Mère Eglise. Its importance to the operation lay in the fact that two roads crossed at its centre. One road is the highway from the port of Cherbourg to the north, and the regional centre of Carentan to the south. The second road led directly from the town square to Utah beach, about three miles east. The plan was to take the town and set up a roadblock that would act like a two-way valve on the fluid battlefield – it would keep the Germans bottled up and away from the battle, while at the same time letting the invasion forces flow free and fast into the French interior.

It had been intended to take the town by stealth. But in the event, the entry of Americans into Sainte Mère Eglise could not have been more public or spectacular. The normally sleepy town was wide awake in the small hours of the night because a large barn had caught fire. The villagers, led by the mayor and chaperoned by the sullen German garrison, were passing buckets from hand to hand from the village pump to the burning building.

This was as much excitement as the town had seen since the Germans had arrived four years before. It would have been a night to remember even if nothing else had happened – even if, to the open-mouthed astonishment of both Frenchman and German, parachutists had not begun to drift out of the sky like sharp-toothed snowflakes.

The Germans soon recovered themselves to the extent that they began to shoot into the sky at the descending paratroops. The Americans had not meant to come down in the town – the ones who scored a bull's-eye on the town were off target. They were supposed to arrive at a drop zone just west of Sainte Mère Eglise. And in fact, as the shooting started in the village, many men of the 505th Parachute Infantry Regiment were gathering in silence on the outskirts.

Paratrooper John Steele found himself drifting towards the steeple of Sainte Mère Eglise's Norman church. His experience that night has entered the mythology of D-Day. He hit the church's stubby pyramidal roof and slid down the slates. His parachute caught a buttress, and saved him from

All the aircraft that took part in the invasion were painted with three stripes on each wing. This was to make them identifiable to anti-aircraft gunners in the Allied fleet, who in previous operations had shot down too many of their own planes by mistake.

tumbling to his death. This was his precarious ringside seat for the night. Suspended, helpless, he watched the fighting below. Deafened by the clanging bells, and bleeding from a wound in his foot, he hung there and watched the Germans shoot his comrades as they came down or struggled to throw off their parachutes.

There was a machine-gun post in the belfry merely a few feet from where he was hanging. Steele played dead to avoid the attention of the gunners, and was eventually taken prisoner at about 04.30 in the morning, shortly before the Germans were driven out of the town by the 505th. Many paratroopers were killed taking the town, and still more died defending it from counter-attack over the next couple of days. But perhaps the most pitiable deaths were those of the men who, in the first moments, were sucked into the flames of the barn fire. Paratrooper RR Hughart saw what became of one man.

A fellow in my outfit, a tall, skinny fellow, went into this flaming building, chute and all. Nobody knew about it at the time. But, the next day, when the fire was out, one of the officers and another fellow got a long plank and they were carrying him out. He was burnt up so bad that he broke in two. And that doesn't go too well with some people, I know. But, after being in the Mediterranean and seeing the things we saw down there you sort of get toughened up to it. But, it's a horrible thing to see one of your buddies, that you lived with in England and knew for quite some time, have that happen to him.

Sainte Mère Eglise was quiet by dawn. It now claims the honour of being the first town in France to be liberated, and an effigy of paratrooper John Steele hangs with its parachute from the roof of the church. This latter-day gargoyle is one of the strangest war memorials in all of Europe.

Paratrooper James Eads landed just outside Sainte Mère Eglise – in a manure pile. He saw the burning barn, but circumstance immediately forced him away from the town rather than into the battle. All the same, he spent a night filled with drama, valour and death. Here is his own long and lucid account of an eventful first day in France:

Our C-47 had been hit by both flak and machine-gun fire. We were off target. The green light came on and the troopers started out of the plane. The fifteenth man had equipment trouble. After some delay trying to fix his rig I, being the sixteenth and last man to go, bailed out on a dead run.

My opening shock was terrific. First, I saw all the tracers coming my way. Second, I tried to guess how high I was. Third, I checked my chute. I also saw flame from a fire ahead of me which was reaching as high as I was in the air.

A tracer had gone through my chute canopy like a cigarette hole in a silk handkerchief, smouldering and fiery red. The hole was getting bigger by the instant. I grabbed my front risers and brought them to my waist. I was in a hell of a hurry to get down before my chute became a torch. The bullets, in which tracers intermingled, were still snapping all around me. It seemed as if they would curve to one side just as they were going to hit me. I became so fascinated by this that I forgot to release my risers and

I was plummeting to earth extremely fast. Just as I checked the burning hole in my chute and saw it was now about eighteen inches in diameter, I hit the ground, plowing through the limbs of a tree. I bashed into the ground. I took most of the shock with my hind end. My chute then draped lazily over the tree.

I could hear shooting and yelling all around me, and saw a glow of light from a huge fire to my front and left of where I was laying. From this glow, I could see troopers coming out of the C-47s only three or four hundred-feet high. As I started to sit up to get out of my chute, I promptly slid flat again. After two or three more attempts and a sniff of the air, I finally discovered that I was lying in cow manure. I recall that I even snickered at my own predicament.

Suddenly from my right front, three men came running towards me, the first one about 100-feet away. I could see the coal-bucket helmets and thought 'Oh hell, out of the frying pan into a latrine – now this.' As my tommy gun was strapped to my chest, I gave up trying to get it out and reached for my .45 automatic that was strapped to my right thigh. I always keep a round in the chamber and seven in the clip. I thumbed back the hammer and started firing. The third man fell with my eighth round right at my feet.

I gave a huge sigh of relief and tried again to get up. This made my chute shake the tree. Then from my direct right about seventy-five yards away, a German machine nest opened up at me. I could hear the rounds buzzing and snapping through the leaves of the tree and into the ground beyond me. Again, I thought: 'Dammit, is the whole Kraut army after me, just one scared red-headed trooper?' I tried once again to rise up and bullets ripped into my musette bag and map case strapped to my chest, rolling me on to my left side.

I rolled back and tried to unstrap my tommy gun. Just then a loud boom came from the area of the machine gun, and all I could hear was the shooting and yelling coming from the direction of the glow of the big fire about 300 yards away.

I finally got out of my harness, grabbed my tommy gun, and started moving for the scene of action. All this took place within five minutes, and hearing a sound behind me, I dropped flat and tried to see what or who was there. Taking a chance on a hunch, I snapped my cricket. An answering two clicks came back at once, then up crawled a trooper, whom I didn't know but I could have kissed him for just being one of us. His first words were: 'I got those Kraut machine-gunners with a grenade, but it blew off my helmet and I can't find it. Holy cow, you stink!'

Moving to the edge of the orchard, we came to a hedgerow. As we were attempting to get over through this grove, we heard a click and answered it at once with two clicks. Another trooper, ready to go. Assuming a hedgerow to be about four-feet high, I slid through and dropped about ten feet down to a narrow roadway.

The three of us prepared to move across fields to the fight going around the fire about 250 yards away. We figured it to be quicker than trying to follow the road and running into some kind of a roadblock. Just then to my left, coming down the road towards us, was a noise of hob-nailed boots running. We crouched down along the bank, and I could hear the other two move to my left and fan out. I told them to wait for an opening burst before firing. The runners had to come around a slight curve in the road and I wanted to make sure all of them had rounded the curve before firing. We then saw there were three of them strung out, the first one now only about forty feet away. I started firing short bursts at the last man, then the second one. All three fell.

We then scurried over the hedge into another orchard. A large two-storey house was to our right, so we circled around it and moved closer to the action, now only a very short distance away. One of the men with me had an M-1 rifle; the other, a tommy gun, same as mine. Hearing running and shouting to our left, we dropped down as about ten Krauts came crashing through what looked like a garden. They were almost on top of us when we opened fire. All fell. Also, the trooper with the M-1 fell. We then moved on.

Suddenly, two figures loomed out of the shadow of a building. I almost fired before I recognized them as being in civilian clothes. The man with me could speak French, so crouching low, we held a hurried consultation. I could understand some of the talk, and the trooper told me the rest. All of us had bailed out right on top of Sainte Mère Eglise, when the townspeople were trying to put out a fire and being 'chaperoned' by a hundred or more Krauts. Our planes were so low that the troopers bailing out were perfect targets and were being slaughtered.

We thanked them, told them to get back in the building, and then moved on.

About seventy-five yards further on, we entered the edge of a large square with a church at our left side. There were troopers lying everywhere, almost all of them still in their chutes. One was hanging from the spire on the church. There was a stone wall around the church. We dropped behind this, just as a troop-carrying vehicle came down the street towards us. We were sitting ducks, so we both started firing, hoping to take as many of them with us as we could.

Out of the corner of my eye I also noticed firing coming from a building across the street at point blank range. One of us got the driver of the truck, and it stopped, and out of it, the Krauts came. I had to put in another clip. I had just accomplished this and began to fire again when I heard my buddy grunt and saw him fall. Suddenly, the firing from the vehicle stopped.

I shot out the building's window area and raced back behind the church, circling around it. I reloaded with just one clip, as I had no more taped together. I had started out with twenty clips, ten on my belt, seven in my knapsack, and three taped together, staggered and reversed. At thirty rounds to a clip, I had 600 rounds. The three taped together, gave me ninety rounds for speedy reloading. I had already emptied six clips.

Starting out again down the opposite side of the square from where we had met the troop carrier, I almost tripped over a Kraut lying on the ground. He had a burp gun. As he rolled to bring his gun around, I fired.

Then in the building behind me, a Kraut carbine let go and numerous Kraut voices began to yell something. Somehow, the one lying on the ground missed me, the bullet hitting the K-ration in my right pocket. I emptied my clip at the front of the building and moved out fast, reloading as I ran. It was now about one hour and thirty minutes since I had bailed out.

Hearing some firing immediately ahead I ran on, figuring on being some help to someone in need. Plus I wanted some company of my own people. I came upon four Krauts undercover, firing in the opposite direction. Sporadic fire came from the direction they were firing. As I looked, one fell, so I dropped the other three. One thing about a tommy gun: it's just like a garden hose. You aim it in the general direction of your target, hold on the trigger, and wave it back and forth. You waste some ammo, but you just can't hardly miss.

There were eight troopers behind a low stone wall and among some bushes. I held a hurried conversation with a sergeant and was told there were six members of the 505th Regiment, also one from the 508th, and one from the 101st Division. Two of the 505 men were seriously injured. One man had some TNT.

I then explained my mission to this sergeant, and asked him to help. We checked the two wounded. One had died and the other lad was past help. We made him as comfortable as we could, and moved out towards Chef du Pont. The sergeant told me it was only a couple of miles away. It was then somewhere around 3 o'clock in the morning.

We skirted a road, keeping to the second hedge from the road. Three men to the left side of the hedge and four to the right. We saw eleven dead troopers, all in their chutes, four hanging in trees. Somehow, we managed to reach the edge of Chef du Pont with only two short battles and without losing a man.

We ran into a group of Krauts at the edge of the village. There must have been a platoon. For some reason, they thought we must have been at least a company, because they broke and ran, maybe because of our numerous automatic weapons, two BARs, three tommy guns, and two M-1s. I was now down to nine clips.

We passed a building on the left side of the street with lots of German writing on it. A heavy machine-gun opened up from behind a low stone wall. One 505 man circled behind and threw two hand grenades and cut loose with his tommy. The nest was silenced.

Across the street was some kind of an important building, and it was flushed out by two of the men, two from 505 and the other 508 trooper. Then one of the men peeked around the corner and reported a train depot just to the left of a long narrow courtyard. He took off for it, with a word to cover him. At the far end of the courtyard or square, a machine gun cut loose and he fell. Then directly ahead of us along each side of the road and across the track, more Krauts opened up. One more man fell.

We concentrated our fire on them, then dashed towards them. They ran, going on down the street, house to house, room to room, we proceeded on towards the river. When we got to the edge of the town, there were only three of us. I had two-and-a-half clips left, so I took the remaining clip from the last man to fall that had a tommy gun. I picked up four more clips.

Of the three men left, one was from the 505, one from the 101st, and myself from the 508. When I jumped, being a demolition man, I had ten pounds of TNT. The man from the 101st had six pounds, plus his BAR. The trooper from the 505 had an M-1. That was our fire power.

Each one of these TNT quarter-pound blocks are tremendous, if set right, packed right, and detonated correctly. Starting across the causeway, I noticed it was flooded on both sides. Suddenly from our right, from an old factory-looking type of building about 400 yards across the flooded area, heavy fire power poured on us. We dove to the left of the offside of the causeway for protection. We immediately drew fire from across the bridge in the middle of the causeway. The 505 man fell.

The other man and myself moved on, firing in bursts at the ones ahead of us. When we came to the bridge, no more fire was coming at us from that direction. However, from the old factory, heavy fire was still coming. We then noticed some rifle fire from the other end of the causeway and to our right. I directed the 101st man to give me his TNT and keep firing at the factory.

I dropped below the left side of the bridge. I laid my gun down, set my eight pounds of TNT, then hand walked under and to the other end of the bridge, set the other eight pounds – and was promptly knocked into the water. I came up and swam back to the starting point, fire from the factory hitting all around me. I retrieved my gun, then noticed my side and my head were bleeding. It was then I noticed my BAR man wasn't firing. He was dead.

At the same time, I heard firing going on again in Chef du Pont. Crawling along the offside of the causeway, I set my short fuses to my charges, connected them with primer cord for instant detonation to the end of the regular two-foot fuse and continued along the offside of Chef du Pont. I had gone about fifty yards when the roadway vibrated terrifically from my charges. I went on into Chef du Pont and met up with fourteen paratroopers, most from the 505, a couple from the 101st, and three from the 508. I told the officer in charge what had happened, and he sent six men back to set up a roadblock. One had a bazooka, and I was sure he was glad to have him stay with us.

The others headed back to Sainte Mère Eglise. Within five minutes, they were shooting at all kinds of vehicles trying to come through Chef du Pont, get over the bridge, and get away from the invasion of the paratroops. We knocked out a big truck just as it reached the causeway and another small one that tried to get by him. We now had a very effective roadblock.

Within the hour, about twenty more troopers came up from behind us, and almost the same number entered the scene from the Chef du Pont side. In the meantime, I lost three more men, as almost that whole hour had been one continual roar of guns. I had fifteen rounds left.

I joined the troops in Chef du Pont and sent eight men back to the causeway to keep the roadblock active. Not seeing any of my men, we returned to Sainte Mère Eglise. I ate, drank a bottle of wine, had the blood washed off my minor wounds, and joined in the civilian celebration that was going on. I was so happy that they were happy. I cried with them.

It was now late in the afternoon and almost dark. An officer from the 82nd came up and told me my group were assembled at Hill 30 and I was to join them. He had another mission scheduled for that evening. I joined what was left of my people at the edge of Hill 30, and after one hell of a battle, we captured it. This lasted until the wee hours of the morning. After the hill was secure, we set up a perimeter defense, and by morning light, June 7, had beat off four counter-attacks. We had started with thirty men for this particular mission; six were left.

I said a silent prayer and slept.

THE 4TH DIVISION HITS THE BEACH

As the American paratroopers gravitated towards each other in the rural darkness, their comrades out at sea were making ready to storm Utah Beach. Utah was the responsibility of the 4th Infantry Division, under the command of Major-General Raymond Barton. Their task was threefold: to get ashore, to link up with Omaha as soon as possible, and then to push west and take the port of Cherbourg.

'At about 03.30 hours, we began unloading into landing craft . . .' said John de Vink, a communications sergeant with a mortar battalion.

> . . . Men in full battle gear had to climb down the cargo nets hung over the ship's side. Some had their arms or legs smashed as they tried to jump into the landing craft. I had a bad time of it, for in addition to my regular battle gear, I had a forty-pound radio and a portable telephone to carry.

The waves were six-feet high in places. Each man had to time his jump into the pitching Higgins boat. To drop into the boat as it was rising like a piston was almost guaranteed to earn a heavily laden GI a broken limb. But to make the leap as the boat was plunging down was almost as hazardous. A few men mistimed the jump completely and were crushed to death as they fell between the transport ship and the landing craft. Many soldiers later said that getting on the Higgins boat was the most terrifying experience of the entire day.

Lindley Higgins, of the 4th Infantry Division, had a novel way of getting on to his namesake's invasion barge. He walked the plank – which was hardly less precarious than the blind leap that most of his colleagues were undertaking.

> The transfer was made by crawling rather awkwardly across the hoisted Jacob's ladders and then dropping into the open boats. The best way I can describe this operation is to say that it was totally screwed up.

The men were loaded into their LCIs (Landing Craft, Infantry) eleven miles from shore. It was still dark and the coast was invisible. The run-in towards the beach was long and rough. 'I don't believe anyone in the history of mankind ever got any sicker than we did . . .' said Corporal Willard Coonen.

. . . Loaded down like pack mules, we were bounced around and thrown about while throwing up everything we had eaten for days. Our guts ached from the dry heaves. Scared as hell and sicker than the devil, we were drenched in salt water, with every dip and bob of the landing boat. My glasses became covered with salt spray, making it difficult to see.

Once inside the landing boats, we had to hang on to its side for dear life, or we'd have been thrown flat on our backs. Each of us had a heavy canvas back pack over our musette bag. This back pack contained two twenty-five-pound mortar shells. Each squad had two two-wheel carts which were on rubber tyres. One cart contained a knocked-down mortar, and the other was loaded with mortar shells packed in wooden boxes. Each loaded cart weighed about 500 pounds and had a long T-shaped handle with extension chains attached to the end so that four men could pull it. Inflated life belts like the ones we wore around our waists were wrapped around each cart so that they and their cargo could be floated ashore.

The LCVPs (Landing Craft, Vehicle and Personnel), with their flat bottoms, were not designed for a sea-going voyage, and certainly not for the rough weather of the Channel on D-Day. Men spent the three-hour chug towards the shore bailing out with their helmets. Water continually sloshed over the side of the boats, many of which were carrying heavy machinery as well as a full complement of fighting men. There was a constant danger of being overwhelmed.

These LCVPs were eighteen-feet long, said John Beck, a mortar man. They were pooled by the English and Americans, and we drew an English boat. Into the boat was crammed twenty men, all of our equipment, mortars and ammunition. The waves were tremendous and the gunwales of our boat were only about six inches above the water. We began passing LCIs – which were larger crafts, and they were sinking. We had to pass them by as nothing could detain us from reaching our destination. We had been issued seasick pills. I took one of them and dropped down and feel asleep. The explosion of shells awakened me as we approached the French coast.

The sight of dry land – even though it was planted with machine-gun posts and sown with mines – cheered the sickened soldiers. Anything was better than the green-faced agony of seasickness.

And then came the deafening overture of the naval barrage. This was a welcome and reassuring development for the men in the barges.

> **Rockets screeched overhead, and the battleship 16-inch guns behind us boomed away,** said Willard Coonen. **Hundreds of planes roared overhead dropping their bombs on the beaches we were headed for.**

As the bombardment started, John de Vink's LCVP was still sheltering like a duckling under the maternal wing of the USS *Nevada*.

> **We circled endlessly, it seemed, under the huge guns of the battleship. I had never heard or seen a battleship firing a salvo. Lo and behold, when they did fire, it felt as though our landing craft was lifted clean out of the water, such was the suction as the huge shells travelled overhead.**

As Joseph Camera headed into shore he remembered some words that General Patton had spoken to him and his comrades before the sea-borne invasion of Sicily – a successful operation comparable to D-Day, except that the French coast was heavily fortified whereas Sicily had not been.

> 'Soon you are going into battle,' he said. 'Some of you have a terrified concern for this. Well, don't let it get you. If you get killed, you'll never know what hit you. And if you get wounded, you'll be darn glad to be alive.' He had a way of making you more inspired than frightened.
>
> I was twenty-one years old. I had just learned to smoke. I don't really think I was frightened. The first battle is the toughest. After that, you seem to acquire a confidence that overcomes fear. When you begin, you wonder how will you ever get used to it, but then it becomes automatic. Then there's that feeling of pride, when you tell yourself: I did it before and I can do it again. I know what to do, and how to do it. And one more very important thing I always told myself: I'm on the winning team.

This young man, who had smashed up a pub for fun when he first arrived in England, had another source of strength and comfort, which he turned to now:

> I thought about the ninety-first psalm, verse seven. *A thousand may fall at your side, ten thousand close at hand, but you it shall not touch. This truth will be your shield and your rampart.* Wave after wave of assault troops were landing on the beach. We were heading towards Utah. Artillery from the German big guns was now beginning to explode. I prayed to God to protect me and – if I didn't make it – to take me into His kingdom.

Joseph Camera was right to be concerned. At this point the assault on Utah was not going according to plan. Waves of bombers had been sent just ahead of the landing to soften up the beach defenders. But the pilots could not see their targets because of low cloud, and were over-wary of dropping their payload on their own troops. The consequence of this was that most of the bombs fell harmlessly inland, well behind the defences.

The weather was also affecting the orientation of the leading LCVPs. Moreover, one of the patrol boats, charged with leading the landing craft into the right beaches, was hit by a shell and went down. The strong winds and the lack of guidance were causing the first wave of troops to drift south of the planned landing zone. When they hit the beach they were nearly two miles off target.

The misplaced landing could have been disastrous. But it turned out to be one of the great strokes of luck of the day. The defences at this point were very light, and the first wave crossed the beach unopposed but for some rifle fire from the trenches behind the sea wall. But it still needed someone to seize on the good fortune and run with it.

ROOSEVELT ON THE BEACH

The highest-ranking officer in that first wave was Brigadier-General Theodore Roosevelt, son of the former president whose name he shared, and a distant cousin of the current one. At 57 he was the oldest American officer to take part in the Normandy landings, and the only general to land with the first wave. He was there because he had insisted on being with his men, making repeated requests to his divisional commander. His requests had been turned down again and again, partly because of his age and the state of his health – he had suffered a heart attack and walked with a stick – and partly because the military feared the consequences for morale if a Roosevelt should be killed on the beaches. The brigadier-general argued that morale was precisely why he had to be there: 'It will steady the men to know I am with them,' he had said in his request.

In the event, Roosevelt's presence achieved much more than that. He was a model of coolness under fire: he refused to wear a helmet because he thought they were uncomfortable, and when shell blasts spattered his uniform with sand he would brush it off with the nonchalance of a Georgian dandy batting at flies.

But Roosevelt was nobody's cupcake. Despite a lifetime of ill health, he had fought and been wounded in the Great War, he had led archaeological expeditions to Asia, he had been with the 1st Division in Sicily, and he had a voice that was once described as 'a bellow only a few decibels louder than a moose call.'

As soon as he hit the beach, Roosevelt noticed that the landmark building of La Madeleine, which was supposed to be to their left, was far away to the right. As he contemplated this, Roosevelt was joined by Colonel James Van Fleet, commander of the 8th Infantry Regiment. They had to make a snap decision: to send a message back to the ships, redirecting later waves to the pre-planned location, or to keep them coming in at the wrong location. They looked around them: German resistance was negligible; amphibious tanks were already coming ashore and engineers were at work blowing gaps in the beach obstacles; and there was an open exit from the beach leading across the inundated areas towards the town of Sainte Marie du Mont.

After all the months of planning, the agonized inspection of maps and the covert surveillance, the success of Utah came down to an unlikely fluke. An unexpected lapse on the part of the Germans, a freak hit on a patrol boat and the subsequent navigational error on the part of the Americans – all these seemed to have combined to give the invasion a great head start.

Roosevelt and Van Fleet decided to keep the momentum going and land the entire invasion force for Utah at the wrong place. 'We'll start the war right here,' Roosevelt is said to have declared. It was the right decision. Utah Beach was peremptorily shifted two miles south.

John Ahearn of the 70th Tank Battalion was one of the first to learn about the new plan:

As dawn broke it became evident that we were going to be the first tanks on the beach. We had all mounted into the tanks. The British commander brought us in on the beach just as far as he could, and we got off in six feet of water. The tanks had been weatherized, and we had shrouds over our engines. Owen Gavigan was the first tank to land on Utah Beach, and mine was the second.

It became evident that the beach area was not the same as it had been planned we would land on. I saw General Teddy Roosevelt on the beach, and got out of my tank and reported to him, and told him who I was and what my mission was. He told me to go ahead to the lateral parts of the beach, north and south, and to take care and to get inland as fast as we could. I then directed Lieutenant Yeoman who was my second in command, and told him to take half of the tanks and proceed up to the north, and I would proceed to the south.

As the second and third waves came in, boatload after boatload of men were disgorging onto the beach. They dragged with them or behind them the vast and varied apparatus of war. John Beck got to work the second he got his feet wet.

We jumped out in waist-high water and began unloading. We set up our mortars on the beach and began firing in support of our infantry. There was only about twenty yards of beach and then there was a levee about twenty-five-feet high. There was a stone wall, and on the other side for about half mile it was flooded about three feet deep. There were German signs reading MINEN, and it was crisscrossed with barbed wire just under the water.

Everywhere men were getting down to their assigned tasks. Some were even moving off the beach and heading inland, over the narrow causeways and past the flooded, mine-infested shallows of the river Merderet.

Resistance was very light, and most of our company made it into shore, said John de Vink. We did not talk much during these times, as we were expecting the worst. Our gas-operated M-1 rifles became jammed on the beach with sand. We field-stripped and cleaned them in record time. We had been trained to do this blindfolded. Company D immediately moved quickly inland behind the 4th Infantry. I dug in behind the four-foot seawall for protection from the shelling, which was heavy now. We set up communications, and began getting crews out, running phone lines to company. We used both phone lines and radio while we were busy laying wire.

Colonel Van Fleet called on us to be stretcher bearers. Four of us carried several badly wounded men to a first aid tent on the beach. This was the first time we were actually under mortar and small-arms fire. We talked only in code, and no idle talk was ever allowed. Somehow, with God's help, we were able to proceed. This observation I now make looking back. It was the greatest show on earth, and also the greatest sacrifice by the men who gave their lives for us.

Only God knows why I was spared and not even wounded. I know I didn't deserve it.

By now the Germans had oriented their bigger guns on the beach and were bringing fire to bear on the invaders. Lawrence Orr, a coastguard, was busy unloading his LCI when he was mugged by a passing shell:

This explosion came and it just cleared out everything that I had in my pockets. I had a pair of Raybans that my wife had sent me. I think I was the only guy on the whole ship that had a pair of Raybans sunglasses, and I was so proud of them. You could put them on in the dark and still see. I had a couple of fountain pens and a pencil and a pad in my pocket, a pack of cigarettes, a cigarette lighter. It took everything out of my pockets, it even took my shoes off. My helmet was gone. My life jacket was only hanging on one arm. Even my pants pockets: they were emptied.

Lindley Higgins also lost what was most dear to him – his smokes.

I had with me a carton of Lucky Strikes. Now this wasn't unusual, except that Lucky Strikes were almost impossible to get overseas. We usually got Raleighs or some other less desirable cigarette, so a carton of Luckys was a prize. They were in the long

A decent foxhole was the key to staying alive on the beach, and later in the countryside of France. Digging in for the night was a ritual every soldier observed. A hole of even a few inches in depth could keep a man out of a sniper's sights or protect him from a shell blast.

pocket at the back of the invasion jacket. The carton was completely saturated. When held in the hand, it simply bent over like a limp rag, and there wasn't a single salvageable cigarette in the carton.

Such are the vicissitudes of war, I suppose.

That so minor a misfortune should stick in the memory testifies to the success of the Utah landings. A far grimmer drama was unfolding down the coast on Omaha Beach, but here at the western end of the landing zone losses were lighter than anyone expected. A total of 23,000 troops went ashore at Utah Beach on D-Day, and about 200 were killed or wounded on the beach.

This is less than one casualty per 100 men. No soldier who landed in France on 6 June would have turned down those odds.

LINK-UP WITH THE AIRBORNE

The beach was securely in American hands by ten o'clock in the morning. And by mid-morning an Aviation Battalion was hard at work constructing the first makeshift airstrip in the vicinity of the battered town of Sainte Mère Eglise. It consisted of great rolls of burlap (impregnated tarpaper) laid out like a red carpet for the supply Dakotas to land on. Paratroopers had found their way through the night to Utah, and were holding the causeways behind the beach, which meant that men and vehicles were soon moving inland.

Tank Commander John Ahearn wasted no time in getting off the beach, but before he left he had a close encounter with one of Germany's lesser-known secret weapons:

> There was a small tank-like object that I had never been informed about, and had never seen in the operations in Africa or Sicily. I was concerned, but my mission was to get inland as rapidly as possible, so we proceeded through. Later on, I read about the fact that there were a number of these so-called 'Little Goliaths' that had been controlled from one of the strongpoints of the Germans. Apparently the controls to these had been severed. Luckily for us, as it turned out.

The Goliaths were little remote-control robots on tracks, like baby Panzers. They were powered by Bosch starter motors and stuffed with TNT. The idea was that they would be driven into the midst of troops and detonated, but more often than not the cable-control failed or was severed. Ahearn was right to ignore it.

> We got inside the seawall, he continued, and proceeded laterally between the seawall and the road, where we saw a number of infantrymen from the 2nd Battalion of the 8th Division who were at this time proceeding northward. As we looked down southward, it became evident that there was another strongpoint of the Germans. Although we saw no activity there, I had our tanks fire some shells into it. With this, a number of Germans – or, as it turned out, impressed soldiers who were not of German nationality – came out, with their hands in the air and began running towards us.

So then I dismounted from the tank and to take them prisoner, and as I did, the most unusual thing happened. They began gesturing me to stay still, and yelling 'Achtung, Minen.' We delivered these thirty or so odd prisoners to the infantry.

A good number of the defenders behind Utah Beach were elderly Austrians or 'volunteers' from the Soviet Union. These were men who had been taken prisoner on the eastern front, and were then shipped west to plug gaps in the Atlantic Wall. There were entire units made up of Georgians, Azerbaijanis, Kazakhs and even Koreans. Most of them surrendered at the first opportunity, and were only too delighted to fall into American hands.

Far more dangerous than these unwilling *Freiwillige* were the minefields and booby traps that littered the land behind the sea defences.

The Germans had all of the open fields mined, and coils of barbed wire seemed to be strung all around us, said Willard Coonen. 'Achtung Minen' signs, with their skull and crossbone symbol, seemed to be everywhere, indicating that the fields were mined – or at least they wanted us to think so. We naturally took their word for it.

As the infantry moved inland they came upon evidence of the paratroopers' night's work. John Beck arrived at a scene of destruction and could easily piece together what had happened.

You could write the scenario: down the road was a German soldier lying dead, stripped to the waist and shaving cream on his face. He had been shaving before going on guard and paratroopers had burst in the kitchen, the German ran out the front door and had been killed further down the road. Also on the road was a German kitchen unit which had been ambushed in the darkness. The Germans used huge draft horses to carry food and coffee to their troops and the horse and drivers were lying there dead, with the overturned kitchen wagon.

Lindley Higgins also saw plenty of death, and found it hard to be indifferent:

Not only human corpses were visible, but the number of cattle, Normandy being quite a dairy country. Cattle were laying dead, and the German army, for all its mobility, had a number of horses carrying ammunition. These were, of course, dead also. Everything in Normandy seemed to be dead at that time.

But there were live and determined defenders too, and not just among the more seasoned German troops. Alfred Allred had a sad and pitiless encounter with a lone German sniper, a teenage boy who would not give up the fight.

He was in this old Frank's barn and kept shooting at us, some little German about seventeen years old. He'd knock several leaves off of the trees around us, I guess he was shooting at me. I went out there and tried to get him out. This old French lady – bless her heart, she was as sweet as she could be – she knew this German and she tried to get him out. But he wouldn't come.
We had to kill him. We finally decided to burn the barn down and burn him up in it. I think he committed suicide: I heard a rifle shot. But he burned up in there, burned to death or whatever. They found his body and the French buried him.

Allred had another, happier meeting on his way to link up with the airborne troops at Sainte Mère Eglise.

Shells were falling everywhere. There was one old French gentleman there. He kept dancing and clapping his hands and saying 'Vive la France, Vive de Gaulle, Vive l'Americain.' He was so happy because at last it had happened. The invasion was on its way.

The character of the fighting changed as the Americans consolidated their hold. Lindley Higgins decided that much of the ordnance that he had laboriously dragged across the sea and up the beach was redundant.

Neither the pole charges nor the satchel charges, which are supposed to be used in the demolition of pillboxes, were used. All the pillboxes had been thoroughly destroyed by the naval fire during the evening before and during the day, so there was no such thing as an intact or armed or manned pillbox in that particular portion of Normandy.

Hence the pole charges, the satchel charges, most of the TNT caps, fuses, and the like, ended up in the swamp waters. The rifle grenades, which like my carton of Luckys were being carried in the horizontal back pocket of the invasion jacket, had a metal tail on them, which was somewhat flimsy. As a result, when you hit the ground at any time, the wings or the guide pieces of the rifle grenades became distorted and useless. Hand grenades, in this type of combat, tend to be somewhat useless too, since there were no people visible at whom to throw them. They also were discarded. In other words, a considerable amount of armament and equipment ended up in the swamps of Utah Beach.

He did, however, keep a tight grip on his M-1, 'the lovely Garand' as one GI called it. This rather old-fashioned-looking weapon, with its rosy wooden stock, bore a distinct family resemblance to the romantic repeater rifles of the Old West. But it was a fine weapon, the best rifle of the war. It had a gas-operated reloading mechanism and was accurate over more than a mile, much further than any soldier was likely to be able to spot an enemy. So if you could see him, there was a chance you could hit him. And it was sturdy:

> During the traversing of the swamp and the mud the barrel of my rifle, unknown to me, had become totally encrusted with mud and water. On emerging from the swamp, I accidentally fired it into the air. It fired immediately without any problem. Speaks well of the M-1.

Now that it was light, more and more lost paratroopers emerged from the hedgerows and entered the fray. The ones who were still a way inland were heartened by the sound of the naval bombardment of the beach, and the knowledge that the 4th Infantry were on the march. Many of the troopers made their way to a village – any village – because there was bound to be someone there to fight and someone to fight alongside.

'As it began to get light, we found three more from my platoon . . .' said Robert Flory, who with his two comrades had wiped out the German patrol foolish enough to march in tight formation.

. . . We started moving west and shot three Germans who had been sleeping in a barn. Up ahead of us we could see a familiar church steeple. We knew that we were approaching Sainte Marie du Mont. Then we ran into a group from my company. We must have had a force of about seventy-five men in all, a general hodge-podge of people from the 506th, 502nd, and a few from the 82nd. We had no idea how many Germans were in the town, but our training paid off. We played the leapfrog by squads as we moved into the town. One squad would dash forward, while the other squad provided covering fire. A machine gun was on each flank, also giving covering fire.

Two fellas with a bazooka dashed down the street, stopped, aimed, and blew the front door off the church. Shortly after that a white flag appeared and a dozen German soldiers surrendered. We cleared the town in less than an hour. We found one of our buddies hanging in a tree. His parachute got caught in a tree, and he was still in his harness

A lieutenant and two GIs found a battery of three 88s about a thousand yards east of town. Two of their guns had been wrecked. The third one was still serviceable. They turned the gun around and sighted on the church tower. One round was fired and the church tower disappeared with all the snipers. In the meantime, we had found two equipment bundles in a pasture outside of town, and we replenished our supply of ammo and grenades.

The naval bombardment had long since stopped, and we were wondering about the beach, the beach named Utah. Colonel Sink, our regimental commander, finally arrived in a Jeep. He conferred with Colonel Turner, our battalion commander, and soon learned that the beach people were finally making their way inland.

Paratrooper Leland Baker was one of the first to see them coming.

I saw a platoon of men coming up the road way down in the distance. I was unsure who or what they were. It turned out they were friendly. I let them get close enough to me until I could see the shape of the helmet. That was an old telltale sign that we learned in a hurry, the distinctive shape of that Kraut helmet. So I let them get close, then I stood straight up and made sure they could see me because we had already heard that some of our people were killed since we had on jumpsuits instead of the regular traditional uniform. Not all of the invasion forces were aware of this, and some of our people had been mistaken for Germans.

They got closer; I could very easily see that four-leaf clover on their left shoulder, which was the insignia of the 4th Infantry Division. They got on closer, and their lieutenant called out to me: 'How're you doing there, paratrooper?' I said, 'Fine, sir, how are you doing?' He said, 'Well, I don't know yet. This thing just started for us.'

In fact, this thing was going remarkably well, and there were similar happy encounters between airborne paratroopers and seaborne infantry everywhere between Ravenoville in the north and Sainte Marie du Mont in the south.

By way of an added bonus, the German artillerymen, who were out of sight of the shore, had not realized that at Roosevelt's command the Americans were veering to the south as they approached land. Consequently the German gunners were raining huge quantities of shells on an empty beach as the Americans poured equally huge quantities of equipment on to the new location of Utah.

By mid-morning the flow of men and *matériel* off the beach and down the causeway was unstoppable. Now the 4th Infantry Division got a chance to see the price that the airborne had paid for their relatively easy ticket:

Our dead and wounded were scattered along the roads, said Willard Coonen. On D+1, we reached Sainte Mère Eglise and met with the paratroopers and glider troops of the 82nd and 101st Airborne Divisions.

Parts of their chutes were still hanging in the trees, and gliders, or what was left of them, were scattered around. Many had the wings broken off from hitting obstacles such as trees or posts. A number of them were standing on their nose.

Many soldiers found it hard to look into the face of a corpse. It was easier to limit yourself to checking out the colour of their boots – black meant German, and brown was one of their own.

> **The view of American dead was always to me one of the most inhibiting factors of war,** said Coonen, **since they were people with whom you had been associated. Or at least were dressed and looked like people you had been associated with, even though you might not know them.**

Of course, it wasn't just that the dead looked like people you knew or might know. It was that they looked like you personally. Any corpse could be you, or maybe would be you if your luck ran out. And every living, breathing soldier was trying to keep that thought out of his head.

The 4th Division were off the beach, but it was still a very long way to Berlin. A lot more GIs were sure to be killed before the war was over. The 4th didn't know it, but a great many were dying even now – fifteen short miles away on the blood-soaked sands of Omaha Beach.

4
BLOODY OMAHA

As our boat touched sand and the ramp went down, I became a
visitor to hell.

So said Private Harry Parley of the 16th Infantry Regiment, which
spearheaded the assault on Omaha Beach. It was 6.30 in the morning. The
assault was beginning at the same moment as the attack on Utah to the
west. Two regiments made up the first wave on Omaha. The 16th Infantry
came in on the left in Easy Sector, which was divided into stretches of
beach codenamed Green and Red. The 116th Infantry came in on the right
in Dog Sector, which had three sub-divisions: Red, White and Green.

The men of the first wave stepped off the boats into a murderous
blizzard of gunfire. In that moment, the first seconds of the battle, they
could no more avoid the bullets than they could have dodged the wind.
The German gunners had zeroed in on the lead boats. They opened up on
the invading soldiers as soon as they showed themselves. Some of the
enemy guns were positioned in such a way that they could shoot straight
into the opening maw of the landing craft, cutting the Americans down as
they stepped up to the ramp. Entire platoons were shot dead before they
could even get off their boats.

Alan Anderson saw 'machine guns ripping into the ramps, and men
tumbling just like corn cobs off of a conveyer belt.' As his boat hit the
beach, Anderson turned to look at the naval officer guiding them in.

He was standing there on the bridge and there was a flag
alongside of his head. A barrage of machine-gun fire came along
and cut that flag off. He had that kind of bewildered look that
sometimes comes on men's faces when they're first under fire,
when he realized how close he had come to being killed.

I also noted when we got close to shore that there was a man
who was part of the crew removing underwater obstacles. He was

The US soldiers underwent an ordeal before they even reached the beach. 'All our equipment was wet,' said Private Harold Baumgarten. 'Our TNT was floating around the boat. We were dead tired from bailing out water with our helmets. Our feet were frozen blue.'

badly wounded in the water and he was raising his hand for someone to help him. We were trying to find a rope or a buoy or something we could throw over to him. Then the officer received orders for us to put back out to sea, because they were afraid of losing all of the vehicles. I remember with horror this poor man, as he lay in the water raising his hand and waving to us and then sliding under. The water was tinted red with the blood that was flowing from his wounds.

The Germans had held their fire until the first landing craft reached the shore. Up to the moment when the barrage started, Sergeant Harry Bare, 29th Division, 2nd Battalion, 116th Regiment, was hoping that the defending guns had all been knocked out by the sea and air bombardment.

This hope died 400 yards from shore. The Germans began firing mortars and artillery. To try to explain the absolute chaos to anyone who wasn't there would be impossible. Fire rained down on us, machine-gun, rifle, rockets from the bunkers on top of the cliff. I saw assault boats like ours take direct hits. The boats were zig-zagging to avoid being hit, which fouled up all the plans. Our boat dropped its landing ramp somewhere near Les Moulins, and my lieutenant, the first off, took a shot in the throat, and I never saw him again.

As ranking non-com, I tried to get my men off the boat, and make it somehow under the cliff. I saw men frozen in the sand, unable to move. My radio man had his head blown off three yards from me. The beach was covered with bodies, men with no legs, no arms – God, it was awful. It was absolutely terrible.

In many landing craft the men hauled themselves up the sides and dropped into the water rather than make the suicidal jump off the ramp. But this was hardly any safer. Often the LCIs ran aground on sandbars two or three hundred yards out to sea. The water was deep, and the men were as heavily encumbered with their gear as medieval knights in armour. Some sank like bricks and drowned. Charles Zeccola of the 16th Infantry survived only by abandoning all the equiment he had brought over from England.

As I made a running jump into the water, I went over my head. I think I had seventy pounds on me. I had a rifle, eight rifle grenades, plus bandolier and backpack. I got out my knife, and cut away everything. I went in there with just my rifle and rifle grenades which I had strapped to my leg.

Many of the men were poor swimmers. They had been assured that they would be landing in ankle-deep water, and in any case they had their Mae West life preservers. But even these proved deadly for some overladen GIs, as coxswain Robert Adams witnessed:

I could see bodies of soldiers and their rumps were sticking out of the water, because they had their lifebelt around their waist and not their chest, and they couldn't keep their head up when they hit deep water, and so they drowned. All the belt did was to keep their ass up out of the water.

Among those going in with the first wave was the American photographer and war reporter Robert Capa. A veteran of many wars, he had been with the 1st Infantry Division in Sicily, and so decided to hitch a ride with them to Omaha. His guess was that it would be interesting without being too dangerous. He got it very wrong.

The coast of Normandy was still miles away when the first unmistakable popping reached our ears. We ducked down in the puky water in the bottom of the barge and ceased to watch the approaching coastline. The first empty barge, which had already unloaded its troops on the beach, passed on the way back, and the boatswain gave us a happy grin and the V sign. It was now light enough to start taking pictures, and I brought my first Contax camera out of its waterproof oilskin. The flat bottom of our barge hit the earth of France. The boatswain lowered the steel-covered large front, and there, between the grotesque designs of steel obstacles sticking out of the water, was Easy Red beach.

My beautiful France looked sordid and uninviting, and a German machine gun, spitting bullets around the barge, fully spoiled my return. Then men from my barge waded in the water. Waist-deep, with rifles ready to shoot, with the invasion obstacles and the smoking beach in the background – this was good enough for the photographer, I paused for a moment on the gangplank to take my first real picture of the invasion. The boatswain who was in an understandable hurry to get the hell out of there, mistook my picture-taking for explicable hesitation, and helped me make up my mind with a well-aimed kick in the rear.

The water was cold, and the beach still more than a hundred yards away. The bullets tore holes in the water around me, and I made for the nearest steel obstacle. A soldier got there at the same time, and for a few minutes we shared its cover. He took the waterproofing off his rifle and began to shoot without much aiming. The sound of his rifle gave him enough courage to move forward, and he left the obstacle to me. It was a foot larger now, and I felt safe enough to take pictures of the other guys hiding just like I was.

I finished my pictures, and the sea was cold in my trousers. Reluctantly, I tried to move away from my steel pole, but the bullets chased me back every time. Fifty yards ahead of me, one of our half-burnt amphibious tanks stuck out of the water and offered me my next cover. I sized up the situation. There was little future for the elegant raincoat heavy on my arm. I dropped it and made for the tank. Between floating bodies I reached it, paused for a few more pictures, and gathered my guts for the last jump to the beach.

Now the Germans played on all their instruments, and I could not find any hole between the shells and bullets that blocked the last twenty-five yards to the beach. I just stayed behind my tank, repeating a little sentence from my Spanish Civil War days. *Es una cosa muy seria. Es una cosa muy seria.* This is a very serious business.

I didn't dare to take my eyes off the finder of my Contax and frantically shot frame after frame. Half a minute later, my camera jammed – my roll was finished. I reached in my bag for a new roll, and my wet shaking hands ruined the roll before I could insert it in my camera.

I paused for a moment . . . and then I had it bad.

The empty camera trembled in my hands. It was a new kind of fear shaking my body from toe to hair, and twisting my face.

An LCI braved the fire and medics with red crosses painted on their helmets poured from it. I did not think and I didn't decide it. I just stood up and ran toward the boat. I stepped into the sea between two bodies and the water reached to my neck. The rip tide hit my body and every wave slapped my face under my helmet. I held my cameras high above my head, and I suddenly I knew that I was running away. I reached the boat. The skipper was crying. His assistant had been blown up all over him and he was a mess.

Seven days later, I learned that the pictures I had taken on Easy Red were the best of the invasion. But the excited darkroom assistant while drying the negatives, had turned on too much heat and the emulsions had melted. Out of 106 pictures in all, only eight were salvaged. The captions under the heat-blurred pictures read that Capa's hands were badly shaking.

A terrible misfortune for a news photographer, but in the grander scheme Capa was lucky to find a boat, lucky to get off Omaha with his life, and lucky to make it back to England with some kind of scoop. Many boats did not even make it as far as the beach. W Garwood Bacon of the 7th Naval Beach Battalion was in an LCI which hit a mine on the way in.

> Without warning a blast shook our craft from stem to stern and a sheet of flame shot some thirty or forty feet in the air directly forward of the conning tower. A fire broke out below and smoke poured out of the gaping hole torn by the flames. As if the explosion were a pre-arranged signal, the Jerries opened up with everything: 88s, mortars, machine guns . . . Terror seized me as I gazed horrified at the burned and bleeding frantically rushing and stumbling past me, trying to get away from the blinding fire and smoke.

Bacon decided his best bet was to get off the burning ship and head for shore in a rubber raft.

> We dropped the raft over the side. I climbed over and dropped seven or eight feet and landed on all fours into the pitching, rocking craft. Machine-gun and rifle bullets whined past our ears, or plunked into the water near our craft. We pushed our way through the iron and wooden ramps and poles to which were wired Teller mines. As we reached more shallow water, where three- and four-foot waves were breaking, I marvelled that we were not dashed against some mine or reeled to pieces by gunfire.

Roy Arnn, as leader of a demolition unit, was one of the first to make it, soaking and exhausted, to the shallows. He was wounded almost as soon as he crawled out of the water.

> I must have been one of the first ones hit. I was trying to get the mine detector out of the box but couldn't as the lid was jammed. There was no place to hide in the open, and a sniper shot me. The bullet kicked sand in my face and passed under my left armpit. Then a shell from a German 88 artillery piece exploded near my feet. The shrapnel hit my right shoulder and leg. The

explosion and concussion knocked the breath out of me. The force of the explosion blew my helmet off and cut the corner of my left eye. I soon lost sight in my eye because blood was running into it.

As I lay there wondering just how badly I had been hit, the incoming tide water started to go around me. I tried to get up and run or crawl to the high water mark, but I couldn't get my leg to work. I fell back down a couple of times. The Germans were firing everything they could. Lieutenant Ross told me to stay down and he would come out to get me. He crawled out to me and I put my head on his butt and grabbed his leg. He crawled and dragged me to the high-water mark where I stayed for most of the morning. As he left he was wounded in the leg.

I prayed to God before we hit the beach that morning. Also, after I was hit and a few times more while lying in the sand and rocks, unable to move. Things on the beach did not look good. There was one soldier near me that was crying and asking for his parents.

Richard Merrill was a captain in the 2nd Ranger Battalion. He too was dismayed by the strength of the German opposition. It was not what he had been led to expect.

We thought getting across the beach would be no problem – but it didn't turn out that way. The tide was lower than we thought. There was a longer area to cross, and it was cross-stitched with fire. Small-arms fire, machine-gun fire, mortar fire, artillery fire. I was the first one off the craft. Captain Frank Corder, from Texas, was the next man off. And I remember Frank's exact words: 'This is no place for Mrs Corder's little boy Frank.'

You knew the shortest path was a straight one right across the beach. You'd hear 'zip-zip', just strings of machine-gun bullets and automatic weapons criss-crossing paths. You're soaking wet; everything is heavy. You'd try to time it to run and you'd fall. You'd run on a dry piece of sand and then hit water and immediately tumble, get up and keep going. I don't remember anyone right with me; I was just hoping the others were coming behind me.

There were bodies around in the water, and there were others once you got across. One of the men from my boat, we saw him get hit and tumble and get up, and we were hollering: 'Keep going, Rusty! Keep going!' I saw Frank Corder too, but he was tough to recognize because he'd lost an eye and teeth.

I was the first one out. The seventh man was the next one to get across the beach without being hit. All the ones in-between were hit. Two were killed; three were injured. That's how lucky you had to be.

The firepower trained on the beach was awesome. The geography naturally favoured the defenders: the beach was flat and wide, enclosed at both ends by high cliffs – once on land, there was nowhere for the soldiers to go but onwards into the guns.

The sloping bluff at the back of the beach formed a kind of grandstand overlooking the sea. So the Germans, like spectators in a gladiatorial arena, had a clear and uninterrupted view of the American soldiers as they disembarked. Some of the German gunners could not believe that the invaders would be so foolhardy as to meet them head-on. 'Are they going to swim in under our muzzles?' said one incredulous defender as the Americans struggled ashore.

And there were so many guns! There were thirty-five pillboxes on top of the bluff or embedded in the slope, and on D-Day they were so well camouflaged as to be invisible. The boxes were manned with infantrymen who were bristling with small arms and hand grenades.

Then there were eighty-five machine-gun posts equipped with MG-42s, the gun that the Allies called a Spandau. This fearsome weapon caused hundreds of casualties on Omaha. It was usually mounted on a long-legged tripod – it looked like some kind of mechanical mosquito, sinister and utterly deadly. They were capable of pouring fire onto the beach at a rate of 1,200 rounds a minute. The machine-gun posts were positioned in such a way that they could shoot across the beach, parallel to the shore. Together with the guns on top of the bluff pointing out to sea, they constituted a gruesome cat's cradle of firing lines; any soldier attempting to cross the beach could not help but pass through the gunners' sights.

There were eighteen anti-tank positions. Since very few tanks made it to the beach, the German gunners fired their 88mm shells straight at the landing craft. A direct hit would obliterate an LCI and all its men: many survivors of Omaha describe seeing whole boatloads of men vanish in a mighty waterspout. There were six mortar posts: the German *Nebelwerfer* had six barrels – it looked like the chamber of a revolver writ large – and the mortars that it fired were known to the Americans as 'screaming mimis' because of the terrifying noise they made in the air. There were also thirty-eight rocket batteries and four artillery positions overlooking the beach.

All along the bluff there were 'Tobruks' which consisted of concrete chambers buried deep in the earth. On top was a cylinder about five-feet high, also made of concrete. A man could stand within this one-man trench and peer out or shoot. Some Tobruks had gun turrets set atop the cylinder, so they were like sunken pepperpots. The man inside was almost impervious to enemy fire, but could wreak destruction on any attacker.

All these defences were linked by a network of concrete trenches running parallel to the beach. Perpendicular tunnels allowed for reinforcements to be brought up. The men manning the defences were not, as the Allied planners believed, inferior *Osttruppen* – 'volunteers' from Poland and Russia. They were fighting-fit men of the 352nd Infantry division, and there were far more of them than anyone expected. They were rested, dedicated, well-trained and fresh; they had been manning the Normandy defences for less than a week.

The beach obstacles were designed to ensure that all these guns had plenty of targets when the invasion came. Most of the obstacles were designed by Rommel himself. Like a kind of martial couturier, he would make sketches of his concepts in a notebook, which he then passed on to his engineers to turn into something workable. Among his little ideas were the 'Czech hedgehogs', which consisted of three pointed girders welded together. They were placed in such a way that they would be submerged at high tide, with the result that the sharp tip would rip the bottom out of attacking boats. There were also wooden stakes set in the sand and pointing seaward to skewer advancing landing craft. This could hardly be called an invention, since Henry V had used the same device against the French cavalry at Agincourt. Rommel's refinement was to tip each of these stakes with anti-tank mines.

Donald Erwin was the skipper of an LCT. He had terrible difficulties getting near enough to the beach to get his troops away.

> As I tried to get in close, I remember seeing the water starting to splash ahead, and I thought the battleship firing behind us was

firing short. But no such thing. The Germans had started to open up with 88mm guns and mortars.

We dropped our ramp to get our troops and equipment off, and then all hell did tear loose. We came under intense fire, as did the LCTs to the right and left of us. Most of the fire seemed to be rifle, machine gun, and mortar fire. But I found I still couldn't get the soldiers and equipment off because the water was too deep. We spent about an hour trying to get our landing craft closer to the beach, and then as I recall, a couple of bulldozers were driven off our ramp in pretty deep water. They did reach the shore, only to be blasted by German gunners with phosphorus shells which started them burning.

Then some of the soldiers, with a couple of the commissioned officers leading, took off from the ramp in water up to their armpits, with rifles held high over their heads, and headed for shore.

And then a series of things happened and sights I saw I'll never forget. As soon as a few more of the soldiers left the ramp, two of them got shot just as they stepped off the ramp. They were quickly pulled back on board ship. One was shot in the back, but it appeared to be more of a grazing type wound and not serious. The other was shot in the stomach, a more serious type wound, and I recall a bullet just missing a rifle grenade on his belt. Had it hit the grenade, it would probably have blown him into bits.

Now I had a problem. The rest of the troops refused to leave, and I had orders that I should disembark these troops and equipment here and now. It had been stressed that to fail to do so could jeopardize invasion plans and an officer could be subject to court martial. It was even suggested that if necessary, orders were to be carried out at gunpoint. But I could in no way force human beings to step off the ramp into almost certain death, because by now the situation had grown much worse. The shell fire had become even more intense, and the sea continued to get rougher. The pandemonium seemed to be everywhere, with lots of smoke and explosions. There were bodies floating in the water.

There were two soldiers nearby that were trying their best to survive. One of them had his arms around one of the large wooden obstacles that the Germans had driven into the beach. Hanging on to his waist was another American soldier. They were using the post as protection against the German rifle and machine-gun fire. So accurate was this fire that the bullets were splintering the post on the sides. The incoming tide was raising the water ever higher on the post, and sooner or later they would have no post left for protection. I often wondered if they survived.

We could see US soldiers huddled at the base of a cliff. They weren't moving inland. The Germans were firing at them from the front and the tide was bringing the sea ever closer to them from behind. At this point, we ourselves had come under intense rifle and machine-gun fire. Bullets were pinging and ricocheting off the ship. The men in my crew were now flattened out against the ship as if they were a part of it. I recall a couple of my crew yelling 'Skipper, let's get out of here.' Believe me, I was ready.

Finally, a reprieve came. Orders came over our radio from our command ship to retract from the beach. When I gave the command to raise and secure the ramp of the landing craft, I noticed a German mine bobbing in the water close to the end of the ramp, but it never quite made contact with the ramp. If it had, we never would have made it out of there.

With the ramp up and secured, we attempted to retract from the beach by winding in the anchor cable with our gasoline engine-driven winch and backing down or reversing with the three screws or propellers on the stern of the landing craft.

At about this time, we rescued four or five sailors from drowning near our landing craft by pulling them out of the sea. They were completely fatigued, and as I remember, as blue from the cold water as any living human being I've ever seen. The one thing I'll never forget is that they were so exhilarated and so very thankful at having their lives saved, that they completely emptied their pockets and gave my crew everything they had in their possession, including their Colt .45 pistols. They had had their LCVP blown out from under them while they were trying to get ashore.

We still had most of our troops and equipment aboard. Finally, around two o'clock that afternoon, we got the orders that we should proceed to the beach and attempt once more to get our troops and vehicles off. This time around, the German shelling and gunfire had been much reduced.

We still had trouble getting in close enough. We never did get all of our troops and vehicles ashore. One US sergeant I had aboard said he was sure he would lose his Jeep and trailer in the water, so he chose to stay with his Jeep and trailer until we beached again. But we didn't beach again on the American beaches. Not until we were at the British invasion area did he and his equipment get ashore over the beach. I wonder how many weeks it took him to get back with his American outfit.

The sea defences had certainly had the desired effect on the day. First they slowed the attackers, which made them much easier targets for the machine-gunners on the bluff. The Germans did not even need to be good shots, because their guns were pre-sighted on the obstacles. A couple of clicks of a ratchet, and it was like shooting tin ducks in a fairground – the gunners knew a target was going to pop up, they just had to pull the trigger at the right moment. This meant that even after the attackers had forced a route through the obstacles they were still in mortal danger; the Germans could concentrate their fire on the gaps in the defence, mowing down each new boat load as it disembarked. 'The bullet hit them and their craft to good effect . . .' said Ludwig Weiner, an inexperienced but efficient Spandau gunner defending the Normandy coast.

> . . . I was a little surprised to see them falling, I don't know why. Never having seen a real battle it did shake me to be hurting those men, even though they were enemies. Even then, in my stupidity, I thought I was only hurting them, not killing them.

The killing was real enough down at the waterline. Private Leo Nash saw his lieutenant, Edward Tidrick, get hit in the throat as he came off the boat. Tidrick stumbled to the beach and raised himself up to give one last order: 'Wire cutters! Advance with wire cutters!' Then a volley from a machine gun cleaved the lieutenant in half – he was split like a log from his head to his waist.

By the end of the first hour of D-Day, Omaha was turning into something very like a massacre. On any other battlefield the attacking army would have fallen back, but at Omaha there was nowhere to retreat to. The soldiers had to advance or die in the water. Many suffered just that fate: some of those who had been wounded in the sea just made it to the beach, only to drown later when the tide came in. Others deliberately withdrew into the water, keeping just their heads above the waves, bobbing like seals so as not to present a target to the gunners. Even then they remained vulnerable to snipers, who were picking off individuals in the water and on the beach. Men drifted into shore 'in a dead man's float' so as to avoid their attention at least until they could make the perilous dash across the sand. Some could only shelter behind the bodies of their comrades, clinging like shipwrecked sailors to the human flotsam all around them.

Private Henry Basey was one of the few black soldiers to hit the beach. Black soldiers were segregated at this time, and none of the African Americans in the US Army were in combat units (most belonged to the Quartermaster Corps). But they took full part in the invasion. Basey, Private First Class, was a driver.

> I was supposed to drive the commander's Jeep but he got killed. So many of the leaders got wounded and killed that mostly you had to use your own judgement. And that's what we did. There was lots of confusion. The ground was vibrating. Just shaking something awful. You couldn't hear anything – just the big guns and mortars and small-arms fire.
>
> What I remember was Pure D Hell. The smell of the bodies and the gunpowder is something I will never get out of my nose. There were guys falling all around me, hollering, and there was no one to help them. I didn't think I'd live through it myself.

Private Harold Baumgarten of the 116th Infantry was on a British LCA. The bow doors were wide enough for only one soldier at a time. 'Many of my thirty buddies went down as they left the LCA,' he said. He managed to get off the boat unscathed, and then had a series of incredibly lucky escapes as he headed for shore.

> I got a bullet through the top of my helmet first, and then a bullet aimed at my heart hit the receiver plate of my M-1 rifle. I waded through the waist-deep water, watching many of my

buddies fall alongside of me. The water was being shot up all
around me, and many a bullet ricocheted off the water-top at me.
Clarius Riggs, who left the assault boat in front of me went
under, shot to death.

A little in front of me, I saw Private Robert Ditmar hold his
chest, and heard him yell, 'I'm hit, I'm hit!' I watched him as he
continued to go forward. He tripped over a tank obstacle and as
he fell, his body made a complete turn and he lay sprawled on the
damp sand with his head facing the Germans, his face looking
skyward. He seemed to be suffering from shock, and was yelling,
'Mother, Mom . . .' as he kept rolling around on the sand. There
were three or four others wounded and dying right near him.
Sergeant Barnes got shot down right in front of me and
Lieutenant Donaldson. Sergeant 'Pilgrim' Robertson had a
gaping wound in his upper right corner of his forehead. He was
walking crazily in the water, without his helmet. Then I saw him
get down on his knees and start praying with his rosary beads.

At this moment, the Germans cut him in half with their
crossfire.

The scenes of carnage in the first wave were reminiscent of the British
experience on the Somme, a generation before. As on that day in 1916,
there were units made up of men who had signed on and trained together,
and who now were dying together. Company A of the 116th Regiment was
effectively wiped out on D-Day. Twenty-two men from Bedford, Virginia,
were among the dead. Of the three sets of brothers in A Company, five were
killed that morning on Omaha and the sixth was wounded.

In those first moments it was hard for the American soldiers to see how
anyone could run the gauntlet of the MG-42s and survive. Harold
Baumgarten, for example, had gone only a few more paces before he took
his first hit.

Fragments from an 88-millimeter shell hit me in my left cheek. It
felt like being hit with a baseball bat, only the results were much
worse. My upper jaw was shattered, the left cheek was blown
open. My upper lip was cut in half. The roof of my mouth was
cut up, and teeth and gums were laying all over my mouth. Blood
poured from the gaping wound. I washed my face out in the cold,

dirty Channel water, and managed somehow not to pass out. I got rid of most of my equipment. I was happy that I did not wear the invasion jacket. I wore a regular Army zippered field jacket, with a Star of David drawn on the back and 'The Bronx, New York' written on it. Had I worn the invasion jacket, I probably would have drowned.

In order to get my equipment off, I had to try to unbuckle the life preserver, which was under my arms and going up near my neck. I accidentally squeezed the carbon dioxide capsules and my life preserver pulled my arms up and I was out of the six inches of water that I was in, and made a perfect target.

The water was rising about an inch a minute as the tide was coming in, so I had to get moving or drown. I had to reach a fifteen-foot sea wall, two hundred yards in front of me. I crawled forward, trying to take cover behind bodies and water obstacles made of steel. I got another rifle along the way. They were zeroing in on me though, and a bullet went through the thick steel rails of the tripod-shaped obstacle that I was behind. I continued forward in a dead-man's float with each wave of the incoming tide. Finally, I came to dry sand, and there was only another hundred yards or maybe less to go, and I started across the sand, crawling very fast.

Baumgarten made it to the sea wall. Small knots of men were gathering here. Some were wounded, some were shell-shocked, all of them were dripping wet, spattered with other men's blood and vomit, weak with fear and seasickness, and numbed by the horror of what they had just come through. As they caught their breath they looked back at the water's edge, where the carnage went relentlessly on.

It was now apparent that we were coming ashore in one of the killing zones, recalled Lieutenant Charles Cawthorn, also of the 116th. The havoc they had wrought was all around: bodies, weapons, boxes of demolitions, flamethrowers, reels of telephone wire, and personal equipment from socks to toilet articles.

Hundreds of lifebelts were washing to and fro, writhing and twisting like brown sea slugs. There was a wide stretch of sand being narrowed by the minute by the tide, then a sharply rising shingle bank that ended at the sea wall. Against the wall were soldiers of the first assault team. Some were scooping out shelters; a number were stretched out in the loose attitude of the wounded; others had the ultimate stillness of death; but most were just sitting with their backs against the wall.

But the sea wall was no safe haven. The Germans up above were raining down mortar fire and dropping the distinctive wooden-handled grenades with the tin-can-shaped fragmentation head known as 'potato mashers'.

While I was resting a young soldier named Gillingham fell in beside me, white with fear, said Private Warner Hamlett of the 16th Infantry. His look was that of a child asking what to do. I said, 'Gillingham, let's get separated as much as we can because the Germans will fire at two quicker than one.' I heard a shell coming and dove into the sand, face down. Shrapnel rose over my head and hit all around me, blowing me three or four feet.

My rifle was ripped from my hand and my helmet went twenty-five or thirty feet in front of me. When I started to jump up and run, a sharp pain hit my spine from my neck to my lower back. I pulled myself by my elbows to my rifle and dragged myself into the hole the shell had made. The shell that injured me took Gillingham's chin off, except for a small piece of flesh. He tried to hold his chin in place as he ran. Bill Hawkes and I gave him his morphine shot. We stayed with him for approximately thirty minutes until he died. The entire time, he remained conscious and aware that he was dying. He groaned in pain, but was unable to speak.

THE SECOND AND THIRD WAVES

As the first men struggled up the beach, others were still making their way in on landing craft. A dreadful scene awaited the second and third waves. The water's edge was already strewn with debris and dead bodies. Shattered landing craft lay askew in the shallows; half-tracks and Jeeps burned in the oily water. Men took what small shelter they could behind the beach obstacles which had been put there to kill them. Bullets fizzed and plopped into the sea like raindrops, and mortar fire raised plumes of sand and water everywhere. And the spilt blood of the soldiers dyed the sea and the spume red. The incoming tide left a pink water-mark on the sand – like a slowly advancing line on a map – with each new breaking wave.

The better coxswains used all their seamanship to get the troops as near to the beach as possible. Robert Adams had friends aboard his LCI, men of the 1st Division that he had put ashore in the invasion of Sicily. 'The ship's crew had great respect for the soldiers we carried. We were proud to have the 1st Division aboard. We all prayed for their safety.' As well as praying, Adams did everything humanly possible to keep them safe up to the moment they left his boat.

> There is almost always a sandbar out from any beach, and our routine was to cut the motor for a second, and let our backwash carry us over, and I must have unconsciously done this, because I was able to get my boat right up to the edge of the beach. Some boats just didn't go in, whether they were inexperienced or what, they were circling round and evidently thought the conditions should be a lot better. But by God, we did plow in.
>
> When you hit the beach, you keep your boat in forward gear at low speed because you must keep enough steerage on so that your boat will be perpendicular to the beach. If your boat got just a wee bit broad side, you would be broached, washed up sideways on the beach. Keeping too much forward motion was touchy because you could end up high and dry on the beach.
>
> Backing the LCVP away from the beach could be just as perilous. You had to back it out, keeping your boat as straight as possible. I was lucky enough to back out without mishap. Backing out I saw something I will remember all my life: my boat grazed a telephone post placed by the Germans as a hazard, and on top of it – I could almost reach out and touch it – was a Teller mine. It could have blown us all to bits.

Not all the boat leaders were so fearless or so conscientious. Their orders were to deliver the troops and get back out as quickly as possible with their boats intact. Some coxswains took that to mean that they were entitled to drop the troops hundreds of yards out to sea, beyond the range of the German mortars. There were angry confrontations in some LCIs between American officers and British boatmen. One sailor who wanted to make the drop far out was persuaded to go close by an American who held a

Colt .45 to his head. Something similar happened on the boat where Private Ray Voight was waiting to make the leap:

Lieutenant Kernsey was with us, and he just got married in England. He told the coxswain 'Listen, you hit bottom, or I'm going to leave a grenade for you.' And he meant it.

Well, we hit bottom. There's no doubt about that. But when they opened the front, the shorter people couldn't touch bottom. A sandbar is what we hit. So the water was six feet or over when we came off. Some of them had to pop their Mae West's and they were sitting ducks. They just bobbed around like corks out there, and I guess they were all of them killed.

I stayed down as much as I could. Being six-foot-two, I could bounce up and get some air and go forward. I stayed and used the cover of water till it was about three-and-a-half feet deep, and then I made a break for it. Things weren't so good then: there were people laying in front of me, most of them I could name.

I lay between four people, and they were hit by a 20 millimeter. I could see the 20 millimeter hitting the crowd, and at the same time an 88 went off over our heads, and I couldn't hear. My ears were ringing. I noticed I was bleeding, so I rubbed my head: it was blood, but it wasn't mine. It was from the people sitting in front of me.

Voight had in fact been hit in the arm by a shrapnel fragment. The wound was so deep he could clearly see the bones of his wrist. He knew that his life depended on moving forward, and his progress was a series of strange, dream-like encounters with one soldier after another – each of them doing what they could to stay alive.

The first man he came upon after being wounded was trying to dig a hole with his helmet in the wet sand. Each new wave washed away the beginnings of his foxhole, but the desperate man continued pointlessly and frantically to dig.

So I left him, and I went by another man, and he was on his knees praying. I rolled up, and I started thinking about those detonators in my pocket. I had let go of the pole charge in the water, and I had forgotten about the one on my back. If that was hit by anything, we'd all blow up. So I took off my combat assault jacket. I was jumping and rolling and running and zig-zagging.

I got up behind my flame-thrower, Eddie Saucier. He was behind one of these wooden poles. This is hard to say: he wanted me to cut his pants open so he could relieve himself. I guess he was having a bowel movement. So I did: I cut his pants open, and then I made a run. I looked back: Eddie was coming through it standing up. He put up his arms sideways, and then just went round in a circle and slowly just went right on down and that was where he stayed.

I promised Eddie that if he got hit, I would get a letter from his wallet and send it back to his fiancée in Harper, Connecticut. But I wasn't going to go back down the beach, not till it quieted down. I think you can understand that.

Private John Zmudzinski hit the beach at 07.30 and was stranded, unable to advance, among the beach obstacles. He was struck by the varying reactions of his comrades as he took time to weigh up the hazards that he would face in the dash to the sea wall.

Some people simply froze and didn't do anything. I saw one GI just lying there calmly taking his M-1 apart and cleaning the sand out of it, he didn't seem to be excited at all. Everybody reacted a little bit different.

On our section of beach, the machine gun and mortar fire was so heavy that everyone was pinned down, shoulder to shoulder, on the beach. You could have held your hand up and probably stopped a tracer bullet. You could see the tracers going over your head.

It was a very funny thing, that you can't explain. You could pretty well duck the machine-gun fire but you could not hide from the mortars. It was a matter of Russian roulette. You didn't know whether to stay where you were or go down the beach. It was just a matter of chance, who got hit.

John Peck was on the deck of the destroyer USS *Herndon*. He was a medical officer, and he was waiting for his first casualties to come in. As he watched

'The water was turning red. I noticed a GI running – an enemy gunner shot him. One of the aid men moved to help him, and he was also shot. I will never forget that medic lying next to the GI and both of them screaming. They died in minutes.' Robert Slaughter, 116th Infantry

the battle on the beach and the waves of aeroplanes passing overhead he saw the luck run out for an entire platoon of paratroopers.

I shall never forget it. It has meant so very much to me since those days. It happened early in the morning. I stood on the deck admiring the huge troop transport planes and their glider planes flying in to drop parachutists behind the shore. All of a sudden, one of the planes exploded with a great flash of white and blue and red lights, which was itself a striking sight by itself against the clear blue sky. All that was left was a large, soft, white cloud of smoke.

Just at that point, the early morning sun struck the cloud and had turned it to a beautiful golden pink, and that's all that was left of that beautiful big plane and all those beautiful men in the plane. Strangely enough, I was struck with a strong emotion of awe. It seemed strange to say, but it was truly a beautiful sight and a fitting tribute to all those men. It seemed to me that I almost heard the Lord speaking, 'To hell with this stuff, fellows. You're coming home with me.'

Lieutenant-General Omar Nelson Bradley, commander of the American invasion troops, was watching the situation develop from the bridge of his command ship, the cruiser *Augusta*. His ears were stuffed with cotton wool to dull the noise of the *Augusta's* guns; his binoculars were glued to his eyes; a sticking plaster covered a huge and unsightly boil on the general's nose.

There was very little radio communication with the shore, but coxswains such as Robert Adams were coming back with snippets of information which they passed on to the top brass:

> We approached a support boat and picked up a one-star general and about four or five people on his staff. He said to me 'Son, how is it on the beach?' I responded, 'Pretty hot, sir.' And he said, 'Well, take us in as close as you can.' I remember as a kid reading cowboy and Indian stories as to how the enemy, whichever side, liked to kill the leader, the man in control, usually obvious by his insignia. I kept thinking, here I've got the man with the star on his helmet. I'm going to get killed just because he's a general: they'll blow this boat out of the water.

Reports from men such as Adams and his one-star general were enough to convince Bradley that the battle was going horribly wrong. But there was almost nothing he could do about it. He seriously considered calling off the attack on Omaha and redirecting later waves to the British beaches. But, given the lack of radio contact – most radio sets had been shot to pieces on the beach – he could probably not have done that even if he had wished to. Yet to stand there watching the destruction of his men was, he later wrote . . .

> . . . a nightmare. I gained the impression that our forces had suffered an irreversible catastrophe, that there was little hope we could force the beach. I agonized over the withdrawal decision, praying that our men could hang on.

Part of the problem was the almost total lack of motorized support for the infantrymen on the beach. Most devastating was the loss of the DD swimming tanks. Twenty-nine were launched, of which twenty-seven sank before they fired a shot. Recent archaeological evidence indicates that they did not go straight down as soon as they were launched, as has often been suggested. They put to sea successfully and got in sight of land, but then the drivers noticed that they were drifting off course in the current. They tried to tack towards the church spire of Vierville, which was their orientation point. It was then, when they were broadside to the high waves on the open sea, that their canvas skirts were overwhelmed and the tanks went down. So it was an understandable lack of seamanship on the part of the tankmen, not a design fault or a tactical error, that left the men on Omaha with so little tank support.

More heavy support was lost closer to shore. The amphibious DUKWs, floating trucks fitted with artillery intended to give close support to the infantry, were top-heavy and capsized out to sea. Twenty big guns went down with them.

Rhino barges carrying bulldozers and Jeeps came adrift and impeded the landing craft heading for the beach. The tricky business of getting a vehicle down a ramp and into deep water was rendered almost impossible by the harassing fire from the bluff. JC Friedman was with the 747 Tank Battalion attached to the 29th Infantry Division.

> The tanks on the LST were landing in eight feet of water.
> They never had a chance. The Germans were zeroed in on us,
> knocking out our tanks before they could even hit the beach.
> The halftracks, Jeeps and trucks were being blown up by
> landmines. There were tank obstacles waiting to be blown up by
> our infantrymen. The noise of gun fire as well as the smell of
> death and gunpowder seemed to be all around us. Everyone in
> my tank was praying. I kept thinking: is this the end of me? Will I
> ever see my family again? God give me strength to go on and see
> this day through. There was constant shelling and shrapnel
> flying off the tanks. It seemed like the earth was crumbling
> beneath us.

Sergeant Alan Anderson, driving a halftrack, made it to shore with his life – but without his vehicle, his gun or any of his equipment:

We hit an anti-tank ditch and the vehicle submerged. I remember looking over at my driver, John Howard, and seeing the water fill the cab and engulf his head so that he was under water. I was trying to urge him at all costs not to take his foot off of the foot pedal because we would lose our momentum. It did no good, because we went down deeper and deeper into the hole, and finally the motor stopped as the water went over the top of the breathing pipe.

John and I had to wait inside the cab for the water to fill in completely because we were unable to get the doors open. As I stood up, somehow or other my life belt became inflated, and I got caught. I had a terrible time pushing myself through. I tore some of the skin off of my side, but managed to extricate myself and get out of the cab. John was able to do the same.

When we got up on top, we came under withering machine-gun fire, and the men were just barely holding on in the back of the halftrack treading water. The vehicle was kind of listing to one side, and it was obvious we couldn't stay there, so I gave them the word: 'Over the side! Let's head for shore!' We had to abandon everything else so we could get upright in the water, and then swim for it. The undertow was absolutely terrible, and it was very very difficult to make any progress.

Anderson got to shore within site of one of the exits from the beach. But without a weapon, or even a helmet, he felt hopeless and useless. He considered making a dash to get off the beach, but everything he could see going on around him made this seem utterly futile. Like hundreds of soldiers along the length of Omaha, he saw no way that he could even move from the spot, let alone press inland.

We were coming under tremendous mortar and machine-gun fire. I noticed that the Germans had zeroed in on this exit route, so anyone who tried to go out through was just committing suicide. Mortars were coming in. There was rifle fire, machine-gun fire, and everything imaginable directed on that exit. Every time somebody tried to make it through that exit, they were getting killed. One man near me who was encouraged by an officer to get off the beach, and this man stood up and tried to go forward, and he got shot right between the eyes. Several other men were killed in like manner.

I decided then that it was best to dig in and stay put for the time being, because there was no place to go and I had no weapon or anything else to do anything with. I then proceeded with my hands to dig into the sand, and I found a helmet and I used that helmet to dig further and dig myself down.

Anderson shovelled the sand out in front of him. He was now lying in the lee of something very like a child's sandcastle; this was all the protection he had from the raking German gunfire. Nevertheless, it probably saved his life, because it was enough to slow a couple of machine-gun shells that pierced his sand wall and fell spinning into his cupped hand. In the din of battle, he took a moment to inspect the spent bullets, suddenly as harmless as dead wasps: 'They were hot. I remember looking at them and thinking how odd that was.'

'I was wearing a pair of white coveralls,' said one medic. 'They had become red from the waist down from handling the wounded. One officer came to me with a slight wound in his earlobe, and told me he wanted to be sure it got in his records for a purple heart.'

All Anderson's memories from that moment are bathed in an air of the surreal. His experience of being levitated by passing shells would have been almost magical were it not so horrible:

> The navy started firing against the pillboxes in our area. Big
> 12- or 16-inch shells were landing thirty yards or less in front of
> us. They created such a vacuum that they pulled you right out of
> the hole. I remember being just lifted up when these shells went
> over, and slammed back down in the ground after they exploded.
> The concussion was beyond belief. I was deaf for about three
> days afterwards.

Anderson was joined in his foxhole by some other soldiers trying to find their unit. Together they made the dash across the beach.

> I heard some fellow ask about his buddy and one of our fellows,
> Luther Winkler, said 'He's dead. His whole head is blown away.' I
> went over to see how Winkler was, and his face was just exactly
> like raw hamburger.
>   Some man came running holding his intestines in his
> hands. He had been hit by shrapnel, and he was hollering
> 'Help me! Help me!' and his intestines were kind of hanging
> and running out through his fingers, and the next thing I
> knew he fell, probably dead, within maybe five or ten feet of the
> aid station.

This was mid-morning, and the fact that there was an aid station at all means that, by this point in the day, the mechanisms of logistical support were beginning to function. Doctors got to work in a captured pillbox as soon as the German dead were cleared out. Men with chest and abdominal wounds were treated here, on dry land, because they could not be moved far. Those who had been hit in the arm or the leg were sent back down to the water's edge to be ferried back to hospital ships.

Stretcher-bearers performed miracles of courage, running into the line of fire to rescue men who were calling for a 'medico' or (more often) for their mother. Medics wore army uniform but were unarmed, as stipulated in the Geneva Convention. They were identifiable to friend and foe alike by the red cross worn on their sleeves and painted on their helmets. Though casualties among medicos and stretcher-bearers were high, Captain Richard Fahey of the Army Medical Corps felt that the enemy were, on the whole, obeying the rules of war. 'There is always a bad apple in every crowd. But our medics on the beach were within point-blank range of the Germans, and they were honourable enough to respect the Red Cross bands – I am sure of that.'

Captain Fahey had come in on the second or third wave, picking up some passengers along the way.

> Our craft came upon a bunch of American soldiers floating helplessly in the water. They had been blown out of their craft. We fished them out and, since they had nothing but the clothes on their back, we told them that we would transfer them on to some crafts that were travelling back to England. To a man they protested, and insisted upon going in. They had nothing, no guns, nothing! We each had a supply of six boxes of K-ration which was to last us for the first two days. So we each shared two boxes of our K-rations with them and these men came into the beach with us.
>
> There were virtually no army vehicles or Jeeps on the beach, and the ones that had arrived were blown up by the Germans. There were many wounded and dead. I saw one man whose remains consisted only of a sheet of skin flattened on the sand. There was a circular place in the middle of the skin, apparently where the explosion had occurred. The only part of his body that remained were his hands, the calvaria of his skull and his feet.
>
> I remember a lieutenant who was hit on his steel helmet with a shrapnel fragment. The shrapnel knocked a large flap into the front of the helmet, bending it under his scalp in the frontal area of his head. Blood was streaming down his face. I took hold of the rim of the helmet and by slowly wiggling it side to side, managed to get it off his head and dumped his dirt-filled hairy scalp flap out of the helmet.
>
> I cleaned the wound as best I could, and repaired the scalp with sutures and more sutures. When I finished, he felt so good that he began shouting 'My men need me, I am going back out there, let me go!' I had to tell him that he was going back to England, and that was final. He was a real nut – no, a real guy.

AT POINTE DU HOC

The sheer promontory of Pointe de la Percée is drawn like a curtain around the western end of Omaha Beach. Beyond it, out of sight of the beach itself, is a second headland called Pointe du Hoc. From the seaward side they stand out like twin exclamation marks on a blank page.

In 1944 the most formidable German gun battery in the American sector was sited on Pointe du Hoc. From these heights the great guns, with their fifteen-mile reach, could easily shoot down on the gentle golden curve of Omaha; they could lob 155mm shells into the armada that crowded the sea to the horizon; or they could turn their cyclops gaze on to the wide-open beach at Utah Beach, stretching away to the north and west.

The Allies had decided that the battery had to be put out of action on D-Day. Aerial bombing might do it, but it was rightly considered too hit-and-miss an approach. The guns would have to be captured and disabled by a specially trained force. The 2nd Ranger Battalion of the US Army was given the job.

The plan was that three companies of the 2nd Battalion would make a direct assault on Pointe du Hoc. They would land on the narrow shingle beach, scale the cliffs and take the guns while the defenders were still stunned by an accurate and precisely timed naval bombardment. They would hold the guns while three more companies of Rangers, landing at the far end of Dog Green sector on Omaha, swiftly proceeded up the Vierville draw to the coast road, turned right, and attacked the fortifications at Pointe de la Percée. If their comrades at Pointe du Hoc had succeeded, then the Rangers from Omaha Beach would link up; if they had failed, then the Omaha Rangers would attempt to capture the big guns from the landward side.

So there were three separate chances to take the six great guns out of the battle: the bombardment from the air; the assault from the sea; and the smash-and-grab raid across the land.

But this carefully laid plan started to go wrong even before D-Day dawned, when one of the officers of the 2nd Battalion experienced a spectacular loss of faith in the plan. Sergeant Frank South, a 19-year-old medic, witnessed the kerfuffle:

> Late at night on the 5th there was a great deal of shouting going on in the gangway outside the surgery. It appeared that our newly appointed battalion commander had become a bit drunk and

was convinced that all the Rangers were being sent on a suicide mission. He was complaining loudly about it. Word got back to Colonel Rudder that things were going haywire with this officer, whereupon he left the ship he was on and came over to the *Ben Machree*, relieved the officer of his command, and assumed command of the task force, which was to assault the cliffs at Pointe du Hoc.

Colonel Rudder took this chance to step into the breach, even though he was under orders from General Huebner not to make the assault. This was certainly a blessing in disguise as Rudder would play a decisive role in the events of the coming day.

But at the time it was unsettling for the men. Frank South spent the night obsessively checking his gear; as a fighting medic he was equipped both to take lives and to save them.

> I compulsively worked on my Colt .45 automatic: cleaning it, re-cleaning it, checking it, working the slide, and making sure that the clips and rounds were in order. Next I turned to sharpening my fighting knife, and again inspected my medical pack. It had everything from bandages to morphine to plasma, and anything else I could think of.

In the morning the men were loaded into British LCAs. From here, a mile or two west of Omaha, Frank South had a magnificent view of the entire invasion fleet, and of the first minutes of the campaign to liberate Europe.

> Dawn broke with leaden overcast skies. The seas were gray and white-capped, and it was cold. Planes were overhead giving us air cover and the big guns from the warships were firing – to what effect, we couldn't tell. It was extraordinarily spectacular. The noise of the ships' fire, the huge armada on our left, warships as far as our eyes could see.

The Rangers were scheduled to touch down on the beach below Pointe du Hoc at 06.30. The naval bombardment of the heights was due to lift at the same moment. But as the LCA approached the shore it became clear to Colonel Rudder that his craft was heading for the wrong Pointe. Perhaps it was the spectacular distraction of the events on Omaha, or maybe it was the strong eastward current, but the British coxswain was heading for Pointe de la Percée, three miles east of the objective. Rudder ordered the sailors to make a sharp right turn.

> This meant that we had to come in more or less parallel to the cliffs, and started picking up fire from the German positions along the top. On our boat, one of the British sailors returned fire with a Lewis machine gun, to little or no effect, of course. As we began to close with the shore the battleship *Texas* and the British destroyer *Talybont* could see the action on top of the cliffs and started laying down some very effective shell fire.

The detour via Pointe de la Percée had made the Rangers late. Despite the efforts of the naval destroyers, the Germans had had time to get out of their bunkers and back to their gun emplacements. When the Rangers arrived at the beach they were waiting.

The Rangers were equipped with rocket-propelled grapnel ropes. They fired these at the clifftops as they hit the shore. But the ropes had become wet and heavy on the way in, and many fell short. Sergeant Leonard Lomell was in charge of the second platoon of D Company. As their boat touched ground he let loose his six rockets and careered off the LCA. He did not see how many of the grapnels found the clifftop:

> The ramp goes down, I'm the first guy shot, machine-gunned through the right side. I don't know if it was a machine-gun bullet or a rifle bullet. It just went through my right side, through the muscle. And then I step off into water over my head. Believe me, I wasn't counting ropes. I came out of that water and I have my arms full of gear and stuff. The guys pulled me out, my platoon, and I just rushed to the base of the cliff and grabbed any rope or thing that we could get in our hands to get up that cliff. I couldn't tell you if they were my ropes or F Company's ropes or E Company's ropes.

Sergeant Frank South saw a Ranger carry his rockets on to the shingle and let them off at point-blank range to be sure they reached the top.

US Rangers bring prisoners down from Pointe du Hoc, the dogtoothed outcrop of which can be seen in the distance. The Americans have hung the stars-and-stripes on the rockface as a signal to the Allied naval gunners. It is telling them not to shell this part of the coast.

Sergeant Cripps hand-fired them while standing only three feet off. In the process of firing the first one, he was partially blinded, with carbon particles embedded deeply in his face. Nevertheless, he went on, and again, in almost direct line of fire from the machine gun, was able to get the second one in position, fired it, again taking a terrible blast. It took extraordinary courage, determination and self control. I still feel this act of bravery was never properly recognized or rewarded.

Some of the Rangers had ladders that they had borrowed for the occasion from the London Fire Brigade. The ladders were heaved into position on the cliff face with their feet in the boat. One soldier who attempted to scale the cliff by this method was seen pitching from side to side 'like a metronome' as the German tracer bullets whizzed either side of his head.

Most of the Rangers opted to attempt to go up by rope, using their combat knives to carve out handholds in the soft rock of the cliff face.

Some were still struggling at the bottom, trying to heave themselves up. The naval shells had knocked chunks of rock out of the cliff, creating a pile of slag at the bottom ten-feet high. This was a kind of head-start, but it was still a daunting climb.

> **Bill Petty, one of our more assertive combat types, was standing and cursing at the bottom of the rope,** said Frank South. **The rope was slippery, muddy and wet. Captain Block, also an assertive type, said 'Soldier, stop fooling around and get up that rope to the top of the cliff.' Petty – a buck sergeant at the time – turned to Captain Block and said in his Georgia drawl: 'I've been trying to get up the goddamned rope for five minutes and if you think you can do any better, you can fucking well do it yourself.'**

But the Rangers knew how important it was to move fast: they were at their most endangered when they were on the way up, unable even to shoot back. Some of the soldiers were clever enough to tie burning short-fuses to the grapnels before they fired them; the hiss and sparkle of the fuses made the Germans think they were bombs about to go off, and they kept away from the cliff edge. All the same, some got close enough to roll stick hand grenades over the precipice: all the Rangers could do was tuck in their heads and hope for the best as the *Stielhandgranate* tumbled down the cliff face and detonated around them.

The braver German defenders went up to the edge and sawed through the ropes with knives and bayonets. The confrontation was like something out of the Hundred Years' War, a full-frontal attack on castle battlements. All the Germans lacked was boiling oil – and all the Americans needed was an old-fashioned siege engine.

Despite the Germans' best efforts, the first of the Rangers made it to the top, spraying machine-gun fire as they hauled themselves on to the level ground. There were plenty of crater-holes, a helpful consequence of the earlier aerial bombardment, and soon the Rangers had enough men on the clifftop to push forward.

Sergeant Lomell was completely focused on the task. Disabling the dangerous guns was far more important than hanging around and killing Germans.

We played it like a football game. Charging hard and low. And when we got over the top, nothing stopped us. We depended on speed. We went right into the shell craters for protection, because there were snipers around, and machine guns firing at us. We wait for a moment, just a moment. If the fire lifted we're out of that shell hole into the next one.

There was an anti-aircraft position off to our right and machine guns off to the left of us. Maybe a hundred yards away. We were charging out of a shell crater and machine guns opened up on us. And there was another machine gun that we destroyed on our way in. We did have some fire fights, little skirmishes. When we were confronted, we'd drive them out and fight them and they'd run like rabbits, you know, right into their holes, and out they went. But we never stopped. We kept firing and charging all the way through their buildings. 'Find the guns' was our big objective.

But the guns weren't there. When the Americans entered the great casemates which had been built to house the guns they found that the long gun barrels had been replaced with wooden logs.

To some of the Rangers this was a bitter disappointment – had they stormed the heights for nothing? – but others thought that the immense artillery pieces could not be far away and that, until they were destroyed, they represented a real danger to the men coming in on Utah and Omaha. Sergeant Lomell scouted around the hilltop, thinking that there could not be many places to hide six huge guns.

We saw these markings in this sunken road. It looked like something heavy had been over it. We didn't know if it was a farm wagon or what the hell it was. We had to go looking for the guns, because we couldn't hear anything big firing nearby, just the mortars and 88s coming in. And God, we were surrounded by troops, a combat patrol of about forty or fifty Germans walked in front of us not more than twenty feet away. I've got about ten or twelve Rangers: I'm not about take on fifty Germans when we've got a mission to perform. Finding the guns comes first. The Germans were headed in the other direction, so we let them go.

Leaving most of his patrol to set up a roadblock and destroy telegraph lines, Sergeant Lomell set off down a dirt path between two high hedges. This was bocage, the typical Norman countryside that had caused so much trouble to the gliders in the night. It was like walking down a wooded railway cutting. The Rangers could not easily see into the fields either side of the road.

Jack and I went down this road not knowing where the hell it was going. But it was going inland, and at that point in time we had actually made deepest penetration on D-Day. We came upon this vale, or this little draw with camouflage all over it. And lo and behold – just pure luck – I peeked over this hedgerow and there were the guns. They were all sitting in proper firing condition, the ammunition piled up neatly, everything at the ready, pointed at Utah Beach.

But there was nobody in this emplacement. We looked around cautiously and about a hundred yards away or so in the corner of a field was an officer talking to about seventy-five of his men. We assumed that they would be back to their gun positions as soon as they got their instructions straight. And that's why we had to act with such speed.

I said 'Jack, you cover me, I'm going in there and destroy them. Keep your eyes on these people because I won't know if anybody comes.' All I had was two thermite grenades. I put one in the elevation mechanism and the second grenade in the traversing mechanism. There's no noise to a thermite grenade that could be heard a hundred yards away. These grenades were used especially for this sort of job because they melt the gears in the mechanism. Then I broke their sights with my rifle butt. And that knocked out two of them.

Then we ran back to the road, which was a hundred yards or so back, and got all the other thermite grenades from the remainder of our guys. We stuffed them in our jacket and we rushed back and we put the thermite grenades, as many as we could, in traversing mechanisms and elevation mechanisms.

Jack and I were scared to death that we couldn't get this mission accomplished fast enough. Maybe in another ten

minutes those guns would have raked Utah Beach. But we caught
them unawares. I don't think they dreamed there was an
American soldier anywhere near those guns until they found
them destroyed.

This individual act of creative vandalism completed the Rangers' mission
for the day, and earned Sergeant Lomell the Distinguished Service Cross. It
was not yet 08.30 in the morning.

The Germans, presumably infuriated to find that the big guns had been
destroyed under their noses, counter-attacked ferociously. Colonel
Rudder's three companies were now in effect besieged in the strongpoints
that they had taken from the Germans. Their comrades should by now
have been coming up from Dog Green Sector to relieve them, but
A Company of the 2nd Rangers Battalion had been practically annihilated
down on Omaha Beach. There was still a long day ahead for the Rangers.

Frank South was kept busy tending to the casualties.

I don't recall how many we treated. It was just an endless, endless
process. Periodically I would go out and bring in a wounded man
from the field, carrying or leading one back, ducking through
the various shell craters. One time I went out to get someone,
and was semi-carrying him back, more or less on my shoulders,
when he was hit by several more bullets and killed. I didn't
realize he was dead. Remembering that is still bothersome, a
burden of some weight.

Colonel Rudder was directing the battle from a command post he had set
up in a German pillbox. As if the Rangers did not have enough ordnance
coming their way, a shell from a British warship landed right next to the
post, killing one officer and wounding another who was in there with
Rudder. He stormed out of the bunker in a rage, only to be shot in the leg
by a German sniper. Though he was wounded and concussed, he continued
to lead his men. Many of them attest that it was this inspirational example
that kept them going, even though they were hit by attack after attack after
attack. By the time they were relieved on 8 June, more than twice as many
men had been killed or wounded holding on to Pointe du Hoc as had been
lost in the taking of it. Only 90 of the 225 men who climbed the heights
were left standing.

MOVING OFF THE BEACH

'No one can adequately describe Omaha beach around H+5 hours . . .' said Ralph Steinway, a signalman who landed on the Dog Green sector in the middle of the morning.

> . . . the beach littered with equipment vehicles, some abandoned, some burning. The bodies, two and three deep, on the beach. Others floating near the ships. It seemed the sea was full of them. Occasionally a shell would explode, you didn't hear it. It just exploded. Whether it was mortars, or from the anti-tank guns in the bunkers, or 88s, who knows.
>
> We were the last to leave our ship in our weapons carrier, which held our duffle bags, test equipment, and some spare parts we thought might be needed for repair.
>
> The beachmaster was shouting at us to get our butts in or we'd end up like those in the water. Our ship was hit by what must have been fire from one of the beach bunkers, and the coxswain who had come up to the bow sea gates to watch the fun, as he called it, was killed.

Landing craft were queuing up to get to shore, or cruising back and forth along the beach, dodging the fire and trying to find a safe place to put down their men – somewhere that was not clogged with smashed or burning vehicles. 'I made a mistake by looking in the water . . .' said Raymond Bednar, whose LCVP was stuck in the jam.

> . . . there were American GIs with their heads off, their arms off, their feet off, they had either been shot, or had hit a mine or obstacles, and these large ships had come by and cut them up. 'My God,' I said, 'This is it.' That's all Omaha Beach was: the dead and dying and the people coming in to replace them.

But by now, the men arriving in LCIs had a rather less hazardous time of it. Some of the beach obstacles had been blown by engineers, and some of the pillboxes and machine-gun nests had been put out of action by the men of the first wave. These later arrivals on Omaha had to grit their teeth and advance past the dead and the wounded. Private Goebel Baynes saw a dead GI in a foxhole holding a photograph of his family in his hand, and was haunted by the memory of it for ever after. Corporal Arden Benthien had to suppress all his compassionate instincts:

> I passed a good many guys who had been hit. But it had been drilled into us that our job was to get going, not to stop and help people who were hurt. It seems pretty cold-blooded, but if everybody stopped and went to try to help everyone, all we'd accomplish was to have a big bunch of people on the beach getting no place.

Benthien 'ran and flopped, ran and flopped, ran and flopped' across the beach. His unit made it intact and unharmed. At the sea wall he linked up with his commanding officer, Captain Bienvenu, and encountered some shell-shocked and frightened GIs from an earlier wave:

> Captain Bienvenu had been poking around a little bit and asking questions and eyeing the scene, and he eventually said 'Come on, let's go.' I was all ready to go. I didn't think this little bit of shelter was any place to stay very long. We tried to talk some of these other lads along there to go with us, but they were not about to leave there. They somehow had a feeling they were safe there. But our bunch, not one of them was hurt. We headed off with the captain down a little gully through the bluff. Right at the first corner of that exit there was a pillbox that had been very neatly knocked out. It was knocked to smithereens. I don't know whether it was naval gunfire or some of our lads who had blown it, but it was blown and no danger to anybody.

Some of the equipment that had been abandoned in panic first thing in the morning was being salvaged and organized into ammo and munitions dumps. Other gear was being left behind by the new arrivals because it was superfluous. Lieutenant Richard Hopkins Conley, who hit the beach at 11.30, 'directed that the pole charges and satchel charges and bangalore torpedoes be discarded, because I could see that the beach wall had been breached, and we wouldn't need them.'

Lieutenant Conley, did he but know it, had set foot in Normandy in the same manner as the Norman conqueror William had arrived in England a thousand years before – by falling on his face:

When the ramp dropped, as the leader, I ran off first. I charged off. It was knee-deep water, and when I hit it, my feet didn't keep up with the rest of me, and I went down flat. But I didn't get any wetter than I was before.

But by this time groups of men on Omaha Beach were coming together and beginning to carry out their assigned tasks. More and more Americans were gathering at the sea wall. More and more of them were ready to carry the fight inland. And more and more officers were rallying their troops, rekindling their warrior spirit.

W Garwood Bacon, whose orders were to set up a command post on the beach, gathered his strength, picked up an abandoned M-1 rifle, and set off along the sea wall to find his commanding officer.

The sea wall was about three-feet high so I crouched low, ran about ten yards, hit the dirt for a few seconds. In this fashion I covered some three hundred yards without mishap. I got up again for the umpteenth time and dashed another few yards. Suddenly I found myself in the midst of 50 to 75 men, all prostrate on the sand or rocks. Thinking they were lying there held down by gunfire, I threw myself down between two soldiers and buried my face. Suddenly I realized there was no rat-a-tat-tat of a machine gun or rifle bullets whining overhead, so I lifted my head cautiously and looked around. The sickening sight that met my eyes froze me on the spot. One of the men I had dropped between was headless, the other was blown half apart. Every last one of them was dead.

All along the beach, men like W Garwood Bacon were screwing up their courage and getting moving. One or two pioneers had found their way past the sea wall and were pleased to discover that the fire was a little less intense there. A short walk was all it took to take a man past the daunting concrete massif of the Atlantic Wall and into the green and open countryside of France. It was still swarming with Germans, of course, but it was a better place to be than the bloodstained beach.

It was as if the attackers had reached the critical weight needed to push on with the war. Individual soldiers no longer felt like victims of a disaster, but were once again part of a fighting army. They drew strength and courage from each other, and from their officers. One of the inspirational leaders on the day was Brigadier-General 'Dutch' Cota. He was moving up and down the beach, urging huddled groups of men to get up and get moving. One of the men on the receiving end of some encouragement from the general was Bernard Feinberg, whose main concern on the way in was not to be killed on 7 June because it was his niece's birthday:

> Cota said something like this: 'No sense dying here, men. Let's go on up the hill and die.' And with these words, he started to tap soldiers on their butts saying, 'Twenty-Nine, let's go!'

The fact that General Cota was exposing himself to enemy fire, proving that it was possible to stand up at the sea wall and live, helped to hearten the men who had been crouching there for hours. Cota came upon another group and, on being told that they were Rangers, bellowed: 'Godammit, if you're Rangers, get up and lead the way!'

The general tarried while bangalore torpedoes – long tubes of explosive – were brought up to blow gaps in the barbed wire. Once through the wire, men began to seek out new routes off the beach, away from the well-defended gullies.

Richard Conley, who on the crossing had been so worried about not showing his fear, was now among those advancing gingerly up the bluff. Mortars were still falling all around him. Some of the men took advantage of the smoke cover provided by brushfires in the scrub, and by folds in the terrain. Slowly and surely they were getting away from the sea and behind the defences of the Germans. Minefields, not machine guns, were now the main danger.

> We were moving in single file between engineer tape that some brave soldiers who preceded us had strung, and we were alerted for 'schuhmines', small anti-personnel mines designed to just blow off half your foot. Sure enough, part-way up the hill, there was a GI lying just off the trail with the front half of one foot gone. But he was smiling. He knew he'd be going home.
>
> We all moved slowly but steadily, and continued on. When we finally got up on the high ground, we stopped while the company assembled. I was shivering, shaking uncontrollably, and I was ashamed of it, until I noticed that all of the combat veterans of

North Africa and Sicily were shaking just as much as I was. And I immediately felt better, to see that we all shared the same fear.

As men reached the top they linked up with other groups of GIs. Bernard Feinberg found an officer from his own unit.

> Major Bingham and I were standing on a hill. He was looking for snipers. One had just killed our new colonel, Phillip Doyle. All of a sudden I heard a ping, a bullet. I dove to the ground. He never moved. He said 'What a lousy shot.' That's what I call cool.

Harry Bare reached the top, but was nearly killed as soon as he got there.

> On top of the cliff a burst of machine gun fire made us duck behind the ridge. There they were: two bunkers, about twenty yards inland. We couldn't advance, so I crawled forward, circled wide, and came down between the bunkers, and destroyed both with grenades in the gun slots. I was very lucky. My canteen was torn to pieces by at least six rounds. Why I wasn't hit, God only knows.

Hal Baumgarten, the defiant Jewish New Yorker who had drawn a Star of David on his combat jacket, was one of those still at the sea wall. He sat there spitting his shattered teeth into the sand. A medico came up and began to bind up his face with a bandage.

> While Sergeant Breden was dressing my face wound with powder and cleaning me up, shells started to land all over. I grabbed him by the shirt to pull him down. He hit my hand away and said, 'You're injured now. When I get hurt, you can take care of me.'

Patched up and woozy from the loss of blood, Baumgarten now joined the remnants of various companies as they moved up through a captured beach exit towards Vierville. On the way up, at about ten o'clock in the morning, he was hit for the second time that day.

> I was wounded in the left foot while crawling. I tried to bandage it myself, I took the shoe off and saw a big hole in the dorsum of

my left foot. Shells started to land, so I ripped the bandage off and pulled the shoe back on, and dove for protection in a hedgerow. Sergeant John Frazier of Company A seemed to be shot in the back and was paralyzed, couldn't move. I later found out his legs were shattered. While leaning over him, a mortar shell landed, and I got shot in the left side of the head through the helmet into my scalp. I guess the helmet saved my life. Blood came streaming again over my left ear and down on to my face. I dragged Sergeant Frazier to cover behind a wall.

As it got dark I became very trigger-happy and started to fire at anything that moved in front of me. I got another bullet through the face. I was not in any severe pain, though, because we were the first American troops ever to be allowed to carry our own morphine. We each carried a grain of morphine in a little toothpaste tube. All you had to do was shoot yourself under your skin and squeeze and you could be relieved of pain.

Alan Anderson, who had been pinned down on the beach since losing his halftrack and all his equipment first thing in the morning, was moving up the hill at about the same time that Baumgarten was picking up his fourth wound of the day.

I went up on the hill just above the exit; there was a ditch off to the left-hand side. I saw four or five soldiers there, Rangers. I said to them: 'Where is the front line?' He said, 'This is the front line. There are Germans over there and they've got machine guns, so stay down.'

I was overtaken by fatigue. You have to remember I had not slept for two nights and all of the day. My clothes were still wet, and that chemical-impregnated material smelled to high heaven. My lips were parched, and I could hardly close my mouth because it was full of sand and other debris from the artillery pounding we had taken on the beach. One of the Rangers said 'Sergeant, why don't you catch a little nap here. I'll stay awake for a couple hours, then I'll wake you and then maybe I can get a little sleep.' So, I lay down. There was a burst of machine-gun fire, and it was pretty close to my head. I just moved over a little bit and thought 'Well, he can't get me here.' And I fell sound asleep.

As evening fell, W Garwood Bacon was still stuck on the beach, witnessing yet more horrors.

> Our demolition squad were stringing wire in preparation for blasting open a passage through which landing craft might pass. They were grouped together fixing the fuse to a detonator; a small shell came hurtling out of nowhere and landed plumb in their midst sending their bodies flying in all directions.

The balance of the battle had now turned in the Americans' favour, but from Bacon's vantage point the situation still looked hopeless. It seemed that the trucks, tanks, men and artillery pieces that crowded the beach were merely providing the Germans, concealed in pillboxes, buildings and dug in cliff positions, with more things to shoot at:

> By 6pm the entire beach was a mass of men, supplies, and equipment. The Germans opened up again in a terrific barrage on the troops and supplies sitting helplessly on the narrow beach. To make matters worse, the tide was on its way again, covering the mounting mass of vehicles and supplies.
>
> During this a wounded soldier and I shared a foxhole. Closer and closer the shells came, blasting the cluttered beach every few yards. The last couple I remember hearing showered us with loose stones, and metal and debris. Then blam, something exploded in my head making crazy patterns of dancing lights. My head swam and my body seemed to be vibrating. Everything continued to whirl and with a fading of the flashes of blinding lights and tremors through the body I opened my eyes to find everything black.
>
> From far away I could hear my foxhole buddy asking 'Say buddy, are you hit?' It was all I could do to mumble 'I don't know. I think so.' With extreme effort I raised my hand to my neck, the back of my head and felt a warm stickiness that could only mean one thing. I had been hit but how badly I could not know. I was blind.
>
> Throughout the remainder of the bombardment lasting about an hour, I prayed silently and fervently that God would spare my eyes.

Bacon spent the night among the wounded.

> It was a weird feeling lying there blind, listening to the jerky
> movements of the chap on my left and the heavy breathing of
> the soldier on my right, breathlessly trying to identify any
> unusual sounds such as might be caused by German snipers
> prowling about. I dozed off to sleep many times for short
> intervals and it seemed that the night would never pass. Guns
> began firing more regularly, so I turned to the soldier on my left
> and whispered 'Hey Joe is it daybreak yet?' After receiving no
> answer or movement from him I rolled over and nudged the boy
> on my right. He too was unresponsive. Thinking out loud I
> mumbled, 'What's wrong with these guys anyway?' 'They're
> dead, buddy, lost too much blood . . .' came the answer from
> further down the row.

The wounded Hal Baumgarten was brought down to the beach during the
night. Like Bacon, he lay there waiting to be taken aboard ship and treated.
It was here that he acquired his fifth and final battle wound of the
Normandy campaign.

> They took me out and put me in a stretcher, and I saw a huge
> statue – I think in retrospect it was a church silhouetted in the
> darkness. They then laid me out on the sand in a stretcher,
> amongst a line of stretchers containing some of my wounded
> buddies. They gave me some more morphine and I went to sleep.
> The next morning German snipers opened up on the beach,
> including the wounded. I got shot in my right knee, in the
> stretcher. Finally at about 3pm on June 7, I was taken off the
> beach out to an LST. There, a Navy doctor took my clothes off
> and cleaned up my wounds.

By the time that Baumgarten was shipped out, the beachhead was secure
and the fighting was moving inland. The invasion plan had teetered on the
brink of disaster at Omaha. Only two of the five beachheads were secure by
nightfall, the Americans had not advanced far inland, and even now they
were desperately vulnerable to a strong counter attack. But the bridgehead
was there, and the momentum was with the Allies.

In the aftermath of battle, a young American soldier lies dead in the wet sand of Omaha.
Someone has taken the trouble to lay crossed guns at his feet as a kind of makeshift marker.
American forces suffered nearly six thousand casualties in all on D-Day.

At Omaha, Rommel came tantalizingly close to fulfilling his aim of driving the invaders straight back into the sea. If the Americans had been forced off Omaha, there would have been a huge gap in the invasion front between Utah Beach to the west and Gold Beach to the east. Panzers could have poured into the gap and prevented a link-up between the American and British forces. The invasion timetable, indeed the whole second front, would have been placed in jeopardy.

But the Americans clung to Omaha, and clawed their way past it. Little by little, they seeped through the cracks in the German defences and attacked the enemy from the rear. They overcame the defenders and breached the unbreachable Atlantic Wall. They did this in one day.

It is strange to think that many of the soldiers who stormed Omaha were eighteen or nineteen years old. They were boys, and had they not been hurled into battle, they would have been graduating from high school that very week.

Nearly three thousand men were killed on the three-mile strip of Omaha Beach. Many of them are buried on the high plateau at Laurent-sur-Mer that they fought and died to capture. The American Cemetery there has a commanding view of the landing ground. Tide and time have washed away all trace of the carnage, but many of the German gun emplacements, set immovably into the bluff, are still there, staring blindly down on the empty strand. Ralph Steinway was one of the men who made it past those machine-gun nests. The last word on Omaha goes to him:

> General Bradley said that anyone who was on the beach on D-Day was a hero. I don't mean to disagree with the general, but we never felt heroic. We were, for the most part, pretty ignorant until we got a little combat-wise, and we did some very stupid things and lived. And we did our jobs.
>
> The men who were heroes were the guys of the 29th Infantry Division that lived and died going across Normandy. The guys that took the bunker at Vierville. The guys that were floating in the water with their hands outstretched as if they tried to grab on to God's robe as He went by. The men who didn't quit. The guys from the 5th Ranger Battalion who were going on up to fight again. I feel honored to have been in their company.
>
> I must stop now. Thank you for listening to me.

5
ON GOLD

The invasion of Europe crept east with the rising tide.

The optimal moment for landing was when the water was not so high as to cover the obstacles, but when the beach was not so wide as to render the dash for cover suicidal. This moment came an hour later on the British beaches than on the American ones.

Gold Beach was a full ten-miles long. But the western half, from the fishing village of Port-en-Bessin to the holiday town of Arromanches, was backed by cliffs as sheer and unassailable as castle battlements. The attack on Gold would concentrate on the eastern end, from Arromanches to Ver-sur-Mer, where the beaches sloped into a hilly but easily negotiable foreshore.

This necessary gap in the invasion front meant that there would be five clear miles between the Americans on Omaha and the British on Gold. And on top of the cliffs, staring straight down on the broad chink in the Allied armour, was the formidable artillery battery of Longues-sur-Mer. So it was vital for the attackers of Gold Beach to get ashore and link up with the Americans as early as possible on D-Day; the Germans were not to be allowed to drive a wedge between Omaha and Gold and split the invasion force in two.

Major Iain Macleod knew a great deal about the plan for Overlord – more than he was supposed to, in fact. As a planning officer on Montgomery's staff in London he had happened upon the knowledge of where the landings would come. Hitler would have sacrificed armies of spies to know what Macleod found out by accident in the spring.

> Thumbing through a file in the Headquarters of the 2nd Army I saw a receipt for a map marked 'TOP SECRET OVERLORD'. To most people the receipt would have meant nothing, but I had just come from the Staff College and recognised the map sheet number as one based on St Lô, which we had used in a staff

exercise. So we were not to land in the Pas De Calais, but in Normandy. I took the receipt away and burned it.

Now, on the morning of 6 June, Major Macleod found himself bobbing through the night on a restless sea. He was not supposed to be going along on invasion day, but both his immediate superiors had burned out in the frantic stress of planning Overlord, and so Macleod found himself promoted to Divisional Assistant Quarter Master General of the 50th Division. This was a job that came with a ticket to Normandy. At first light on the 6th, Major Macleod got up and went on deck.

> The day was becoming warm, and the coast of Normandy began to take shape through the haze. Then, as full light began to come, one saw the ships and the planes. It was a sight so paralysing that tears came to my eyes. It was as if every ship that had ever been launched was there, and even as if the sea had yielded up her wrecks. It was as if every plane that had ever been built was there and, so it seemed in fantasy, as if the dead crews were there too.
>
> There had never been since time began such a rendezvous of fighting men; there never will be again. And I remember reciting, not in scorn, but out of sheer delight at being part of that great company in such a place: 'And gentlemen in England now abed . . .'

All around the fleet that morning, bookish Englishmen in uniform were mouthing the words of Henry V's Agincourt speech. Back in England, one bomber pilot declaimed a different snatch of Shakespeare's play over the radio to his crew as he set off for his second raid of the day: 'Once more unto the breach, dear friends, once more, or close that wall up with our English dead . . .' he said. 'That's fine,' responded his navigator, 'So long as I am not one of the English dead that they close the wall up with.'

Austin Baker, of the 4th/7th Royal Dragoon Guards, was on a landing craft heading for the beach. He was a tank crew wireless operator, temporarily serving on an ARV (armoured recovery vehicle), a turretless Sherman tank fitted with welding equipment, towing bars and all kinds of fitter's paraphernalia. He saw the beginning of the naval bombardment.

The first sight of the French coast gave me a queer feeling. Everybody stared at it without saying very much as we slowly drew towards it, passing the big troop ships which lay at anchor, having sent their infantry on towards the beach in small assault boats. There were several cruisers lying out there too, firing broadside after broadside inland. We passed within a couple of hundred yards of the *Belfast*. The noise of her guns was ear-splitting. There was a battleship firing in the distance – the *Rodney*, so the skipper announced over the loud hailer on the bridge.

   There were destroyers right in close to the beach, firing like mad. They must have been almost aground. Rocket ships – LCTs carrying batteries of rocket guns – and self-propelled guns firing from LCTs added to the general din. Smoke hung over everything and we could see the flashes of exploding shells on land. We couldn't tell which way they were arriving. About half a mile from the beach a Navy motor-boat drifted past with a dead sailor lying across the foredeck. I'd never seen anybody dead before.

   We were still two or three hundred yards offshore when a big spout of water shot up near our starboard side, followed by another in almost the same place. 'We are now being shelled,' the skipper said dramatically. It was very novel and unpleasant.

Jack Danby of the 5th Battalion of the East Yorkshire Regiment saw two separate acts of heroism as he went in with the first wave. Both involved the kind of combination of skill, know-how and improvization that often made the difference between life and death.

There were frogmen engineers on the beach a few minutes ahead of us, clearing away as many of the mined metal obstacles as they could to make things easier for the landing craft. They were up to their armpits in cold, rough water with mortar bombs exploding all around them, working to defuse intricate mechanisms, getting rid of bombs and booby traps, knowing that failure could mean disaster for dozens of men. Those engineer soldiers were the most courageous of us all. They deserved more recognition than ever they were given.

   On one of D Company's craft, the steering gear was damaged.

The Marine corporal in charge steered by hanging outside the
stern and holding the rudder steady with his foot. We found out
months later that he got it back the same way, after about fifteen
miles and five hours in the water.

Carter Barber was an American film cameraman, sent to record the day for
the newsreels. He watched the unfolding drama with all the elation of a
hack who knows he is on to a great story. His prose, written ten days later,
is still aquiver with the excitement of a once-in-a-lifetime scoop.

At five, the barges were circling round in the water off their
looming mother ship, and the terrific barrages started from the
battlewagons that had preceded us into the Bay of the Seine.
One of the most beautiful sights ever was the quadruple balls of
fire that streaked across the sky with their salvos. Blue-azured
little roman candle stuff; it was hard to realize there were tons of
high explosive behind them.

It was like a review, the way we took those barges into the
beach. You couldn't see the heads of the troops over their sides,
just the coxswain's helmet sticking up from the stern. I looked
aloft, saw our cutter's flag twisted around the mast, and in a
spurt of patriotism, climbed aloft, to free the banner.

Just as I came down from the mast, we saw our first bunch of
men. It was light then, and the scene was quickly changing from
one of an even line of boats knifing in orderly rows behind their
leaders towards the beach to a scene of carnage. One Higgins
boat was completely disintegrated by a direct hit from
shore. There were no survivors, and I couldn't even see the
dismembered parts of the troops aboard come down after they'd
been blasted sky high.

The noise was terrific as we neared the beach. For the first time
I felt no need to kind of talk myself into 'This is IT! D-Day!
What we've been waiting, working and worrying for months and
years. This is going to be terrific.' I knew it WAS terrific when the
noise started, and the fact that the invasion had rushed upon me
so swiftly in the past 24 hours didn't seem strange then.

When we saw the LCT get hit, and rushed to her aid, I noticed
plenty of men already floating face down in the water. They

might have just been stunned, sure. But I had to agree with the skipper that we couldn't stop for them just then, but must keep on to get the other men floundering about. We passed one boy floating high and dry on a raft and nosed alongside the first big bunch of men, and started to haul them aboard.

The first bunch I took pictures of with my borrowed camera. Three minutes was enough, and I put the camera down and went forward to throw heavy lines to other men in the water. Twos and threes of them were screaming 'Oh, save me . . . I'm hurt bad . . . please, please, please!' And I yelled back 'Hang on, Mac, we're coming' and looked astern at the guys on our boat hauling other wounded men aboard, and wondered at the inadequacy of everything. We needed ten pairs of hands more.

One big fellow, who afterwards admitted he weighed 230 pounds stripped, had two legs broken, and was in intense pain. We had a hell of a time getting him aboard because his clothing was waterlogged and he was weighted down with helmet, rifle, pack, ammunition, et al. The man screamed as we helped him aboard, but we had to be a little callous so that we could get the man on deck and move to another group of survivors.

I watched one man from the bow. He shouted 'I can't stay up, I can't stay up.' And he didn't. I couldn't reach him with a heavy line, and when we came towards him his head was in the water. We didn't stop, and went on to seven or eight more men who were just about ready to sink too.

Although it seemed like hours, we quickly got all the men aboard, including one old man who was so soaked in water that he was almost drowned. His head was laid open almost to the brain. It took five of us on our boat's fantail to hoist this man aboard, by placing boat hooks under his armpits.

This was when the transport surgeon looked at the boy in the lazarette and pronounced him dead. This kid had crawled into the lazarette by himself, although vomiting blood the while. He laid there for an hour while we picked up his mates, and had apparently gone into a coma. Four hours later, the kid reappeared from the lazarette and went aboard the LST. 'You were supposed to be dead,' said one of our boys. 'Yeah,' said the kid querulously, spewing blood from his mouth.

We disposed of our only casualty. This man had died with his eyes open, apparently from shock. Rigor mortis had already set in and we couldn't close his eyes. When we searched his pockets for identification, I thought it was the first time and last time anyone ever rolled this guy right under his eyes. He had a wallet tightly secured in a condom, with hundreds of pound notes, and an American silver dollar round his neck. Been in the Navy five months, thirty-nine years old.

We stripped him to his underwear, tied him to a rusty piece of steel, and prepared to bury him. I tried to cross his arms over his chest, but they were too stiff. His flesh was green. McPhail, the skipper, reappeared on deck with his Bible, intoned the words, and we stopped the cutter's engines. I took off my helmet and the rest of the boys followed suit. We slid the body into the sea.

We called a wee time out. 'What time do you think it is, Barber?' asked McPhail.

'Way past noon at least. Maybe four o'clock.'

'It's nine-thirty this morning.'

We looked around at the heaps of clothing strewn on the deck, gear of the rescue, some abandoned and some cut off. I went below to look around, and it was even worse. There were clothes in the galley sink, on the stove, in the focsle, in the head, on the bunks. I stepped on a soggy bunch and blood oozed out. The whole boat below decks stank of blood, vomit, and urine.

By now the infantry were going in, or waiting to go in. Some were queueing to get aboard their landing craft, others were already afloat in choppy water. IG Holley used the time to dispense a small tot of compassion to his younger comrades:

With the Middle East behind me, and aged 20, I felt like an old soldier. I was answering the usual question – 'What's it really like in action?' – from the ones that hadn't been. I tried for the last time to reassure 'Brakey' (eighteen years old), one of the young reinforcements who had attached himself to me. He was very apprehensive about going on his first op.

On our craft we had a small keg of naval rum and a couple of bottles of whisky put there by some unknown person or authority – I never found out who – probably with the intention that we might need a little Dutch courage. One drink was enough for me. I hoped it would settle a queasy stomach caused by the flat-bottomed craft tossing about in the swell.

Things were becoming hot now. 105s or 210s were coming in on us. There was a sharp crackling of machine-gun fire and I quickly got my head down after taking a quick look. The long line of beach lay ahead and immediately behind hung a thick pall of smoke. There were flashes of bursting shells along the whole front. We were in range now of mortar fire, a weapon we had grown to respect in the past.

The tension was at its peak when we hit bottom. Down goes the ramp, out goes the captain with me close behind. We were in the sea to the tops of our thighs. Floundering ashore we were in the thick of it; to the right and left the other assault platoons were hitting the beach. Mortar bombs and shells erupting the sand and the brrr . . . br . . . brrurp of Spandau light machine-guns cutting through the din. There were no shouts: everyone knew his job and was doing it without saying a word. There was only the occasional cry of despair as men were hit and went down.

To my right I spotted 'Laffy' crawling on his hands and knees with the radio floating in the water behind him. I thought he had been hit; later I learned that he was in the middle of a relapse of malaria – a legacy quite a few of us had from the Middle East.

The beach was filled with half-bent running figures. We knew that the safest place was as near to Jerry as we could get. A near one blasts sand over me and my set goes dead (during a quiet period later on I find that shrapnel has riddled my set). A sweet rancid smell is everywhere, never forgotten by those who smell it: burnt explosives, torn flesh and ruptured earth.

The German defence of the beach was nothing like as murderous as on Omaha, but still there was plenty of danger. There were no safe beaches on D-Day. Everyone knew that the first seconds were the most hazardous, when you were near the easy target of a stationary landing craft, or moving slowly through the shallows. You were quick, or you were dead. So Private WH Edwards was horrified to be lumbered with some cumbersome extra luggage on the way in. He kicked up a fuss that probably saved his life:

I landed with the 2nd Battalion The South Wales Borderers, the only Welsh battalion to land on that day. When we started to go down the steps of the LCI, a sergeant informed me that every man in our platoon was to take a bicycle with us. This came as quite a shock, and my protestations were heard by an officer. When I informed them I couldn't swim, he accused me of holding up the invasion. I was relieved of the bicycle.

We proceeded into the water. I grabbed the rope which a sailor had attached to a disabled tank. All went well until a buckle of my pack got entangled with the rope. A large wave caught me, my steel helmet went one way, and my rifle went the other way. I was about to go under for the third time when my friend, knowing my fears and seeing me in difficulties, came out and dragged me ashore. He started to pump the water out of me until I had recovered sufficiently to realise that the open beach, with shot and shell flying around, was not the healthiest place to stay.

Sergeant Mackenzie was offloaded in reasonably shallow water, but nearly succumbed to unexpected hazards beneath the surface:

We kidded ourselves that as we were on an LCA, we would land straight on the beach without getting our feet wet. At about 100 yards from the beach, the bloke in charge of the LCA called out 'Sorry lads, this is the best I can do. Mind how you go off the ramp as it might crush your feet.' Well off we went: bed roll on shoulder, kit on back, rifle slung round neck, and fingers crossed.

The water struck cold at first, but I soon forgot that in frantic efforts to keep my feet. The sand was like a quagmire underfoot. As you put one foot down, you had the devil's own job to get it out. And when you did, you kept your balance by a miracle. Although the water probably wasn't more than four-feet deep, shell holes and bomb craters made it eight-feet deep in places. You never knew when you were going into one. Also there were bodies under water, and these could throw you over.

At that moment Private Jim Daly was trying hard not to become a dead body underfoot. At first he had thought the landing was like 'another

'I stepped down into only a couple of inches of water. By the third step I was on to dry land and running, bangalore torpedo in my left hand and rifle in my right. My way lay close to a burning tank; I felt the heat of the flames on my face.' Frank Wright, Royal Marines

practice in Bournemouth,' but as men fell dead or wounded to the left and right of him, he was suddenly full of despair. He felt sure that the invasion had already turned to catastrophe – until he saw an inspirational sight on the beach.

> The chaps who had fought in Africa had their heads down. I knew the whole thing was in earnest. Even at nineteen years of age you catch on quickly. On our LCT we had four SPs, a Bren carrier and a Sherman tank. When we came off the ramp, the halftrack that I was in was hit by an 88mm shell. We were now blocking the ramp, so nothing else could get off. We swam out and managed to fasten a tow rope to the front. A tank that had backed up pulled us on to the beach.
>
> At this moment, with dead and wounded on the beach, I felt that the whole invasion must have been a failure. I was drenched

to the skin and very miserable, but then the sight of our troop commander – riding a white horse along the beach and urging everyone on – cheered me no end.

It is a complete mystery where the commander got a horse, or what made him think that a trot across the sand was a good idea. Higher ranks were always targeted by gunners and snipers (American officers went to great lengths not to display easily visible insignia), so a commander making such a grand chivalric gesture would have been an irresistible target.

All along the fifty-mile invasion zone, machine guns were the main danger faced by the troops once they got out of the sea. Most menacing of all were machine guns in pillboxes. They caused more Allied deaths than any other weapon or tactic. The Allied planners knew the power of the pillbox, and there were units specially trained to neutralize them.

Our job was to clear the beach of machine-gun nests before the main infantry landings, said Ivan West, one of the first commandos ashore on Gold. **The Navy began silencing the enemy guns by firing shells through the pillbox slits. Later we saw the guns inside, twisted like pipe cleaners, the bodies blown to kingdom come.**

But many gun-nests were left untouched by the naval bombardment. And a pillbox with a machine gun could cut like a scythe through advancing infantry. On the other hand, they were peculiarly vulnerable at close quarters. A gunner in a pillbox has a strangely blinkered view of the battlefield: he can see for hundreds of yards ahead, but does not know what is happening five yards directly to the left or right.

One man who understood pillboxes was Colour Sergeant-Major Stanley Hollis of the Green Howards. He won the Victoria Cross on Gold Beach – the only person to be awarded Britain's highest honour for bravery that day – for a single-handed action against a pillbox at Mont Fleury. His citation for the medal tells the story:

During the assault on the beaches and the Mont Fleury battery, Sergeant-Major Hollis's company commander noticed that two of the pillboxes had been by-passed, and went with Sergeant-Major Hollis to see that they were clear. When they were twenty

yards from the pillbox a machine gun opened fire from the slit, and Sergeant-Major Hollis instantly rushed straight at the pillbox, recharged his magazine, threw a grenade in through the door, and fired his Sten gun into it, killing two Germans and making the remainder prisoner.

He then cleared several Germans from a neighbouring trench. By his action he undoubtedly saved his company from being fired on heavily from the rear, and enabled them to open the main beach exit.

Later the same day, in the village of Crépon, the company encountered a field gun and crew, armed with Spandaus, at a hundred yards' range. Sergeant-Major Hollis was put in command of a party to cover an attack on the gun, but the movement was held up. Seeing this, Hollis pushed right forward to engage the gun with a PIAT from a house at fifty yards' range. He was observed by a sniper who fired and grazed his right cheek, and at the same moment the gun swung round and fired at point blank range into the house.

To avoid the falling masonry, Sergeant-Major Hollis moved his party to an alternative position. Two of the enemy gun crew had by this time been killed, and the gun was destroyed shortly afterwards. He later found that two of his men had stayed behind in the house, and immediately volunteered to get them out. In full view of the enemy, who were continually firing at him, he went forward alone using a Bren gun to distract their attention from the other men. Under cover of his diversion the two men were able to get back.

Wherever fighting was heaviest Sergeant-Major Hollis appeared, and in the course of a magnificent day's work he displayed the utmost gallantry, and on two separate occasions his courage and initiative prevented the enemy from holding up the advance at critical stages. It was largely through his heroism and resource that the Company's objectives were gained and casualties were not heavier, and by his own bravery he saved the lives of many of his men.

Hollis's magnificent feat of arms began half a mile inland: the Green Howards had met little resistance on their slice of King sector. The East

Yorkshire Regiment, who were just to the left of them, hit trouble straight away. Jack Danby was one of them.

> We reached the shore opposite a high sea wall and a line of fortified buildings. Pre-bombing by the RAF had put a lot of the Nazis out of action but they were still lively along our seafront. There was small arms fire from every building. Barbed wire barriers were strung all along the sea wall. It was very formidable. Tucked in under the wall we were out of range, except for mortar bombs exploding on the beach, and we managed to cut some of the wire and clear a narrow way up a concrete ramp.
>
> When we had crossed the promenade behind the wire we were able to get into the shallow communication trenches which the Germans had made around the buildings, and could shoot into the window spaces left in the fortified houses.

To the right, things were going pretty much according to plan – and only a few minutes behind the stopwatch precision of the schedule. Major ARC Mott was company commander with the 1st Battalion of the Royal Hampshires. He was due to land on the stroke of H-Hour at 07.30, but was eight minutes late.

> At 07.38 we touched bottom and stopped, some way from the sea's edge on this flat beach, as we expected. Down went the ramp and out I jumped, no doubt starting to shout 'Get up them beaches,' as ordered. This ended in bubbles, for the water was about seven-feet deep. My Mae West saved me and brought me to the surface, with the LCA about to pass over me. I caught hold of a chain and was towed ashore. After a moment I saw an aerial, then a steel helmet, then the astounded eyes of Private Dossor, my batman, who was the only man to follow my example. We had hit a sandbank and the LCA had gone over it, and could continue the run-in.
>
> We all disembarked safely. I noticed all five of B Company's LCAs had fanned out to line abreast some way out. Five columns of men began to make their way over some 300 yards of sand after wading the last eighty yards knee-deep. I was soaked to the skin. My watch had stopped at 07.48. My map case had floated

Not many men got ashore dry-footed. Most fought in dripping wet clothes, which dried on them over the following days. These men are disembarking from a British LCA. In the background, a tank is about to roll down the ramp of LCT 858 and trundle into the fray.

away and for all I knew my Sten and ammunition were useless. My binoculars were misty.

We could see tanks and a flail-tank ahead of us and toiled on, walking rather than running. I found myself in the lead, going between the obstacles and up to a large, shallow pool which I waded through. I could not get any wetter and I was keen to get off the beach, which was starting to become less safe.

At last we reached a thin belt of wire. We paused for a moment and I joined 11 Platoon and told a man with wire cutters to get busy and a tape man to follow. The latter rather slowly and crookedly went forward, paying out tape to mark a safe route through a field of reeds some five-feet high. We stayed on the edge, waiting for something to open up at us. Eventually it did, mortars I think, with a little whistle and small explosion. I got my men away from the shingle, but some of company HQ crouched down behind a tank and got a direct hit, as did another lot close to me. I saw a steel helmet lobbed into the air, and this may have been the luckless Private Dossor's, who died from his wounds next day.

As soon as the tape man was well out in front we followed in a long snake. Only a direct hit could have done much damage in the reeds. There were other snakes on either side and we got safely to the hedge. We were through the defences with surprising ease, for ladders and bangalore torpedoes were not needed, and though there were notices saying 'Achtung Minen' everywhere, I do not think anyone had touched off a mine. The grass was burning and smoke obscuring the view.

Major Mott realized he was in the wrong place, some distance to the west of his objective, the village of Asnelles.

I knew we could not go wrong if we edged westwards, as there were rocks and I knew these were west of Le Hamel. We went along the hedge and the whole company was in a long snake with gaps between platoons. It seemed safe as we were defiladed, unless something opened up in front of us. I noticed birds singing rather hesitantly in the hedge. Soon the smoke cleared enough for me to see Meauvaines ridge and church, and looking over the hedge, I identified Asnelles spire.

I made a little plan to get into Asnelles: 10 Platoon giving cover, while 12, followed by 11, went up a hedgerow near which we knew the enemy post was – indeed it had started to fire at us.

12 Platoon came up in savage mood, out for blood as they had had some casualties. They went in single file up the hedgerow. Then snipers and at least one Spandau opened up on them as they came into view. Lionel Bawden was hit early on and killed instantly. Sergeant Smith, a tough man, was also hit and wounded. This left them rather helpless, so I told Graham Elliott to get 11 Platoon on in any way he could.

I went back to Charles Williamson. At this point mortar bombs started pitching among us, though the troops thought they were mines. I went into Les Roquettes and saw D Company coming

through and the Devons following them, all delayed and anxious
to get off the beach and on with their tasks. I said that as far as I
knew there were no enemy around except at Asnelles, and we
were looking after them.

So off they went. There was a block of men in Les Roquettes,
some of them bewildered by the explosions all round and among
them. I found Charles, who was doubtful about getting to
Asnelles direct, owing to the minefield, but a flail came and set
off a number of mines, which was fun to watch.

Major Mott could afford to enjoy the spectacle now that he was off the
beach. Many soldiers had gained the impression from their briefing that
their sole objective for the day was to shake the sand from their boots, and
so they stopped to make a cup of tea as soon as they were on the landward
side of Rommel's Atlantic Wall. They could fight the Germans, but they
could not fight the overpowering British instinct for making a cuppa in a
crisis. Some historians claim, only half in jest, that the British serviceman's
inalienable right to declare a teabreak actually slowed the Allied advance
on the first day.

Major Iain Macleod, the officer who had spent so many months making
plans for this day, was at this moment still out at sea. At last the time came
for him to go ashore.

I climbed with elderly dignity down the scrambling nets and into
our LCA. We began to circle a few hundred yards away from the
beach. Quite a long time passed, the sun grew hotter, and I began
to doze. Suddenly, and for no reason I could see, we stopped
turning and ran straight for the beach.

The beach was alive with the shambles and the order of war.
There were dead men and wounded men and men brewing tea.
There were men organising for a battle advance and men doing
absolutely nothing. There were some German prisoners waiting
patiently for heaven knows what. There was a graveyard of
wrecked ships and craft and tanks of every size.

This was a little later in the morning, after the first wave had already begun
to move inland. Kenneth Rees, a signalman driver, came in at about the
same time.

Our vehicle was not well enough waterproofed, and spluttered to
a halt before reaching the shore. The officer on board was being
about as typically nonchalant as a British officer could be, sitting
on top of the vehicle viewing the scene through binoculars as if
on holiday, despite our efforts to pull him down.

  We landed just opposite a huge pillbox. I remember a
particular feeling of pathos at seeing the seemingly unmarked
body of a British soldier with every stitch of his clothing,
including his boots, blown off by a blast, lying face down
in the sand.

Kenneth Rees's other memories of the day take the form of a series of
emotional snapshots, the last of which contains a disturbing presentiment
of the scenes that would greet Allied soldiers when, eventually, they
reached the concentration camps of Germany and Poland:

  . . . The sense of amusement I felt at the cartoon-like spectacle of
  a short, bandy-legged German, with a great helmet almost down
  to his shoulders as it seems to me, and looking like a half-brother
  to Goebbels, or a chimpanzee, marching disconsolately along the
  shore, presumably under orders to report to some post. I
  thought: what a comical example of the master race!

    . . . My distress at seeing a badly wounded British soldier,
  tossing and turning, lying for a long while in the shade, near a
  low wall where someone had obviously dragged him. No one
  seemed to know how to help him.

    . . . My sense of astonishment at seeing dead Germans thrown
  up on a truck like cattle or sardines, at all sorts of angles.

The first dangerous German that Don Cowlan encountered on the beach
was a German shepherd dog.

  I landed at Arromanches, one of a naval landing party of
  commandos attached to the Royal Marines. My first memory is
  of a large Alsatian dog running towards us and frightening the
  life out of me.

    It was our job to establish communications between ship and
  shore, and we took over a small hotel in the town as our HQ,

after checking it for booby-traps. Later we found two German soldiers, absent from their units and living with local French girls. The girls were not happy with their liberation, and were not slow to tell us so in no uncertain terms.

Wilf Blackwell of the Hertfordshire Yeomanry had the reverse experience. This was the sight that greeted him as he went inland, still very much under fire.

> As we progressed up a small lane leading from the beach, two teenage French girls were walking down the road, waving like mad, and obviously so happy to see their liberators arriving that you would have thought that they were on holiday.

A mile away, another young French girl was aching to catch her first glimpse of the liberators. Mlle Genget lived in the little village of St Come on the high ground above Arromanches. Fizzing with the excitement of it all, she scribbled down impressions even as the German soldiers that she pointedly refers to as the 'tenants' beat a hurried retreat.

> Suddenly a big gun was fired from the sea and the smaller cannon of the Boches were answering. There can be no doubt that big battle is about to commence. We dare not move and we put cotton wool in our ears.
>
> The noise was terrific and we wondered how it would all end. The hours seem long – very long – but after a while the firing ceased and we heard our front door open and a voice call out: 'It is finished, we are free, the English are at the crossroads.'
>
> Our tenants came out of their trench in the garden next door and GL arrives. Everyone is well at his house. He tells us of the great victory of the English. He tells us we should go and look at the sea. We got ready in spite of being still very upset and afraid and got to the Villa St Come. From there what a sight met our eyes! As far as we could see there were ships of all kinds and sizes and above floated big balloons silvery in the sun. Big bombers were passing and repassing in the sky. It is marvellous and an unforgettable sight – a very consoling sight for the suffering of the last few hours.

Whilst we were waiting at the Villa we could see tanks and armoured cars passing on the road to Asnelles. We saw a sort of boat which can sail on the seas and travel on land. There is so much to see and all so interesting! Finally we go back home, and leaving the civilians to show the way to the English soldiers. We learn that the first soldiers had to swim ashore with water up to their shoulders before they safely landed on the French soil they had come to deliver.

The English had thought that all civilians had been evacuated from the coast and were very surprised to find the inhabitants had stayed in their homes. Our little church had received a direct hit on the roof. Fire broke out, but with the help of the villagers it was soon overcome. Guns were firing on the big blockhouse between Belle Vue and Arromanches and the underground trenches leading to the munitions stocks belonging to the Germans. Soon all was wiped out. What a noise everywhere and smell of burning! We returned to our rooms and from the window we see a file of tanks passing through the fields opposite and leaving on their way to Bayeux. Are we dreaming? Is it all really true?

THE TANKS ADVANCE

Back out to sea, second Sergeant Miller of the Royal Marines was manning twin Oerlikon guns on the quarterdeck of a LCF (Landing Craft, Flak). His job was to provide close support to the infantry. His fire was directed by the signals from the men on the beach:

> A lamp flashed from the beach followed by coloured smoke. We closed and raked gun emplacements and machine-gun nests with pom-pom and Oerlikon fire until another signal: 'Thanks!' It was impossible to hear orders over the noise of explosions and gunfire so orders were passed by messenger. 'Check Firing' by a thump on the back of the gunner. The air was filled with smoke of battle and cordite, the din of light and heavy gunfire.

Trooper MG Gale was also out at sea providing artillery support, but from a Sherman tank. He drove into the water with his regiment, but had an accident that left him way behind his comrades.

Sitting in the driver's seat, I began to move our Sherman fitted with its new 17-pounder gun. I moved very slowly down the ramp and began to ease her off the end, waiting for the drop into what we had expected to be about six feet of water. We were all battened down, and well waterproofed – which as it turned out, was just as well: we fell into twelve feet of water. We had pulled in right on to a shell hole, and there we were, well under water.

The lives of Gale and his crew were saved by the extension on the air intake. This chimney-like protuberance was designed to keep the engine dry while the tank was in the water. It was to be blown away with a small pre-set charge once the tank was on dry land – which in this case was quite some time.

Before I could decide what to do, voices were reaching us over our radio telling us not to try to move as the water was almost to the top of our air intake. I was told to cut the engine and wait for instructions. We were able to follow what was going on by radio, but we sat there for almost two hours, waiting for the tide to go out, seeing nothing except water through our periscopes.

Gale felt he had let his comrades down somewhat by spending the first hours of the invasion marinading gently on the seabed. But he found a way to redeem himself later in the day.

Having re-joined the troop, we moved very slowly inland. We were on the top of a hill looking over a valley, when we received instructions over the radio to engage a tower some two miles away with our high-explosive shells. We were told snipers were troubling our troops.
   This was the first time we had brought our big gun into action that day. The gun was loaded and the gunner fired, having taken very careful aim. Looking for the fall of our shot, we saw nothing except for a burst in the ground – 100 yards or more to the right of the tower. We were all quite sure it was not ours. The gunner fired the second time: still no hit on the tower, but again that burst almost on the same spot as before. We then realised to our horror that our sights were out. We tried a third shot, making

allowances for the sights and this time our shot fell almost the same distance to the left of the tower.

Then the gunner had an idea: he would open the gun's breech and try to sight the tower looking through the barrel. After a lot of trial he was able to do this. He then raised the barrel to allow for the distance. With fingers crossed, we waited for our shell to land and, more by luck than judgement, we were right on target. We received a 'Good show, lads' over the radio from the commanding officer, and took the very first opportunity to correct our sights. No one was ever told how we fired that shot.

Most of the tanks and armoured vehicles destined for Gold Beach had made it to shore. This made life much easier for the infantry. As well as taking on the vicious MG-42 machine guns in their pillboxes, the tanks provided physical cover for soldiers as they scurried up the beach. There were men on Omaha who would have been glad of a fraction of the armoured support that the British had here.

The elephantine herds from Hobart's mechanical zoo vindicated their inventor on Gold – and later on Sword. Emerging from the sea like iron krakens, the strangely mutated Shermans and Churchills had the additional effect of spooking some of the less hardy German defenders. The flail tanks fulfilled their primary function with particular aplomb, merrily thrashing a path like metal-clad carpet beaters through the first belt of minefields.

But the British tanks were not impregnable. There were complaints from British commanders that they tended to 'brew up' – explode – much too readily. And the German anti-aircraft gun known as the 88mm, which was being used to such deadly shellburst effect against infantry on Omaha, was just as lethal against British armour. A good few tanks on Gold were put out of commission before the seawater had drained from their skirts. IG Holley, a wireless operator in the Royal Hampshires, was on his way off the beach when he saw one that had been knocked out. He also saw what happened to some men of his regiment who sheltered behind the wreckage for too long.

High up the beach a flail tank was knocked out. B Company HQ group paused to take cover behind this mass of steel. A shell whipped in, scored a direct hit on them and they were gone in a blast of smoke, out of which cartwheeling through the air came the torn, shrieking body of a stretcher bearer – the red cross on his arm band clearly discernible.

There were other hazards awaiting tanks at the exits to the beach. Lieutenant Michael Barraclough was first in a column, but was overtaken by a colleague as he crossed the sand. As he watched what happened to that tank and its crew, he knew that it should have been him:

The tank behind me went over the top of a sand dune directly ahead. What none of us knew, and what we couldn't see from our tanks, was that beyond the dune was a culvert which the Germans had flooded. The tank drove straight into the culvert and sank. Two of the crew drowned but the rest escaped only to be cut down by mortar fire. There was only one thing I could do. With Doug Arnold, the tank captain who had escaped, I built a bridge on top of the submerged tank from rubble, while under continuous mortar fire.

There was never any room for fear except perhaps in the quieter moments. That evening, I learned that my best friend, John Allen, had been killed. As a joke he had painted a cross on his tank turret saying 'Aim here.' A shell had gone right through the cross. They couldn't even identify which body was which in the tank.

GETTING OFF GOLD

The infantry made deep inroads in the afternoon. IG Holley of the Hampshires had a little local trouble on the beach, but was on the road and moving parallel to the sea by lunchtime.

We made the sea wall, and a pillbox to our left flattened us with its Spandau. It was silenced a few minutes later, and we got on. We were on the road. Now we turned right and ran as fast as our equipment would allow us. A Sherman tank tried to make it along the road which collapsed beneath its enormous weight. It lay in a great hole, undamaged but unable to get out. The tank commander had his head stuck out of the turret and was going mad with rage.

The reaction of German soldiers to the invasion varied widely. Some gave themselves up at the first opportunity, and found themselves in open-air cages in Portsmouth by nightfall. Others, like these infantrymen in Arromanches, fought hard and inflicted high casualties.

We turned off the road through the wire fence with the plaques saying 'Achtung Minen'. A long white tape ran straight across the mine field, this corridor opened up by some assault pioneer or engineer, God bless him.

We were about half a mile inland. Our contact with Jerry so far had been dead ones, a number with no fight left in them walking around in a daze, and several make-and-break running fights that had developed as we advanced and they retired.

Without a wireless we had no idea how things were going except in our immediate vicinity and we were moving forwards all the time. Men and equipment were pouring in as the tempo of the invasion increased: Bren carriers, Jeeps, tanks, artillery – it was all coming. We lost another two men, took a few prisoners. This colossal punch had slammed into the Western Wall, and we stood and watched with a great feeling of pride.

The British were moving through German strongpoints like ink through blotting paper, soaking up resistance all along the way. The beach was secure, but as yet no British soldier from Gold had linked up inland with an American soldier from Omaha. The chink in the armour had not yet been closed.

But by evening there was a steady flow of surrendered German troops moving through the Allied front line and down to the beach. Among them were many foreign volunteers, 'a miserable looking lot, apparently of Mongolian type,' said one British soldier. They were in fact Soviet citizens from the Central Asian republics – and were probably delighted, after serving both Stalin and Hitler, to be in the relatively gentle hands of the British Army.

But not all Wehrmacht prisoners were pleased with their lot. Ralph Crenshaw, a US Army pharmacist on a hospital ship off the British beaches, encountered two very unhappy German POWs who impressed him in different ways:

> A German officer, a colonel, I believe, was brought aboard into my area. By his demeanor, he was obviously a hard-core Nazi. He postured, demanded this and demanded that, and acted as though he was in command, and didn't consider himself a prisoner. He demonstrated an egomaniac personality. Even as a prisoner, he was awesome and frightening. I could only imagine the fear he must have brought to anyone unfortunate enough to have been his subordinate or even worse, a captive.
>
> A German prisoner brought aboard on a stretcher had a body cast extending from his ankles to his chest. He was a pitiful human being, pleading with me and our ship's doctor for help. He called us 'Comrade, comrade.' Our ship's doctor, with my assistance, opened the cast, only to find this pitiful human being was being eaten by hoards of maggots. We removed the cast, cleaned him, bathed him, gave him painkillers. We were too late. He died peacefully that evening.
>
> Even though an enemy, he was human. To this day, I think about this soldier, and wonder about his civilian life, his family, his hopes, and the hopes that never came true, and his dreadful end.

This wounded Wehrmacht soldier is a renegade from Soviet Georgia. The uniform patch on his sleeve declares his origin. In some German units, a quarter of the men were from Eastern Europe. A few, when captured, turned out to have no idea what country they were in.

Major Mott, who had been so pleased to land on the beach on time, remained efficiently at work throughout the day. One by one his men and his fellow officers were killed, but he stuck to his task with the imperturbable ennui of an old-school professional.

I told Graham to take his men into the orchard. We could see one of the Boche in a trench taking shots at us, but the troops were slow at answering. They were reluctant to follow Graham, who dashed forward into a crater. As no one went with him, I did. We went to a gap in the corner of the wall, I with a grenade in my hand. I saw two Boche in a trench, so threw the grenade, but it did not go off. Back came a stick grenade, which did explode. Graham bravely hurled his body on top of me. He did not get hurt. I lay by the wall, feeling very exposed, while Graham went back and called up some of his men. I peered round the wall and saw no enemy, just an underground system of trenches.

We went cautiously along the orchard wall, looking through gaps to try to locate our opponents, which was chiefly done by them shooting at us. Bisson was outstanding, shooting through gaps and rallying his men. He got a bullet through his helmet which nicked his skull, but he carried on. At one time I saw two Boche through a gap, so fired single shots at them, and the next day found two corpses with bullets through their heads – only twenty yards range. At any rate my Sten was still working.

I took my men into Asnelles without seeing anyone. Suddenly I felt a blast and heard a loud crack. I didn't know what it was, possibly another mine or stray shell. Then came another blast and another, and it dawned on me that there was an anti-tank gun in our way. We began to look for another way to Le Hamel. This was probably when Graham was fatally wounded. I heard that he had had his jaw blown off by an anti-tank shell.

I collected what men I could. I got to some high ground overlooking the strongpoint. There was a tank cruising along the edge of an anti-tank ditch. There was the odd sniping shot at the tank commander as I talked to him. I told him to go forward to the strongpoint. Soon he reappeared with fifteen prisoners. He went in again and retrieved some more. Then David Warren appeared with an AVRE which fired several shots into the concrete. Again Bisson went in and brought out some prisoners, but the dose had to be repeated before the position was silenced. I admired the Boche who had stayed on resisting to the last.

It must have been early afternoon by now and at about this time my carrier turned up, so we had a welcome replenishment of all kinds of ammunition. Peter Paul met us by St Côme and showed us a safe way to the battery and radar station. Both had been occupied by D Company without too much opposition. The canteen was undamaged, as were the ration store and the officers' quarters, which contained some useful kit. D Company had collected a good bag of prisoners, including some sailors.

D Company then went to deal with the battery beyond Arromanches. David organised some naval medicine to precede their attack, which was successful. My next job was to take some of C Company into Arromanches. The only opposition was from a dog, presumably a Boche one. Arromanches was full of French people. Flowers came out and tricolours and Union Jacks. I had been told that all coastal inhabitants had been moved inland, but these were delighted to see us.

Major Macleod, the staff officer who had not even expected to go to Normandy, wandered inland with the advancing troops. He even managed to enjoy a passably pleasant evening. And like many of the men who crossed a Norman beach that day, he was overcome at the end of it by an almost mystical sense of invincibility. It was a rather beautiful feeling:

I can't remember when I ate, but I remember what I ate. From somewhere my batman produced both the great delicacies of 1944: tinned steak pudding and tinned Christmas pudding. These and whisky were my food.

Night began to fall. My batman had secured a corner of a barn for me, and I was thinking of snatching some sleep when the door opened and Tom Black looked in. 'What's up?' I said.

'Nothing. I thought we'd have a drink.'

We stood under the trees, looking back towards the sea. A few fast German fighter planes were making a tip-and-run raid on the beach, and the red tracer bullets climbed lazily into the sky after them. I looked at my watch. It was exactly midnight. I had lived through D-Day. I had been convinced that I would be killed. Now, equally unreasonably, I became convinced that I would live through the war. I would see our second child, who was to be born in October. There would be life after the war. D-Day was over.

6
JUNO'S DAY

Juno was Canada's beach. Before dawn on 6 June fifteen thousand Canadians, every one of them volunteers, lay in wait out to sea. On either side of them were the two British strike forces. To the right, the 50th Infantry Division Group destined for Gold; and to the left, the 3rd Infantry Division Group heading for Sword.

Juno Beach itself was flat and sandy with a high sea wall at the back. It was heavily defended, but presented no geographical impediment to the invaders. Offshore, however, there was a rocky bank with only a narrow, mile-wide gap that the landing craft could negotiate at low tide. There were also tricky shallow areas in the run-up to the beaches. It was decided that the only sensible way to overcome these obstacles was to wait until the tide had risen high enough to carry the landing craft over the shoal. This meant that the Canadians would be the last troops ashore, and that the defenders would have long since been alerted to their arrival.

THE FIRST HOUR

Ron Kenyon was a sergeant in the 13th Field Regiment, Royal Canadian Artillery, and his orders were to provide close artillery support to the Regina Rifle Regiment. He would fire his mobile artillery piece from the deck of the landing craft, but could not open up until they were close into the beach. So at first light he was on deck watching the initial bombardment from the fearsome rocket ships. These long barges fired racks of screaming missiles. They had been used in Russia where they were known as Katyushas by the Soviets and as 'Stalin's organs' by the Germans. Mounting them on sea-going barges was a Canadian innovation.

> As day began to break the bomb flashes could be seen far ahead, said Kenyon. Later the coastline came into view. In our sector four regiments of artillery, 96 guns in line abreast, relentlessly approached the shore and at 11,000 yards started to fire,

continuing to fire until quite close.

We then dropped back a little to let the infantry landing craft go through. The Canadian-invented rocket ship also unloaded its bank of rockets on the shore. There were so many rockets it looked like a porcupine.

For some time we had known that we would be the Canadian D-Day division and we were well prepared. Our 25-pounder guns had been replaced by Sherman tanks with a 105mm howitzer in them and we had practised firing them from a rolling landing craft. By aiming the craft and firing when it became level, fair accuracy was possible. But the din was hard on the ears.

JG Baird, an officer with the Regina Rifles, was in one of the landing craft now picking a shorebound route past the bigger ships.

We could see the beaches through the haze. Yes, there was a church steeple and a water tower. That must be Courseulles with Nan Green Beach in front of it.

That was our beach. The Winnipegs on our immediate right would assault Mike Red Beach just to the west of the inlet. The Canadian Scottish in reserve would land on either after the initial assault. Yes, the landmarks were there just as they had been pointed out on the air photos in the briefing. Further along the coast we could make out Bernières, where the Queen's Own Rifles would land, and still further east was St Aubin where the North Shore Regiment would go in.

Our LCAs are getting into position and moving toward the beach. Able company is on the right, Baker company on the left. Charlie and Dog are behind them in reserve. On our flanks are LCTs with the 1st Hussars and their Sherman tanks.

Destroyers, cruisers, monitors and battleships fire on the beaches and enemy installations inland. Now the 12th, 13th, 14th and 19th Field Regiments, Royal Canadian Artillery, open up with their 105 millimeters, firing from the craft. Rocket ships let go their rockets with a blast of flame. We can see the burst of shells on the beaches.

We are getting close now and the bombardment stops. So far not a shot has fired from the defenders on the beach.

> Machine-gun fire and shells now come in from pillboxes
> which are apparently still open for business, despite the terrific
> pounding they have taken. The LCAs of the leading companies
> and the tanks of the 1st Hussars are working into the beaches
> now. There are the underwater obstacles we had been told about
> – 'Element C' they called them – huge iron gate affairs. And there
> are the triangular hedgehogs with land mines tied to them.

Anthony Duke, the American LCT captain, was still seaward of the natural reef and the man-made beach obstacles when he received a message telling him not to hold back for the time being. He could see the landing unfolding and hear the alarming radio chatter coming from the British beaches. He also noticed that the weather was deteriorating.

> Some of us were slated to go on the stretch of beach right near
> the town of Courseulles. I had been given a long panoramic
> picture of what the beach looked like there. It had obviously been
> taken several weeks before by reconnaissance groups going over
> late at night.
>
> At one point we could hear a lot of talk on the radio about two
> German 88mm guns battering the larger ships off Sword Beach.
> Apparently one LST had been hit, two LCTs were hit, and I think
> a Liberty ship or freighter. Until those 88mm were wiped out, this
> would happen again and again with great loss of life.
>
> We were now creeping towards the beachhead and we could
> smell the cordite from bursting shells and see all the shock waves
> from high explosives bursting all over the place. You could feel it
> right through the steel deck plates of the ship. There was a very
> pronounced and strong feeling that you were in war now. That
> you had to do your job. The sea offshore there was roughening
> up a little bit. The wind was blowing around 15 knots, I'd say.

The weather had grown noticeably worse as the landing craft were forming up for the dash to the beach. There were also stronger currents than expected. The bad weather caused a delay of about ten minutes, but those short minutes proved very costly. Instead of landing in front of exposed beach obstacles, the landing craft of the first wave were being dropped by the swell right on top of the mined stakes and hedgehogs.

Several rocket barges were releasing volleys of rockets towards the French coast, said Wilfred Bennett of the Royal Winnipeg Rifles. They were an effective weapon from what I could see. They seemed to be hitting their mark. The sea was a heaving mass of water with thirty-foot waves. We were given a small white pill to help keep our mouths dry. I cannot recall if they worked or not.

We climbed down the side of our troop ship on rope ladders and into LCAs. These small craft bobbed about as the skipper of each craft tried to head for the shore. One moment, we were down in the bottom of a wave which was so deep that as we looked up, all we could see was sky. And the next moment, we were on the top of one of these huge waves, looking down.

Now it was the Canadians' turn to go through paroxysms of seasickness. Everyone who landed in France that morning agrees that the terror of battle was preferable to the green agonies of a storm-tossed sea. 'We were so sick,' remarked one Winnipeg rifleman, 'that we had preferred to be shot on the beaches rather than go back on those landing craft.' Wilfred Bennett was also eager to get off the boat when the word came.

Our commander was a good soldier. His name was Major Rupert Fultz of Winnipeg. The last order I heard from him as our ramp went down was 'OK boys, let's go.' We hit the water waist deep. Men were falling on the water, and they fell on the beach. The machine-gun fire was so devastating.

A buddy who was on my right was shot in the face and the neck. We were told not to stop and help any of our buddies as we too might have been injured, and we were to carry on as best we could to get across the beach. My buddy lay on that beach until 6pm that evening, and was picked up for dead when they discovered he was still alive.

Everywhere the Canadian regiments were struggling ashore under heavy fire and in heavy seas. The danger of drowning was at least as great as the risk of being shot.

At about 8 o'clock, our craft formed a line, and we were going in, said one Canadian officer. I was just on the verge of descending from my point of vantage, when a shell, a quite small one, tore through our rigging, and another burst in the water a few yards away. I almost jumped from the bridge. I was in the cabin and had on my 'light' assault jacket (which weighed at least a hundredweight) in about two seconds flat. Even at that point I was about the last to get ready; most of the fellows were all ready to go in, their Mae Wests giving them an outlandish shape. I was very interested in the expression on their faces – some looked like a wounded spaniel, some were quite nonchalant about it, others made a feeble effort at gaiety. What amused me most was a fat boy trying to whistle, but the best he could do was blow air with a squeak now and then. I was pretty scared myself. Those last few moments were pretty awful, it was the waiting that was hard. We were coming under pretty intense small-arms fire by this time, and everyone was down as much as possible.

At last the gangways were run down, and it was a case of get up and get in and get down. I maneuvered into position to be as near as possible to the front. I wanted to be one of the first to land – not because of my heroics, but because waiting your turn on the exposed ramp was much worse than going in.

A sergeant and a corporal started down, I was third. The sergeant couldn't touch bottom, but pushed away and swam in towards shore. The corporal started to follow and I plunged in, but the weight of my jacket, filled with enough canned goods to start a grocery store, pulled me under in spite of my Mae West. I got back on to the ramp, and the skipper, very sensibly, decided to pull off and try and come in a bit better. I might say that a couple of sharp cracks in the water made me jump onto that ramp in a hurry.

While I was floundering about in the water, the corporal got into trouble; there was a terrific backwash, and only quick action by a brave merchant-navy lad saved him from drowning. The next run at the shore put me in about five feet of water. A naval fellow with a life belt went in with a rope, and I followed. I must have been a ridiculous sight, holding on to my pistol in one hand, and a bag of my valuables (mostly cigs) in the other, as well as trying to hold on to the rope. Some of the men had great difficulty getting ashore, particularly the short ones. One poor chap was crushed to death, when the ramp broke away in the heavy seas and slammed him between it and the side of the ship. A Spandau opened up just when the water was full of men struggling to get ashore.

I didn't lose much time getting to the back of the beach where there was a bit of protection, and wriggled out of my assault jacket. Many of the assault troops had already crossed the beach, and were fighting forward towards their objective, a ridge back from the beach a few hundred yards. The houses along the waterfront were well stocked with snipers.

There is no good entering into the details of those first few hours ashore. If, as the radio announced later, it was an unopposed landing, God forbid that anyone should have to go in on an opposed one. Our beach was littered with those who had been a jump ahead of us. A captured blockhouse being used as a dressing station was literally surrounded by piles of bodies. Many of the lads on our LCI never got ashore.

As the first wave went in, some soldiers were sure that the landings were going wrong. The naval and air attacks had left the defences unscathed. There was a tangled mass of barbed wire the length of the landing grounds. Machine-gunners were waiting to open fire as soon as the ramps went down, and many men were dying in the water. Moreover, there was little tank support for the first wave of infantry. Some DD tanks had sunk on the way in; others had held back because of the impossibly rough seas, with the result that the armoured protection arrived after the infantry.

In those first minutes it seemed to some of the soldiers that the assault on Juno was turning into a massacre. It was beginning to look as if Juno was going to be a repeat of Dieppe, or a Canadian Omaha.

THE THIRD CANADIAN

All the Canadian troops involved in D-Day came under the umbrella of the Canadian Third Division – and it so happened that everything about their plan for D-Day was broken down into sets of three.

The Division consisted of three brigades, each made up of three Canadian regiments. The 7th Brigade consisted of the Royal Winnipeg Rifles, the Regina Rifles, and the 1st Battalion of the Canadian-Scottish Regiment; they were due to land in Mike sector opposite the town of

Courseulles. The 8th Brigade – made up of the Queen's Own Rifles, the French-Canadian Régiment de la Chaudière, and the North Shore (New Brunswick) Regiment – were to land in Nan sector and take the town of Bernières. The three regiments of the 9th Brigade all had a strong Scots tradition. They were the Highland Light Infantry, the Stormont Dundas and Glengarry Highlanders, and the North Nova Scotia Highlanders – who were held in reserve.

The Canadians had three objectives, three concentric lines on the map that they hoped to reach. And these goals all had three-letter code words which were the names of trees. The first objective was codenamed Yew, and described a shallow arc stretching from Bernières-sur-Mer to Langrune-sur-Mer, about three miles to the east; the second objective was named Elm, and formed a curved front about six miles inland – if the Canadians got this far then they would probably be able to link up with the British to their right on Gold, and to their left on Sword. The third objective, Oak, was the main highway between Caen and Bayeux about nine miles inland. If they reached Oak they would be in the suburbs of Caen itself, and they would be on top of the strategically vital airstrip at Carpiquet, just west of the city. All of this was supposed to happen on Day One.

But as the first wave struggled ashore, none of these objectives looked likely to be fulfilled. Jim Wilkins, nineteen years old, was with the Queen's Own Rifles. He was one of the first Canadians to set foot in France.

> I should explain the make-up of the first wave. A division of infantry is made up of about 15,000 men. A regiment is made up of 800 men and there are nine regiments to a division. The generals always like to have reserves so they hold back one full brigade of three regiments totalling 2,400 men. Now we are down to two brigades of six regiments or 3,200 going in. Now the brigadiers of the two brigades want to hold back one regiment each for his reserve, or 1,600 men, so we are down to only four regiments going in. Next the regimental colonel decides to hold back C and D Company for twenty minutes as his reserve – or 480 men. So who the hell is going to make the first assault? Two companies out of four regiments – A and B Companies of the North Shore Regiment, A and B of the Queens Own Rifles, A and B from the Winnipeg Rifles and A and B from the Regina Rifles – and one company from the Highland Light Infantry. Nine

companies in all, plus assorted engineers, medics, signallers. Each company has five boats, so the total was forty-five boats consisting of about thirty men each or a total of 1,350 men out of 15,000 who are to be in the first assault wave on Juno Beach.

At about 4:30 we were ordered to go on deck where sailor guides took us to our appointed stations. Our landing craft were at deck level and we could just climb in. The first section was No 1 of B Company on the port side. They sat facing in. The next group was on the starboard side consisting of odds and sods: our platoon sergeant, Freddy Harris, who had given up a commission to be with us; the company sergeant-major Bill Wallace; company staff such as runners and stretcher bearers; and combat engineers who were to somehow breach the nine-foot wall in front of us, blow up pillboxes and gun positions. Next, came my section – No 2 of B Company. We climbed in and sat on a low bench running down the centre facing forward. I was at the very back. It was not a good position for us – last group in, first group out. The waves were pretty high as we were lowered into the water. The high seas met us with a vengeance. The marine crew had a rough time unhooking the winch lines.

The forty-five boats start in – at about 1,500 yards we can see the wall in the back of the beach. It looks to be maybe eight-feet high. We are told to stand up. Beside us was a ship that fires rockets. The forward deck is cleared and pointing up are maybe a dozen tubes or mortars at a forty-five degree angle. All of a sudden they fire a salvo – great clouds of smoke and flame engulf the boat. Ten minutes later they fire again. You can follow the rockets by eye as they curve upward. We watched one salvo go high over the beach just as a Spitfire came along. He flew right into it and blew up. That pilot never had a chance, and was probably the first casualty on Juno Beach.

Overhead we can hear the roar of large shells from battleships, cruisers and destroyers. Beside us is a boat with pom-pom guns – anti-aircraft – shooting away at church steeples and other high buildings, where observers were spotting for the German troops.

Soon we are only 500 yards from the beach and are ordered to get down. Minutes later the boat stops and begins to toss in the waves. The ramp goes down and without hesitation my section

'The last thing I saw before I ducked my head was one of the craft to our left blown sky high. A few seconds later we felt the scrape as the craft struck the sandy beach, and in no time the door was down and we were leaping into the foam.' Don Doner, Queen's Own Rifles

leader, Corporal John Gibson, jumps out well over his waist in water. He only makes a few yards and is killed. We have landed dead on a pillbox with a machine gun blazing away at us. We didn't hesitate and jumped into the water one after the other – I was last of the first row. Where was everybody? My section are only half there – some were just floating on their Mae Wests.

My Bren-gun team of Tommy Dalrymple and Kenny Scott are just in front of me when something hits my left magazine pouch and brings me up short for a moment. The round had gone right through two magazines, entered my left side and came out my back. Kenny keeps yelling 'Come on, come on!' I yell to him 'I'm coming, I'm coming.'

We are now up to our knees in water and you can hear a kind of buzzing sound all around. All of a sudden something slapped the side of my right leg and then a round caught me dead centre up high on my right leg. By this time I was flat on my face in the water – I've lost my rifle, my helmet is gone and Kenny is still yelling at me to come on. He is also shot in the upper leg. I yell 'My leg is broken – get the hell out of here!' Away he goes and catches up to Tommy. Poor Tom, I've got ten of his Bren-gun magazines and they're pulling me under. I soon get rid of them and flop over on to my back and start to float to shore where I meet five other riflemen all in very bad shape. The man beside me is dead within minutes. All the while we are looking up at the machine gun firing just over our heads at the rest of our platoon and company.

Then Fred Harris, a friend of mine, was killed in front of me.

Doug Hester was on the same landing craft. During the run-in, rifleman Hester was almost unbelievably blasé about the battle that was about to commence.

Doug Reed and I were standing up eagerly, watching for shore. We began singing *The Bells Are Ringing for Me and My Gal* and continued until we saw the steeple of the church at our landing site. I said, 'Doug, there's the church, I thought it wasn't supposed to be there.' It suffered one shell hole in the steeple. Then we saw the five pillboxes mounted on top of the sea wall. These were our first objective.

About five hundred yards out, they had us in the sights of their small arms and began shooting. We had never been under real fire and realized it when bullets were hitting our assault craft. I said to Doug, as if we should be surprised, 'They're shooting at us!' and we ducked down below the armour.

When the craft got into shallower water, the Royal Marines lowered the door. At the same time a machine gun firing from the second floor window of the hotel focused on our down-ramp. The three in front of me, including Doug Reed, were hit and killed. I jumped out between bursts into their rising blood.

Cold and soaking wet, I caught up to Gibby. That same machine gun began to pick him out. The first burst went through his backpack. He turned his head grinning at me and said, 'That was close, Dougie.' 'Yes, Gibby, there goes your lunch.

We'll have to share mine,' I told him.

The next burst killed him. He fell face-down, spread-eagled in front of me. My memory is crystal clear and I can see him now. I stopped to take a silver wristwatch and ID bracelet his wife had sent him a few weeks earlier. His body would be lost in the Channel. I wanted to send them to her. They wouldn't come off. Then the gunner picked me up. I had to leave Gibby.

I arrived alone beside a pillbox. Looking back, I saw Ted Westerby from our section carrying a ladder. It was the ladder we were to use to scale the wall. Ted took two hits before the third one killed him. I decided to scramble up the pillbox without a ladder and drop a grenade in a slit, determined to get someone.

A hand came out and dropped a German high explosive grenade to the ground. It landed about four inches from my left foot. My first thought was to pick it up and throw it. But I remembered our training so just doubled up and waited. It seemed to be a year. I might lose a foot. Finally the explosion came and I was lucky just to get a nick on my Achilles tendon.

About one hundred yards east of me I could see some other B Company people. I got to them. Everyone still on his feet was determined to get over the wall.

A pillbox made of logs and open on both ends housed an anti-tank gun that was shooting our landing craft out of the water. I threw a grenade in one end. Three of the German crew came out running toward the hotel. One of them was a corporal. He had a Luger in his hand shooting at me. But I had my Lee Enfield.

Somehow John (Shorty) Humenyk and I hooked up together and went east to a dory ramp. We had started up the ramp when machine guns firing on fixed lines about eighteen inches above ground opened up. And there was mortar and 88 fire. Shorty, calm as can be, said, 'What do you think Dougie?' I replied, 'Hell, Shorty, there's no shelter, we might just as well go for the hotel and get as many as we can get.'

As we started, something big exploded and somersaulted me down the ramp. When things cleared, my left leg was bleeding. I found out that our cherished commando knife couldn't slit a uniform. I put a field dressing over the top. It stopped the bleeding. A piece of shrapnel had chewed out the breech of

Shorty's treasured Lee Enfield sniper rifle.

Later, when my wound had started to bother me, I sat with my back against the sea wall. Next to me was a wounded German boy. Every time I made a move he cringed, cowering. We'd both been hit. When you're wounded, that's it. It's over. Finally I tried to tell him that. He seemed to get the idea and relaxed a bit. Stumpy Gordon came along collecting Bren gun magazines and spotted me. 'Let's have that Luger,' he said to me.

'No, Stumpy, you'll have to get one the same way I did.'

B Company lost almost half its number in the sprint to the sea wall. Among the wounded was the commanding officer, Charles Dalton. He took a shot to the head which tore off his helmet and his scalp with it. But he pushed on, his head streaming blood, and took his men with him.

Further down the beach was the major's brother, Elliot Dalton. The two men had said their goodbyes as they boarded their separate landing craft early that morning. Charles had searched for some words to fit the occasion, but settled on a laconic 'See you tonight.' But they did not see each other that night. Late on D-Day, Elliot Dalton received word that his brother had been killed in action. He lived with that news and fought on, until he was wounded and shipped back to England. On being wheeled to his hospital bed, he found it already occupied by a man with his head swathed in bandages and the sheets pulled over the top. It was his brother Charles, alive after all.

HEADING FOR ELM

Despite the heavy resistance, some Canadian troops were marching inland within an hour of landing. One teenage French boy, Claude Guillotin, stood in the doorway of his parents' house and watched them pass. He was almost swooning with the excitement of it.

I was all eyes, looking and admiring the soldiers. They were sunburned and their faces were blackened by dust and smoke. I was amused to see them apparently chewing the cud. I was soon to know well and to taste for myself what was in fact chewing gum. I also would learn that the little packet they carried under their helmet nets was a personal emergency bandage.

The soldiers were tall and solidly built. They didn't tremble apprehensively as the Germans did. Their quiet assurance and the personal strength and resolve which they showed indicated that they were fighting in a just cause which would lead to victory. What a contrast to the Germans! The truth hit us that things had changed and these Canadian soldiers already carried an air of victory.

The absence of Germans in the vicinity having been confirmed, the mood became more relaxed, and something happened which is difficult to describe but it was very intense all the same. Everyone realized that the great event had happened – we were liberated! Four years of occupation were over and the defeat of 1940 was forgotten. Men's voices were changed by the emotion and their eyes shone while the women came out of the houses with flowers to express their gratitude to the liberating soldiers.

In return, the Canadians took from their pockets packets of cigarettes, sweets and little bars of chocolate, which they passed among us. I smoked my first 'Sweet Corporal'. They continued to arrive at the cross and sat down on the banks by the road. The soldiers were thirsty. Pierre Heudes and Gabriel Clerambosq went to and fro between the village cross and Mr André Lefevre's cellar, bringing jugs of cider. I think they must have nearly emptied the barrel.

Something which added to the emotion was the old-fashioned accent of the French-Canadians, who made up part of the regiment. We had been waiting for the English or Americans but it was the Canadians who had liberated us. We had a sort of feeling that we were discovering distant relations. Our hearts swelled with joy, and we lived as if in a dream.

But the beach fighting was far from over. As the Queen's Own Rifles took on the pillboxes at Courseulles, the Royal Winnipegs on their right were storming across the beach and into the town of Bernières. This is an extract from the official history of the regiment:

As the landing craft approached the beach, it was increasingly clear that the bombardment had failed to destroy any of the enemy strongpoints. From a distance of less than 800 yards the enemy opened up with everything they had. The 1st Hussars' DD

Tanks had failed to keep ahead of the landing crafts, resulting in the regiment's going in cold. Gripping their weapons tighter, all knew what had to be expected and done once the order 'Open doors' was given.

As the doors were lowered, these companies advanced through a hail of bullets. Spandaus and Nazi rifles spat furiously at the invaders. During the run-in some assault crafts were swamped on the reefs which abounded in front of Courseulles.

Rushing the enemy, B Company encountered heavy enemy fire. Corporal J Klos, badly shot in the stomach and legs while leaving the assault boat, made his way forward to an enemy machine-gun nest. He managed to kill two Nazis before he was mortally felled, his hands still gripped about the throat of his victim.

Lieutenant JJ Moore was with the 8th Battalion of the King's Liverpool Regiment, the Liverpool Irish. His unit's task was to act as a Beach Group for the 3rd Canadian Division on the western sector of Juno. He watched the unfolding battle for the right-hand extremity of the beach.

We were to disembark at the same time as the Royal Winnipeg Rifles, west of the small port of Courseulles. We were to destroy all enemy opposition on or near the beach, and to protect the flanks while the Canadians pushed forward on a narrow front. Speed was essential, for any delay could jeopardise the whole operation. My job as lieutenant was to land with two sections of my Assault Pioneer Platoon and to clear paths through the vast German minefield immediately beyond the beach and the sand dunes.

We were on a Landing Craft Tank, a small flat-bottomed boat which held six self-propelled 105mm cannon on a Sherman tank chassis, two Jeeps and our two 'Weasels' which were small amphibious-tracked vehicles. My two sections were all specialists, and to ensure that as many of us as possible got ashore, we split up between several landing crafts, hoping that at least some of us would survive to carry out the essential tasks.

A large German fortress had been built in reinforced concrete in the sand dunes, so skilfully camouflaged that it was barely visible. It was unscathed by the colossal barrage. When the landings took place, the guns from this fortress opened up fiercely, firing right along the line of the beach at the landing troops and tanks, and sinking many of the approaching landing craft. Some tanks of the 1st Hussars drove toward the fortress and succeeded at very short range in firing a shell directly through the gun-port of the fortress.

Some specially equipped Churchill tanks – AVREs – passed along the track beyond the fortress, heading inland. Here the Germans had altered the sluice-gates of the River Seulles so as to flood the flat land behind the dunes. The first tank dropped its great roof-load of branches and logs. It then tried to cross over the branches and logs, but sank deeply into the quagmire. With great difficulty the crew managed to get out of the sunken tank. But they were caught in heavy machine-gun fire and one of the crew was killed. Then a bridge-carrying tank followed up and laid a steel bridge over the sunken tank and beyond that more branches and logs were laid, now forming a way for other tanks to follow.

As time went on, the short width of the beach, which had been of some advantage, was becoming a handicap: it was cluttered with an assortment of tracked and wheeled vehicles and presented a chaotic scene, with wrecked Jeeps, tanks, lorries and landing crafts. The signals officer of the Liverpool Irish and his driver were badly wounded after moving less than five yards on French soil, their Jeep having run over a Teller mine which had become detached from one of the beach obstacles. It was a strange scene: dozens of vehicles awaiting the opportunity to move inland, while all over the dunes many sub-units of the Beach Group – signallers, military police, first-aid posts and others – set about their tasks with apparent unconcern.

There were bodies of soldiers from the Royal Winnipegs and the Canadian Scottish scattered about the minefield. Plainly it was our duty to bring them in. I sought some stretcher-bearers from the pioneer corps section and explained the position. They instantly volunteered to help. With a detector and a single tape, two of us swept a narrow path to each body in turn so that each could be recovered.

A quarter of a mile away, a member of the Regina Rifles was in the midst of an action that would earn him the Military Cross.

Lieutenant Bill Grayson, a platoon commander, had jumped from his landing craft on crashing the beach and had hurried across the bare expanse of sand through a gap in the wire, to the edge of the first row of houses facing the sea. There, he took cover behind a corner of a house near the German concrete gun emplacement where he could not be observed by the crew inside.

The emplacement was at the far end of an alley from the house behind which he was hiding. Between the gun emplacement and himself was more barbed wire and a German machine-gun post. He noticed that the firing from the machine gun came in bursts at timed intervals along a fixed arc of fire. Grayson checked the timing of the bursts and estimated that he would be able to get past the machine gun and run to the side of the emplacement where he could toss a grenade through the gun slit.

Immediately after the next burst from the machine gun, he made a mad dash for the emplacement only to become entangled in the wire. Miraculously, the next burst of fire was delayed. Grayson tore himself free and tossed in his grenade. On hearing the explosion, he dived in after it through the aperture. He leaped up just in time to see the last of the German gun crew disappearing through the back door of the emplacement.

The rear man, on seeing Grayson, turned and threw a potato-masher grenade at him, which landed between his legs. Coolly, Grayson reached down, grabbed the handle and threw the grenade back at the German who left abruptly before it exploded.

Grayson then followed the Germans into a trench which zig-zagged along to a covered underground protective area. On looking into this dark hole he could make out three or four figures. He heard shouts of 'Kamerad', so he motioned with his pistol for them to come out. Out came 35 men whom he promptly took prisoner. By then, other men from A Company had reached the emplacement, and they disarmed the prisoners and led them away. With the 88mm gun out of action, A Company was able to push on into the town.

The Canadian troops refused to be pinned down on the beach. Despite the heavy casualties they fought their way up to the beach defences, put them out of action, and pushed on inland towards their second objective, the line on the map designated Elm.

> **Bloody fighting raged all along the beaches,** wrote Ross Munro, a Canadian war correspondent, in his D-Day despatch. **On the right, the Winnipegs had to battle their way past five major concrete casements and fifteen machine-gun positions set in the dunes commanding a long sweep of beach. From dune to dune, along the German trench systems, and through the tunnels, these Manitoba troops fought every yard of the way. They broke into the casements, ferreted out the gun crews with machine guns, grenades, bayonets and knives. The Canadians ran into cross-fire. They were shelled and mortared even in the German positions, but they kept slugging away at the enemy. After a struggle that was bitter and savage, the Winnipegs broke through into the open country behind the beach.**

By now the slightly tardy tanks and artillery were making their way up the beach. RS Haig-Brown was the newly promoted commander of a light anti-aircraft battery of the Royal Canadian Artillery. Like a mother duck with her little ducklings, he shepherded his six big guns ashore.

> The tanks were unlashed and all ready to go, the front doors were opened, the ramp lowered, and down into the sea went the tanks.
> To the left and right were other LSTs, some disabled after having hit mines. But we managed our dash to the shore, weaving our way on the sea-bed between steel spikes sticking up at all angles. Like hounds at a hedgerow, looking for a way through, we were soon up on dry land, with guns at the ready to beat off the German airforce which never came, and the drivers pulling savagely at the waterproofing so that the engines could run. I suppose that in all that movement, on something never before tried in world history, to have been only half an hour late was something of a triumph.
> My first real shock was to see perhaps a hundred of our men dead, lying at the water's edge, their bodies rolling unnaturally

The Canadians took bicycles into the battle, hoping to pedal quickly inland. But the soldiers' backpacks were so heavy that the bicycles overbalanced and reared up like wild horses when the men rode them. Most of the bikes were abandoned within a mile or two of the beach.

on the sand as the tide washed around them. Devastation was everywhere. Nothing was in one piece. Tree trunks were snapped off by shells and strewed the road. Every building was wrecked by the earlier bombardment. Cows lay awkwardly, legs in the air, dead or dying. Overhead was the fierce crack of the Navy's 21-inch shells on their way inland. The noise was unbelievable, made worse if possible by Frenchmen in berets running here and there, too bewildered to know what they were doing.

The village street was now in ruins, the road so jammed with debris that we could not see the tar. Bill Lean, my troop commander, met up with me and together we walked down to the church to spy out the land for the best gun positions. The church steeple had been hit by a shell and now there was a gaping hole six feet across. Up there and unknown to us was a German sniper, and before long we heard the familiar crack of rifle-fire going over our heads. But we were seemingly immune, for too often in training had we had live bullets fired at us. That sound was not so unusual. 'Do you know something, kid?' said Bill beaming all over. 'I think someone's firing at us.' But we just walked on and to this day I have no idea why we did not bother to take cover. It never occurred to either of us. A few minutes later a well-aimed Bofors round put a stop to that little nuisance, and I heard no more shots.

Bridges lay on the other side of a minefield. I was told to organize a way through for the tanks. In their methodical way the Germans had every minefield marked with barbed wire and from the top strand was hanging a notice saying 'Achtung Minen'. If the writing sloped to the left it was a dummy; to the right it was an anti-personnel field; upright meant an anti-tank one. I wanted to go through an area with upright lettering, so I knew I was looking for buried mines.

I knew exactly what to do until I came across the first mine. I knew all about German mines, but I was not prepared for this. This and all the others turned out to be British, captured at Dunkirk in 1940. I had no idea how to handle any of them.

When eventually I did clear a way through, no one would volunteer to drive the first tank down my taped path. 'You cleared the way, sir,' said the troop sergeant-major with a huge grin. 'And if you don't mind, perhaps you would prove it is all right by taking No 1 down there yourself.'

On my first run down the lane, it was necessary to turn sharp left. In doing so, a track broke. It could not be easily mended where it was, so I hunted round for a Royal Engineer's road-laying tank, and asked the major with it if he would pull my helpless tank to better ground. To do so meant going down my cleared lane, but the tracks of a Churchill tank differ from those of a Crusader, and although I had managed it successfully, the wider tank ran over a mine, wrecking it and killing the driver.

The Canadians broke through the German sea defences, and following waves mopped up snipers and other pockets of resistance. Canadian troops had achieved the Yew objective by getting off the beach. Now they were streaming towards the Elm line all along the battle front.

A massacre had been avoided, and now it began to turn into a triumph. The Canadian regiments were making better progress inland than the British, or than the Americans away to the west. But they had paid dearly for it: nearly a thousand Canadian soldiers were killed or wounded on Juno in the course of the first day. Jim Wilkins of the Queen's Own Rifles had been hit twice as he stormed the beach. Now, his leg shattered, he dragged himself to the sea wall.

I managed to slip off my pack and webbing, and crawl on my back. I finally made it. In front of me I could see bodies washing back and forth in the surf. Soon, one of my friends, Willis Gambrel, showed up and we each had one of my cigarettes – which surprisingly were fairly dry. A medic came along and put a bandage on my leg. I had forgotten all about the hole in my side. Then two English beach party soldiers came along carrying a five-gallon teapot. 'Cup of tea Canada?' 'Yes sir,' and they gave me tea in a tin mug. It was hot and mixed fifty-fifty with rum. It was really good.

In the meantime, A Company had gotten ashore with their share of casualties and started to take out the various gun emplacements. Presently there were four or five fellows with me. Then at last a Sherman tank from the First Hussars showed up. They had come in too late to help us. All of a sudden he stopped just a few feet past us, ambled up to the wall and commenced to fire. There are things at the end of these gun barrels called recoil deflectors so that the muzzle blast comes out sideways. The muzzle blast came directly down where we were lying. The man beside me had a bandage around his head and eyes and he screamed every time they fired. My leg didn't like it either. Finally, after much arm-waving at the crew commander, he got the message that we didn't appreciate his presence.

I had already got a shot of morphine from a medic and dozed a little. Soon the tide was almost at my boots, and at long last two English stretcher-bearers came and started to evacuate us from the beach. They carried me in water up to their ankles. The fellow at my head lost his grip and said to his pal – put him down for a second. Just then a good wave came in right over me and on the way out picked up my broken leg and threw it at a right-angle to the stretcher. I said 'Would you mind putting my leg back on the stretcher?' 'Sorry, Canada,' one said, and grabbed my boot and put my leg back.

I was put with a group of other wounded and eventually a doctor came along and asked where I was hit. 'My leg is broken,' I said. With that he took a look and said 'You'll be okay, son.'

JUNO IN THE AFTERNOON

As the first waves pressed inland, the reserve began to make its way ashore. It included elements of the 7th and 8th Brigades, as well as the entire 9th Brigade. These men tumbled into France like a human avalanche, using their weight of numbers and their driving momentum to push back the German front line.

The afternoon and evening of D-Day was devoted to 'delousing' the houses behind our beach, said one Canadian officer. And quite a job it was. We were a bit clumsy at first, and lost quite a few because of it, but soon it became more or less a drill. We found ourselves in little groups, nothing intentional or premeditated on anyone's part. I had a small group of two sergeants and six sappers. They had plenty of guts and were simply eager when we formed a plan to do a certain house. By dark, most of the houses in our immediate vicinity were clean. My loot up to that point was a swastika flag which I had torn from the wall of a sort of HQ.

Some of the houses just refused to be deloused so we burnt them down. We set one on fire which had caused us a lot of grief. When it really started to brew, one young Jerry made an effort to escape through a window. He got partly out when a gunner on an LCT saw him. A streak of about 50 Oerlikon rounds hit him. He hung there for a couple of days until a burial party found him.

Troops were streaming past Courseulles, but the town itself was still a battle zone. The Canadian planners had divided the town into twelve blocks, and each one was assigned to a unit of the Regina Rifles. Now that the beach was secure, the Regina Rifles – known as 'The Johns' – moved through the town, clearing the houses one by one.

As we cleared the town of Courseulles, the people who had remained in the town waved at us as we went by, said Captain JG Baird. They offered cider and black bread. The bombardment had destroyed many of their homes and some had been killed. Yet they welcomed us with flowers and tricolor bunting which suddenly made its appearance. The Canadians were there, and they were happy. The expression on the faces of the children as they had their first taste of a chocolate bar was something to remember.

Charlie company moved into the town to clear its designated portion. Dog company, commanded by Major JV Love, lost two craft by mines. Heavy casualties resulted, including the company commander who was killed. The remainder of Dog, now reduced to forty-nine, reorganized and set out to Reviers, two miles inland, to seize the bridges over the Mue River.

Charlie company now reported Block 8 clear and established itself in this area. Charlie then cleared Blocks 9, 10 and 11 in short order. Able company now reported Block 1 in their hands and were ordered to take on Blocks 5, 6 and 7 along the lock which ran through the center of town. Meanwhile, Baker had cleared 4 and was sent on to 12. At this time Able reported they were being fired on from Block 1, which they had just completed clearing. Enemy had returned to the area through tunnels and it was now necessary to begin the disheartening work again. Another troop of tanks was assigned to them for this purpose.

But the day's work was not complete yet. After a hard fight on the beach, the Winnipeg Rifles and one company of the Canadian Scottish were now moving south on our right. The remaining companies of the Scottish had landed and were moving south also. About 17.00 hours we started to advance south from Reviers. About 17.30 hours Baker, squadron commander, reported that an 88-millimeter gun had knocked out six of his ten tanks. Two detachments of our three-inch mortars set up at Reviers and brought down supporting fire. Six Centaurs with their 95-millimeter guns had arrived at Reviers and were able to assist the forward companies.

The Regina Rifles halted for the day on the Elm line, or perhaps a fraction

The Canadians fought from house to house through the seaside towns of Bernières-sur-Mer, Saint Aubin and Courseulles. Their experience here on the first day was a kind of dress rehearsal for the battle of Caen, where they stalked the enemy through smoking ruins.

ahead of it. They were, at any rate, a good four miles inland. It was a magnificent achievement to have got that far, but their position remained uncertain and precarious.

It was night. The Johns were digging in the fields of Normandy – on D-Day and in enemy-held territory. We were on our own now. Some distance to the right were the Winnipeg Rifles and the Canadian Scottish; on our left, no friendly troops. We were out on a limb if the enemy could organize his forces for an attack. But the plan had been carried out – to assault and break through, exploiting rapidly inland. This meant taking chances on being cut off. And we were on our intermediate objective as ordered: get your intermediate objectives on D-day at all costs.

The battalion was now dug-in and waited for what the night might bring. Looking back at the beaches to the north we could see flashes of bomb bursts as enemy aircraft ventured out. Some flew low over our area and dropped flares and incendiaries on areas where troops might be. Soon there were fires burning here and there across the flat beachhead area for miles around.

THE GERMAN COUNTER-ATTACK

Yew and Elm were achieved by late afternoon, but the third objective, Oak, was still some way off. The vital airport at Carpiquet remained firmly in German hands. 'Our instructions were to break through immediately after hitting the beach,' said Stanley Dudka, a sergeant in the North Nova Scotia Highlanders. 'And to stop at nothing, not to fight unless we had to, but to get to Carpiquet.' The Nova Scotia Regiment was part of the reserve 9th Brigade. It was hoped that by keeping them back until the main battle on the beach was over, they would be able to advance quickly through captured territory towards the airstrip. But it was a full ten miles inland.

I was a member of C Company, and I was part of a battle group consisting of approximately 300 personnel with fifty-seven Sherman tanks, nineteen 'funny' tanks, three self-propelled guns, and three flails, up along with machine-gun and mortar support from the Cameron Highlanders.

But there was tremendous congestion all along the beaches. The roads were very narrow, and when we got ashore at Bernières-sur-Mer, we were held up there for three hours.

One of the things that did take us by surprise were these hedgerows. You couldn't get through them and you would stray from your buddies very easy in these hedgerows. The other main obstacle we found was the tall grass and wheat. They were ready to be cut. If you dug in or lay down on the ground, you had no visibility whatsoever, just a bunch of grass in front of you.

By midday the Nova Scotia Highlanders were in the village of Villons-les-Buissons, halfway between Elm and Oak and only about three miles from Carpiquet. Some units of the Highlanders and the Sherbrooke Fusiliers had ventured further to the village of Buron. Here they became embroiled in house-to-house fighting. Machine-gunners from both sides hunted each other through the streets, and anti-tank missiles were sent crashing through upstairs windows where snipers lurked. The battle held up most of the Highlanders for the entire afternoon, but one or two Canadian patrols had pushed on past Buron and reached the edge of the airstrip. But they were too few to mount an attack.

> We got inland to about eight miles, said Stanley Dudka. And then the orders came that we should dig in, that we should not advance any further. However, we should put out continuous patrols and expect a counter-attack.
>
> We were in what we called a tank harbor. It's like the Indians attacking a covered wagon. The tanks would form a circle, and every second gun was manned on the turret, and we would go inside the circle.
>
> We were supposed to contact the British 3rd Division, which was on our left, and they were supposed to take Caen on that day. We had not made any contact, nor had we sent scouts out. There was no visibility of any British whatsoever, and communications between us and them were just not there.

The German counter-attack came, as expected. Stanley Dudka was digging in, concealed by high grass, when the Panzers came rolling from the direction of Caen.

> We didn't have time to dig more than about two feet. There were two of us in this trench. Then another one of our fellows who had been wounded crawled in on top of us. That left us very little room to maneuver. The wheat that we were in was at least three-feet tall. We could hear the German giving orders in front of us, and we could hear that there were two tanks, one about thirty feet from me, and the other, maybe fifteen feet from him, that were firing over our heads. They were not firing at us. They didn't know we were there.
>
> We fired a burst at the Germans that we could hear, but our bullets seemed to be useless against the tanks. Then all of a sudden, this German hollered 'Come on out!' (I assume). So we talked it over, and we figured it best that we give up. That's where we first met the 12th SS Panzer, one of the most ruthless outfits in German history.

The 12th SS Panzer Division were commanded by Standartenführer Kurt Meyer, a zealous Nazi and a star officer of the Waffen SS. His division was a ferocious fighting unit. Many of the officers had been though the frozen horror of the Russian Front, and knew how to fight. The mass of soldiers, meanwhile, were fanatical, superfit teenagers who had grown up in the Hitler Youth. They were hungry for battle, desperate to spill the blood of the enemies of the Reich. They were utterly devoid of fear and mercy.

These Hitler Youth, wrote war correspondent Ralph Allen, **were beardless killers whose highest aim was to die, whose only god was Hitler, who came rustling through the spring wheat, a screaming curtain of mortars just ahead of them, the fearsome clanking of their tanks behind.**

The young Hitler worshippers were a terrifying opponent. 'They look like babies,' said one Canadian soldier, 'and they die like mad bastards.' Meyer's boys and the grizzled veterans captured dozens of Canadians and pushed the rest back as far as the Elm line, where they dug in for the night.

Meanwhile, a disaster was narrowly averted. The German 21st Panzer Division had been stationary all day while its commander, Brigadier General Edgar Feuchtinger, dithered about when and where to engage the enemy – the Canadians to the left of him, or the British Airborne to the right? Now, finally, these tanks rumbled into the fray. One tank battalion headed due north, up the road from Caen to Luc-sur-Mer. This took them straight down the gap between Juno Beach and Sword. At 8 o'clock in the evening, Colonel Rauch of the 192nd Panzer Grenadier Regiment found himself on the coast, staring open-mouthed from his gun turret at the numberless ships of the Allied fleet. Lieutenant Franz Grabmann, who had fought the British in North Africa, was also there.

We were to make a strong thrust directly to the coast, wipe out the enemy, and take over the beaches to prevent further landings. We had heard the great bombardment on the shore and as we went along the road we heard the sounds of battle. We met little resistance and drove on until we could actually see the sea, and then we met stiffening opposition. I was in an armoured car and tried to get off the road several times because of jabo attack. We met a number of our casualties going back and heard our own tanks firing ahead. The situation was confused, and not helped by the great naval shells that came hurtling over at us.

However, a motorcyclist told us that some of our troops and tanks had actually reached the beach, which was heartening news. Then, like a thunderbolt from the sky, came a great aerial column of planes and gliders. We were so disheartened we felt we could not continue.

Had the advance column of German tanks been bolder, and had Feuchtinger been more decisive, they might now have wrought havoc with the Allied beachhead. One thing that Montgomery feared above all was that his troops would be outflanked. That eventuality did not materialize in the gap between Gold and Omaha, but here, between Juno and Sword, it had come to pass. All it needed now was for the Germans to pour armour into the gap. It would have been like driving a steel wedge into the side of the Allies.

But the Germans failed to make anything of this golden opportunity. The flock of gliders that they saw pass overhead, and which so demoralized the German troops, were reinforcements bound for the 6th British Airborne holding out at Ranville. Feuchtinger surmised wrongly that they were about to drop behind the Panzers and cut them off, and so ordered the tanks to retreat to base at the double. Thus ended the only serious German advance of D-Day.

NIGHT-TIME IN THE CANADIAN SECTOR

As they dug in for the night, the men of the Canadian 3rd Division had every reason to be satisfied. They had advanced farther inland than any of the British and American divisions: theirs was indisputably the most successful assault of the day. The troops had consolidated at Elm almost everywhere along the line, and little fingers of Canadian-held territory probed south towards Caen and Carpiquet.

The 7th Brigade, on the right, had driven inland against moderate opposition and was fast approaching its objectives, states the official history of Canada's Highland Light Infantry. On the left flank, however, the 8th Brigade had been engaged in heavy and involved fighting which had delayed the 9th Brigade in its break-out role. But, on the whole, the picture was good. The

Division was ashore, through the beach defenses, and had pushed sufficiently far inland to retain the initiative, and with a beachhead large enough for the build-up to commence.

They did not know it, but the Canadians were about to face some of the most pitiless fighting of the campaign. In many ways, D+1 was a harder day for the Canadians than D-Day itself. On 7 June, in the battle for the village of Authie, the Nova Scotia Highlanders would lose eighty-four men and the Sherbrookes sixty. On that same day, dozens of Canadian prisoners were summarily executed by Kurt Meyer's SS men, an act for which he was convicted of war crimes after the war. When the Canadians finally took Authie, they were horrified to find the dead body of one of their comrades propped against a wall, a German helmet set on his head, a bottle of beer tucked under his arm, and a cigarette drooping from his lifeless mouth. The soldiers of Canada knew that the SS were responsible, and it is no surprise that in later fighting very few SS men were accorded the privilege of surrender.

Back on the beach, Jim Wilkins of the Queen's Own Rifles was being prepared for evacuation. His regiment had suffered the greatest number of casualties of any Canadian unit on D-Day. And in his platoon of thirty-five men, only one lance-sergeant, one lance-corporal and six rifleman came through the day unscathed; all the rest were dead or wounded.

> **Two German POWs picked me up and carried me to a concrete air-raid shelter,** said Rifleman Wilkins. **They placed me on a low bunk. Very quickly the bunks were full and people were put on the floor. A German boy was on the floor right beside me, and he was in bad shape. Just before it got dark a German mortar landed just outside the door, blew it off and filled the bunker with dirt, smoke and chunks of gravel. Eventually a medic came in and gave the German boy a shot of morphine. I said 'I'll take one of those, if you don't mind.' 'Okay,' he said. And as darkness fell on June 6th, I was soon asleep.**

7
CROSSING SWORD

> 'It looks peaceful enough now, doesn't it?' said someone over my
> shoulder.

Early in the morning of D-Day, Lieutenant HM Edwards of the 77th
Assault Squadron of the Royal Engineers was standing on the deck of the
LSA *Battleaxe*, looking towards the coast. Ahead of him lay the town of
Ouistreham and the wide mouth of the River Orne. Casting his eyes over
the long yellow strand from Ouistreham to Lion-sur-Mer he could see
beach huts, cafés and little seaside houses. This pretty three-mile stretch of
shoreline was Sword Beach, the eastern extremity of the invasion area.

On the left bank of the River Orne, away from the coast and out of
Edwards' sight, British paratroopers were already in action. The 6th
Airborne Division had parachuted into France during the night and were
holding bridges across the river. They were protecting the far flank of the
invasion, just as their American counterparts were doing at the other end
of the battlefield, fifty miles away. Detachments of commandos now
aboard the various ships were due to race across Sword and relieve the
airborne by noon.

Lieutenant Edwards made the most of this moment of serenity.

> Everyone appeared casual, almost unconcerned, in those last
> few minutes before going to our LCA. Even the sinking of a
> minesweeper off our port beam roused little comment.

Then the stupendous naval guns opened up. The two great battleships
HMS *Ramillies* and HMS *Warspite*, as well as the rest of the armada of the
Third British Division, poured tons of shells on to the strongpoints and
the big guns of this stretch of the Atlantic Wall. Sword Beach was the most
intensely shelled of all the beaches, and the bombardment was well under
way as Edwards made for shore:

As we were lowered away, no word was passed between those still on the ship and the first flight in the tossing LCA. The moment was too big, perhaps. Maybe they too wondered what it would be like when we touched down. This was to be my first action, in which there would be a sudden transition from comparative peace to war. In front of us the beach was hardly distinguishable in the smoke and dust, but before we could study it we were crouched in the bottom of the craft for the last lap.

Nearby, Lieutenant HT Bone of the 2nd East Yorkshire Regiment was climbing into his boat with the same sombre sense of occasion. He too saw the stricken ship that had so little troubled Lieutenant Edwards, and recorded the moment in a letter home a few days later:

In the mess decks we blacked our faces with black palmolive cream and listened to the naval orders over the loudhailer. Most of us had taken communion on the Sunday, but the ship's padre had a few words to say to us. Then came the loading into craft – the swinging on davits – the boat lowering and finally 'Away Boats'.

As we left the ship our bugler blew the general salute and then again as we passed the HQ ship, the senior officer returning our CO's salute. Whilst this was going on, all around could be seen the rest of the convoy, with battleships and cruisers firing their big guns, and destroyers rushing round the flashes. One had been hit by something and only the up-ended part of its bows remained in view.

As our flotilla swung into line behind its leader we raised our flag: a black silk square with the white rose of Yorkshire in the centre. The Navy had sewn their red anchor into the top left-hand corner and the brass Marine badge was soldered to the blade of the spear on which the flag was suspended. It blew taut in the wind and spray.

Major KP Baxter went in shortly after the first wave. He now heard the disheartening sound that so many men had encountered that morning all along the Normandy coast – the irregular ping and clatter of bullets striking a soon-to-be-lowered ramp.

The DUKW amphibious truck, known inevitably as the 'duck', had a top speed of about 5 knots at sea and 50 mph on land. Some had guns mounted on them, but this made them top-heavy and likely to capsize. They were best used as ship-to-shore supply vehicles.

Closing to the shore rapidly, eyes scanned the clearing haze for familiar landmarks. There were none. Suddenly a burst ricocheted off the front of the craft, telling us that this was no covering fire. The opposition was very much alive and well.

We had still been unable to identify our position but we were by now right on top of the beach. The protective steel doors in the bows were opened and everyone waited, tensed for the soft lurching bump. 'Ramp down' – and out into knee-deep water. Ahead was a line of prone figures just above the water's edge and, some two hundred yards beyond, a tank was nosed up against the small strip of dunes at the head of the beach.

I had not gone far when I was tripped by some underwater wire and, with no hope of retaining balance with the heavy assault jacket pack, went flat on my face. Attempting to rise, I was struck a heavy blow in the back which flattened me again, and suddenly the machine gun opened up on us once more. The fire came from dead ahead and we could now make out the shape of a heavy embrasure in the low silhouette of some concrete fortifications at the top of the beach.

We then realised that, by the narrowest of margins, we had landed immediately in front of strongpoint 0880, code-name COD. Mortar and light artillery fire being now intensified. The still-unspotted machine gun made an instant target of anything that moved. We found the prone figures above the water's edge to be casualties from the leading craft. Our wireless had been lost when the operator, Corporal Roulier, had been hit on leaving our craft, but on White Beach, to our right, troops could be seen to be crossing the beach and reaching the top.

There was a brief lull in the firing and we immediately took this opportunity to make a dash for the top of the beach. Briefly seeking cover behind the motionless tank to count heads, it was found that only the signalman of our group had managed to come through unscathed.

We had hardly jettisoned our heavy equipment when the strongpoint above our heads sprang to life once more. German stick grenades somersaulted through the air, their effects being greatly reduced in the soft sand, whilst we in turn desperately sought grenades from the remnants of other detachments now grouping with us.

Further action was promptly eclipsed by the arrival of Lieutenant Tony Milne with his machine-gun platoon of the 2nd Battalion Middlesex Regiment. The platoon was equipped with Bren gun carriers, having the heavy Vickers mounted above the engine casing. They were the first infantry fighting vehicle to land. Without a moment's hesitation, waterproofing shields were ripped away, gun clamps freed, and the leading carrier drove straight at the trench line above our heads with a long swinging traverse from the Vickers, depressing into the trench as they closed. A brief pause – silence – then at the end of the trench system some fifteen survivors appeared in hasty surrender. Strongpoint COD had been taken.

Not without difficulty did we identify the machine gun that had given us so much trouble. It was co-axially mounted in a small concrete silo sunk flush to ground level. There was a remote-control firing device which, together with periscopic sights, allowed the gunner complete protection at his position at the bottom of the shaft. The top had been covered by a shallow cupola, finely camouflaged with grass, so that the whole above-ground assembly was indistinguishable beyond twenty paces.

JH Patterson was a medical officer with No 4 Commando. Unlike most, he had known for several days exactly where in France he was to land, because he had been with French commandos at the pre-invasion briefing. 'All the Free French recognized the area at once. One used to work the lock gates at the mouth of the canal before the war'.

Before embarkation, Doctor Patterson had taken a bath, 'Washing off the B. Coli in case you stop one, as the naval doctor said.' Now he was about to be soaked to the skin again.

> 'Troops to parade, troops to parade' came over the loudhailer, and we collected in the mess decks. There seemed to be much less room than usual, as everyone had everything with him, probably for the first time.
>
> 'Troops man your boats, troops man your boats' at 06.10 hours brought us out on the decks. It was quite light and the ship rode steadily at anchor, though a big swell made the little assault craft look rather unsteady. We stepped gingerly over the gap with our heavy loads and began to pack ourselves in. As always, the last man couldn't sit down. The last thing I saw as I sat down was the bow and stern of the Norwegian destroyer sticking out of the water a mile or two astern.
>
> Soon 'Lower away' sent the LCAs down in turn to bump and wrench on their davits as the swell took them. But quickly the shackles were cast off and we rode free, very free, in that sea. It certainly was rough. We waved goodbye to the *Princess Astrid* and slipped away to join the flotilla from the *Maid of Orleans*. Quite soon, thank goodness, we were allowed to stand up and look round.
>
> The big LSIs were all anchored and their LCA flotillas, like tiny flecks on the sea, lifted to view and sank between the waves of the huge swell. With their white, grey and blue camouflage they were

hard to see against that white, grey and blue sea.

The various waves of the assault were forming up, the first wave already well on its way towards the shore. The sky was clearing, and full of the roar of aircraft, big formations of them tearing south. Far out on either beam we could see the warships, with the big orange puffs from their guns and the flashes lighting up the smoke. The roar of the guns was fairly continuous and the nearer ones shook us as we slipped past them, and their shells went screaming overhead.

All the landing craft were moving now, with the LCAs forging ahead and the LCIs close on their heels. The LCTs crept in slowly, allowing us to pass them. The artillery and tanks in them were all firing through the camouflage nets, and the din grew absolutely shattering as all the guns neared to their range.

The rocket ships went in closer to loose their streaming sheaves of flame in volleys. These rockets were intended to silence beach defences, but on our sector they overshot and fell harmlessly in marshy land beyond the east-west road. The beach defences were very much alive when the assault went in. All along the coast were flashes of bursting shells and answering coast artillery, and over it all drifted a thick pall of smoke, streaked here and there with dotted streams of tracer.

All the assault craft were together now, ahead of the bigger stuff. It reminded me of coming up to the line at the start of a sailing race. We were rolling heavily in a big swell which broke continually over us, drenching us and chilling us to the marrow.

My hands grew numb and dead and my teeth were chattering with cold and fright. The chaps in the other boats were passing round the rum, and I could hear snatches of song through the hellish din. Hutch Burt's boat went in singing *Jerusalem*. We didn't sing in our boat. My mouth was bone dry, and I was shaking all over. I doubt if I could have produced a note. We passed round the rum, and those who were not too seasick took a good swig. The sea was well dotted with 'Bags, vomit'.

It was H-Hour, 07.25, and the first infantry were going in. I took a look around the boat. My batman Smith was sitting on the thwart. He was looking awful but gave me a big grin through his green. Private Hindmarch beside me, polite as ever and looking surprisingly pink. Little Sapper Mullen, the artist, as grey as a corpse, who died of wounds later that day. Gordon Webb and Peter Beckett in the bows were peering forward, alert and tense. Lieutenant Kennedy, looking rather grim but enjoying his rum. Just as well too, as he was never seen again after leaving the boat.

Doctor Patterson charged ashore like an infantryman. As a medical man he was not allowed to carry arms: his rucksack contained only medical supplies. He got to work as soon as he was out of the water.

Bullets began to rattle against the side of the craft and splinters went whining overhead. 'Ready on the ramp.' We cowered down. The explosions were very near and one threw spray over us as the splinters tore overhead. 'Going in to land.'

We touched, bumped and slewed round. This was no true landing, we could feel. 'Ramp down.' The boat began to empty. My men and I were the last to leave. I heaved on my rucksack and seized a stretcher. No one seemed ready to take the other one so I picked it up too. I went staggering to the bows, cautiously down the ramp, and flopped into the water. It came up about mid-thigh as the craft had grounded on some softish obstacle, probably a body. I struggled desperately towards the shore.

There was a thick fog of smoke over the beach, and the tide was low but flooding. I noticed after a few paces that there were many bodies in the water. One was hanging on the wire round one of the tripod obstacles. The shoals were churned with bursting shells particularly to my immediate right, and I seem to remember an LCI there being hit. As I got nearer the shore I saw men among the dead, pinned down by the weight of their equipment.

The first I came to was Sapper Mullen. He was submerged to his chin and quite helpless. Somehow I got my scissors out and with my numb hands, which felt weak and useless, I began to cut away his rucksack and equipment. Hindmarch appeared beside me and got working on the other side. He was a bit rattled, but soon steadied when I spoke to him and told him what to do.

As I was bending over I felt a smack across my bottom as if someone had hit me with a big stick. It was a shell splinter, but it hit nothing important and I just swore and went on. We dragged Mullen to the water's edge at last, and he was able to shuffle himself up the beach, so we let him carry on, and I looked round to take stock.

The Commando were up at the wire, and clearly having trouble getting through. As there was nothing to be said for standing around up there, Hindmarch and I went back to the wounded in the water. I noticed now how fast the tide was rising, and the wounded men began to shout and scream as they saw that they must soon drown. We worked desperately and I don't know how many we pulled clear, though it wasn't more than two or three.

Then I saw Donald Glass at the water's edge, badly hit in the back and we went to him and started to cut away his equipment. As I was doing so I became conscious of a machine gun enfilading us from the left front. In a minute I was knocked over by a smack in the right knee, and fell on Donald, who protested violently. I cautiously tried my leg and found that it still worked, though not very well. Donald was too bad to move. I looked around for help but the only other standing figure anywhere was my batman, who was working on his own with the drowning wounded in the water. He smiled and waved to me and I left him to get on with it. I tried my leg again and took one end of the stretcher.

Hindmarch is a big strong fellow and between us we began to carry Donald up towards the wire. I had to have one rest, and at the finish I just lay and gasped lay for some minutes. We left Donald in a bit of a hollow in the sand where he had a certain amount of cover.

The troops had by now got through the wire and I stumbled after them and across the minefield. I remember thinking that it might be wise to walk in footprints. I found the unit assembling in some confusion among the buildings. Someone gave me a swig of rum, which did me good, and Lance Corporal Cunningham put a dressing on my leg. It turned out to be a lucky wound through the muscles and tendons behind the knee joint which had missed the popliteal artery very narrowly. The little bit of shell in my buttock made me very stiff but it was not worth bothering about.

I could find no sign of my batman Smith, but later in the day found him badly wounded in the legs at the beach dressing station awaiting evacuation. The last I heard of him was a letter from his wife asking how he came to die on D-Day, so I am afraid he must have been killed by the air strafing during the night.

Doctor Patterson and his medical staff were not the only unarmed men on the battlefield. Reverend Walter Crooks, always known as Mike, was a naval chaplain. He was waiting aboard ship when a signal came from the beach that they needed a padre. The three sailors who ferried him in were, he said, 'cock-a hoop' to be there.

They insisted on carrying me from the boat so I didn't get my feet wet. They were totally oblivious to the mines.

I remember that beach so clearly. I was wearing battledress, but with a dog-collar. I wasn't scared, though I was in the most perilous danger. I just saw it as a challenge to do all the good I could in those circumstances, to get alongside the wounded and the dying. It meant a great deal to them just to have a hand to hold. Most of them had faith; some were very worried about what would become of their families.

I came across a dead German. He had a New Testament in his hand. I hesitated to pick it up because so many things were booby trapped: discarded guns and helmets would often explode when you touched them.

One might think it strange that a Nazi footsoldier should go into battle carrying with him the story of the Jewish prince of peace. But Reverend Crooks was not surprised to find that many German soldiers put more trust in God than in Hitler.

I was there for two days and I came home on an LST crammed with wounded German prisoners, most of whom were Roman Catholics. I would have loved to have helped them more than I did.

Mike Crooks brought the dead German's Bible back with him. Today it is on display at the D-Day Museum in Portsmouth, England.

'Strewn about from the water's edge were sodden khaki bundles, staining red the sand where they lay. But there was no time to be staring at corpses: a mad dash up to the shelter of the sea wall. Find some sort of hole. Keep your head down.' Richard Harris, Suffolk Regiment

THE YORKS AND THE LANCS

Two British regiments were leading the assault on Sword. The 2nd East Yorkshires were headed for Queen Red Sector, on the left-hand side of the beach, while to their right the 1st Regiment South Lancashire were bound for Queen White. The 13/18th Hussars, equipped with floating Duplex Drive tanks, supported them. The tanks were due to go in slightly ahead of the infantry, but they ploughed through the water much more slowly than the landing craft, and were falling behind.

> We were ahead of DD tanks of 13/18 Hussars; they were due to touch down seven and a half minutes before we did at H-Hour, said Captain A Low of the Royal Engineers. All craft were ordered to stop engines to allow them through. Approximately 1,000 yards offshore the LCT opened up with two salvoes, followed by one salvo a little later. Rockets collided in mid-air, and rained down

on the craft waiting to go in. One landed immediately under our starboard bow, showering the bridge with pieces of casing.

The navy had laid down a barrage of smoke as thick as an old-fashioned London pea-souper. It was intended to cloak the armada in a pall of invisibility; there were big German guns at Le Havre capable of dropping shells the size of boulders into the midst of the flimsy LCAs. The smoke blinded the enemy artillery as intended, but it had the same effect on the advancing invaders. In the choking offshore fog, the DD tanks ran into the path of the LCTs carrying the demolition teams. There was almost a disastrous collision, but the tank commanders managed to swerve out of the path of the larger ships and head on in. Of the Hussars' 25 tanks, 21 made it to the beach. It was 7.30, and the infantry was right behind them.

Private Harold Lee of the Yorkshires was one of the first infantrymen on the beach. He followed a flail tank across a minefield, keeping to the ragged swathe it had cut in the topsoil.

> Some yards in front of my section, a tank which had just landed suddenly stopped dead. A puff of dirty grey smoke, then flames belched from it. With a sickening sense of horror I realised men were being burned alive inside, roasted like a joint in an oven.

Lieutenant Alex Sudborough of the Royal Marines was on LCI 518. Impatient to get on with the landing, he went to the ramp at the front of the ship, where an equally horrific sight awaited him.

> I went forward to see if the brows had been shot over their rollers and if we were in for a dry landing.
>
> The ramp crew were a mass of duffle coats, steel helmets, teeth, jaws, brains and blood. These gallant sailors had all been decapitated by a shell or mortar bomb. There was a sweet, sickly smell which was stronger than all the cordite, grease and oil.
>
> I made my way to the stern where my section was waiting. How were we going to land? Passing amidships I saw that we had been hit at least twice by mortars and that there were casualties. My one regard was to get my section off. We had always been told on field training 'never bunch'. On our landing craft we were in one large vulnerable bunch.

Showing, as I thought and had been so trained, officer-like qualities of leadership, I looked around for a suitable exit from this obvious enemy fire-trap. On the port side, slightly aft of the ammunition tanks, I saw a rope trailing into the sea. Shouting 'Follow me,' I seized the rope and swung myself over the side into what I expected to be three or four feet of water.

Alas, in my panic I had not made sure that the rope was made fast inboard, and the untied end snaked across the deck as I, gripping the rope, neatly dropped like a plummet into a six-foot shell hole which the tide had covered. I weighed fourteen stones stripped. Battledress and boots and rucksack and rifle put me in the region of twenty stones. My mouth-inflated Mae West life belt was quite inadequate to support this load and I was well and truly stuck in the sands of Normandy with a full eighteen inches of water over my head. Help was quickly forthcoming in the form of an RAMC medical orderly who, seeing my plight, waded into the water and dragged me ashore.

At the water's edge I could not help noticing the number of battle-dressed bodies, all face down, which were gently floating on the tide-line, vaguely surrounded by a pinkish tinge.

Many men found themselves on landing craft that were stuck or disabled, and so had to make a jump for it into the sea. Major FJ Hoadley saw a shell rip the ramp from a landing craft like a page from a book: 'I saw a sapper swim, loaded like a Christmas tree with assault jerkin and mine detector.' AJ Lane of the Royal Engineers also went in over his head when he stepped from his boat, but managed to save himself from drowning. He saw plenty of men failing in the attempt.

We could see that we were in for a pretty hot reception, for already exploding spouts of water were appearing all around us. We received one hit on the stern of the craft which wounded a few of the troops before we got ashore. Perhaps it was that first hit that altered the Royal Navy craft commander's promise to land us in shallow water.

When I dropped off the ramp, my Bren gun took me down like a stone, leaving me with several foot of water above my head. Only by underwater walking towards shore did I save myself from a watery end. I could see that some people were either drowning or drowned already. Some I could see screaming and waving their arms while going backwards and seawards. Many were wounded in the water and were unable to move in the advancing tide.

The tide was an unexpected problem on Sword. A strong wind was driving the sea inward much faster than had been anticipated. Consequently, far more craft than expected hit submerged obstacles and were torn apart or blown sky-high.

More worryingly for the success of the assault, the fast tide meant that there was a much narrower than expected strip of beach, and this was causing an immense traffic jam of men and equipment.

The high-running tide was also a complication for the demolition teams who, though they expected to get wet, did not think that they would be functioning as frogmen. 'To our surprise and dismay, the obstacles were standing in about seven feet of water.' said Major CH Giddings, troop leader of the 629th Forward Squadron. He had expected to be standing on the dry beach looking up at these devices. Instead he was in deep water, looking down over the side of his boat at the lethal mines on poles.

It seemed that our carefully worked out clearance drills would be useless. We passed through the first row, turned and moved along between the rows, studying the stakes each with a Teller mine or impact-fused shell fixed to its head. I well remember the effort of concentration required to get the craft near enough to make a careful examination, but not to make a bump. I decided the removal of the mines and shells was an urgent matter. The stakes themselves could wait.

Each man wore an assault jacket in which he carried personal kit and rations, a demolition pack containing six 8-pound charges with initiators and fixing wires, an axe or a shovel, wirecutters, pliers, and a cordage sling. I ordered assault jackets and demolition packs to be taken off, Mae Wests to be kept on and men to get the stakes and remove the mines. The attempt was partially successful, but the sea was cold and running too strongly for us, and men quickly became exhausted in the water, or were swept away.

We nosed our way through the obstacles and felt our craft ground on the beach, on the Continent at last. It must have been about five past eight o'clock. Ramp down – door open – and we plunged into water up to our waists.

We took our demolition packs with us, but left the assault jackets in the LCA. We mistakenly hoped to retrieve them later, but the LCA never returned, and we bitterly regretted the loss of the essentials we had so carefully packed.

The demolition teams moved shoreward as the water carried them in. Every crashing wave brought them nearer to the enemy.

What struck us at once on getting ashore was the narrowness of the beach above the water's edge. How was everyone to move about on that narrow strip? Tanks and AVREs were burning fiercely, and there was a continual noise of small arms, mortar and shell fire, and the roar of the sea behind us.

Some of the enemy were holding out just over the sand dune right in front of us, where the houses were burning, machine guns still in action. I saw a British officer leap up and wave his men forward just as a German stick grenade sailed through the air. I watched his men take their revenge with Mills grenades.

I put my first party to work on a row of timber ramps in two or three feet of water, and stumbled through the sand to my other party. They had had casualties but had started work and were coping as best they could, with the high water and the mass of craft continually arriving. I felt a peculiar blow on my upper arm and I thought I must have been hit, but I could see or feel little, so there seemed no need to do anything about it.

Fountains of spray marked the fall of a shell, bullets whipped up the water; the noise pressed on our eardrums; the smell of explosives and smoke filled our noses; and our eyes took in at a glance the debris – human and material – lying everywhere. Above it all we felt the urge to get ashore and start work.

Mortaring on the beach was still heavy. I met our second-in-command. It was a tonic to see him ashore, clean, dry and cheerful. I myself feeling wet, dirty, hungry and a little weary. Half an hour later I heard he had been killed by a mortar bomb.

We were only able to clear some small areas towards the top of the beach, but it heartened us to see the craft nevertheless still coming in. When at high tide we could do no more, we turned to laying the beach-lateral roadway above the high-water mark.

Major M de L'Orme, commanding one of the beach assault groups, decided to give up obstacle clearance as a bad job.

There were shells, mortars and the occasional bomb falling, and a considerable amount of small-arms fire. For a few moments I thought none of the things we had planned had come to pass. We were late and the tide was high. We were all on one beach instead of spread along the whole divisional front. Our task of clearing beach obstacles was obviously hopeless, so I organised our sections into parties for clearing beach exits and laying track to try to clear some of the congestion.

One of his subordinates was AJ Lane, the soldier who had held his breath and walked to shore like a Nile hippo across the seabed. He was now trying to make sense of the chaos on the beach.

I remember my first moments of dragging myself out of the sea holding on to my Bren gun, magazine boxes and other kit. I looked around to see death and destruction all around me. An absolute inferno: burning tanks, broken-down vehicles, and very many dead and wounded lying about in a narrow strip between the sea and the barbed wire at the back of the beach.

I sought cover behind an AVRE which had just been hit. I moved away quickly enough when I realised it was blazing away and that with its Petard explosive charges it could blow up at any second. I succeeded in making for the bank of the dunes at the high-tide mark. I hoped that somehow I could get my Bren gun into position to fire over and beyond the dunes in the enemy direction, wherever he might be.

I remember – damned silly considering the circumstances – my annoyance and irritation at the sea lice or beach bugs that were crawling all over me as I itched to get my Bren gun alive and kicking to some good purpose. Our attacking position was not easy because of the mortars, shells and bullets that were hammering down on to a small and concentrated beach. I saw shells or mortars making direct hits on soldiers moving close to me. They literally disappeared in a flash.

Until that time I had never seen a live or dead German soldier in my life. Here suddenly there were two of them almost jumping over me as I crouched low behind the sandbank at the high-water mark. One of the Germans appeared to throw a hand grenade as he came over the top to land on the beach, although it was difficult to know one explosion from the many others. A British soldier managed to kick the German's behind to send him sprawling, and then blast away with his Sten gun.

I moved to a position to be able to view the ground over and beyond the sandbank. The area all around seemed to be covered by creeping barrages of small fire, raging and rolling over the ground, threatening to overwhelm us all.

Captain Kenneth Wright could see the confusion unfolding, but his main concern was to find a landmark on shore. He was an intelligence officer with No 4 Commando, and he was going in on the extreme left of the beach with the Free French contingent. It was important that he did not get lost on his way in, but he could not see through the smoke, and he was worried that the destroyers of the Royal Navy and the bombers of the RAF had obliterated every identifiable piece of architecture. He set down his experiences in a letter to his parents, written less than a week after D-Day:

The smoke of the bombing had cleared away and I could see the coast quite plainly. There was a very big and quite distinctive chateau on the edge of it. So our one big worry was out of the way: we should know at once where to go when we touched down as we were making for some buildings about a quarter of a mile west. It was after H-Hour and the first troops must already have got ashore. I remember thinking that we were too close for the time of day – one flight was due to beach half an hour after H, and my lot five minutes after them, but it was obvious that we would be early. No one was being seasick now!

The beach was becoming plainer now and was black with objects, most of which were anti-landing devices, though some were the first infantry crossing the sand. There were a few stranded LCTs about on the water's edge, and I asked my naval officer to take us in to starboard of these. There was a very lively village about two miles down the coast. I thought we might as well take all the cover we could right from the start.

By now we were well under fire and stuff was splashing about all round us. Something biggish fell just over the LCT that I was trying to use as cover and I suppose I should have guessed what was coming. But it was too late to alter course anyway as we were on top of the first line of obstacles. The tide was rising fast and there was about one-third flood at the time. We could still see the tops of the first row: big timber baulks about eight-feet high, with the sloping arms facing out to sea. Beyond them were some more, and a row of single stakes.

Just as we got up to the LCT that I had picked out, and just as we were getting ready to disembark, the Boche who had put one into the water at this spot just before, sent another over. There was a terrific jar, and all the first half of the party in the craft fell over on top of each other. I felt quite numb in my right side – no pain, just an absence of feeling really, and a feeling of being knocked out of breath.

At the same moment, the doors of the craft were opened and the ramp lowered and the naval bloke said 'This is where you get off.' So I got off, after a bit of preliminary gasping for breath and struggling free from all the others. Doughty kept on saying 'Go on, sir' and it seemed ages before I got myself up and off the boat. There were quite a few who could not follow me off, including our Padre. I got off into about three feet of water.

We had about fifty or sixty yards to wade, and what with the weight of the rucksack and the waves to push through, I was nearly exhausted by the time I got clear. I realised that I had been hit and was therefore less mobile than usual. So when I got on the beach I just sat down and dumped the rucksack with all my belongings in it. That beach was no health resort, and I thought I'd be better off away from it even without a change of underclothing!

The beach by now was covered with men. They were lying down in batches in some places to avoid overcrowding round the exits;

some were sitting up; most of them were trotting or walking across the sand to the sandhills on the landward side. There were a good many casualties here, the worst of all being the poor chaps who had been hit in the water and were trying to drag themselves in faster than the tide was rising.

There was a huge pillbox right in front of us as we landed and there was a lot of fire coming from there and from the chateau behind it. I think I must have walked through a machine-gun arc at this time, though I noticed nothing then, for a little later I found bullet holes in my right thigh and left calf.

The behaviour of the men on these beaches was terrific. Our Frenchmen came pouring across the beach chattering madly and grinning all over their faces. We all went through the same gap in the wire at the back of the beach, everyone queuing up and taking their turn as if it were a pay parade. I can't think why we didn't suffer horribly then, for it was a bad bottleneck, but not a bomb nor a bullet came near us.

Just beyond were the ruined buildings for which we were making. Here we all sorted ourselves out. The RAF was bombing the big chateau and scoring direct hits every time. I can't understand how they were put on to this target, but the place was going up in smoke and our planes were all round it.

I sat down under a wall and watched the commando file through on to the main road inland. Everyone was happy and full of beans. Gordon Webb who was with me in the last party to move, gave me some rum, and I got going. We were joined by Joe, the doctor, who was twice wounded in the legs while helping others on the beach and we hobbled off down the main road. As we came up to the grounds of our chateau, a mortar bomb burst in the middle of the section in front – so my luck was still in.

About half a mile up the road I came across the CO. He had been hit in the head and leg but was carrying on, although finding it impossible to keep up. He set up his HQ in a patch of open ground between two biggish houses, while the rest went on into the village and cleared it up, finally destroying a coast defence battery.

While all this was going on, the doc had a look at me and told me not to try and go on any more. Actually, I wasn't feeling too good, but recovered quite a bit again when two Frenchmen came up with some rum and a host of good wishes. I got into a house and lay down on a large feather bed. That was the end of my active participation in the invasion.

The first men inland made an important and life-saving discovery. The German artillery aimers and mortar men could not see the beach, but had a clear view of the mass of silver barrage balloons flying from the jumble of vehicles on the sand. These were meant to discourage dive-bombers, but Luftwaffe activity on the day was minimal. Instead they were acting as a beacon to the Germans. They were an open invitation, and might as well have had the words 'Drop your shells here' inscribed on them in German. Some clever officer alerted the beachmasters to what the Germans were doing, and the word was passed round to release the balloons from their moorings.

They floated up to the skies like soldiers' prayers.

THE CAPTURE OF PEGASUS BRIDGE

The first British soldiers in Normandy, like the first Americans, came from the air. On the night of 5 June, even before the US 101st and 82nd Airborne dropped into the area behind Utah Beach, British paratroopers arrived in Normandy by parachute and glider. Their job was to protect the eastern flank of the invasion.

Two parallel waterways, the River Orne and the Canal de Caen, ran from Ouistreham by the sea up to the city of Caen five miles inland. The only crossings were two bridges, one near Bénouville over the canal and one over the Orne near Ranville. The 6th Airborne had to capture the bridges so that the Germans could not bring up tanks and infantry from Caen. But they also had to keep them intact so that Allied forces could break out of the beach area and push south and take the city.

It followed that the paratroopers would be on their own behind enemy lines until reinforcements arrived from the sea. To make sure the link-up happened as soon as possible, commando units were assigned to get off the beach and make a dash for the bridges. The commandos of the Special Service Brigade were under the command of the swashbuckling and eccentric Lord Lovat – 'Shimmy' to his aristocratic friends. Shimmy Lovat was hoping to exorcise the horrific memories of the Dieppe raid, in which he and his commandos had taken part. Now he assured John Howard, commander of the planned *coup de main* against the Orne crossings, that he would be with him in time for lunch on the sixth.

But the Paras had to take the bridges first. Even getting off the ground in England was no mean accomplishment. Flight Lieutenant LH Cullingford was navigating one of the Dakotas that towed the gliders across to France.

> Dakotas were not intended for operational use such as they were now being put to. Basically commercial aircraft, they had no armour protection for the crew, no self-sealing petrol tanks and, of course, no armament – defensive guns, that is. They were therefore very vulnerable both to fighters and to ground fire.
>
> To provide some degree of personal protection, we were offered the use of flak jackets and flak helmets. These flak jackets were very much like the chain mail worn by knights long years ago. There were separate pieces to protect the body front and rear, connected by quick-release shoulder pieces. An additional piece, fastened to the front body piece by large press buttons, covered the lower abdomen. It weighed fifty-six pounds and was worn over one's parachute harness and Mae West. I have since cherished the thought that almost 900 years after the Normans invaded England, I took part in the invasion of Normandy wearing a protective jacket not dissimilar to the chain mail they wore.

On the evening of 5 June, the British paratroopers prepared to set off. One of them was a young officer named Richard Todd. He had put a promising theatrical career on hold for the duration of the war.

> As the shadows lengthened on Monday June 5, the stand-to order was given. The last ceremony that day was a drumhead service in a meadow near Fairford Airfield by our popular padre, Captain Parry, known to us all as Pissy Percy the Parachuting Parson. Parry was a wiry little Welshman with a nature as fiery as his red hair, and a heart and courage to match.
>
> Drawn up in a semi-circle, 610 men faced inwards towards the padre who stood on an ammunition box. A more unlikely or piratical congregation could not be imagined, every man abristle with weapons, his face and hands besmirched with black cream, his helmet on the ground before him, his rifle or Sten gun laid

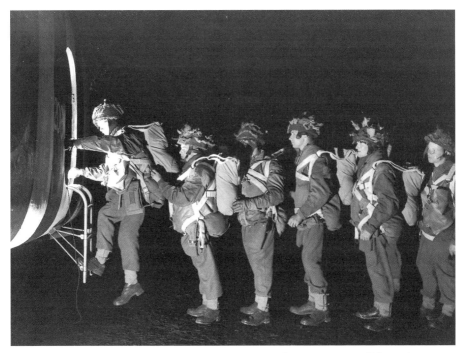

Loaded like packhorses, British paratroopers go to war. Their gear was stuffed into 'jump smocks' which buttoned between their legs like nappies and could be quickly removed on the ground. The airborne wore no spare parachute: they jumped too low to be able to use it.

across it. *Onward Christian Soldiers* went well. *Abide With Me* was rather more ragged. It was not easy to sing that in such a setting and at such a moment.

Just after nightfall, our truck drew up beside the Stirling, silhouetted in the moonlight. We scrambled out, clutching our parachutes, kitbags and arms and formed up in a line in our 'stick' order – with me at the head as I was jumping first.

In the cramped fuselage we sorted ourselves out and sat on the floor facing each other. Only eyes, teeth and bare metal glinted in the dim light. In the crescendo of noise, conversation was impossible. I fell asleep. It must have been about 00.30 hours when I was awakened by the dispatcher: 'Time to get ready, sir.'

We shuffled to our jumping positions. Looking down I could see the crests of the waves. Then the lines of rollers gave way to a blur of land features. The red warning light had already come on, and now I saw yellowy-orange dots floating up towards us. As the normal loading of tracer was one in every five bullets, I realised there must be a lot of lead spraying about.

About a minute after we crossed the coastline, the green light came on. I heaved the jettison bag into the hole, brought my legs together, and was out after it almost simultaneously. There is only so much that the brain can register and the memory retain, but I remember a hell of a lot of what went on in the next few moments.

My exit had been good and I knew that I had less than ten seconds before I hit the ground. The moment I felt my canopy snap open I pulled the rip-cord to release the leg-bag, holding on to its rope with my other hand. I should have let the bag down hand over hand, but I let it slip through my hand and felt it skin my palm and fingers. 'Bugger!' I shouted.

The parachute troops were not quite the first British soldiers in Normandy. That honour went to the glider-borne men under John Howard's personal command. Their orders were to land within fifty yards of the bridge and capture it before the sleeping Germans could get their boots on. It was a lot to ask of the six glider pilots. They could easily get lost; or they could land with such a racket that the Germans would be alerted and ready; or they could crash into the wooden stakes which had been planted in every open field specifically to thwart glider attacks.

All these possibilities were on Major Howard's mind as his glider was cast loose and began its noiseless descent towards the River Orne.

Although we left at one-minute intervals from Britain in the Horsa gliders, there was no telling in what order we would land. Crash-landing was the big fear. My other worry was that we were all carrying grenades that were already primed. If one of those went off and exploded, it would have blown all the ammunition in the glider.

As the aircraft came down, the men linked arms and locked fingers in the landing drill known as 'the butcher's grip'. They also lifted their feet from the floor. At this moment, Howard's gaze was fixed on the pilot, Jim Wallwork, who was struggling to control the glider as it hurtled towards the ground. The commander could see that his friend was covered in sweat despite the cold of the night.

Wallwork tugged desperately on the control column. He could easily have lost his way or, worse, plunged nose-first into the ground. But he managed to put the glider down in the right field and more or less level. It screeched across the hard earth like a fingernail across a blackboard. Then it took to the air again, before coming back down with a huge jolt. The paratroopers sitting in the back raised their legs still higher, expecting the floor to be ripped from beneath them. The glider rattled and skewed, but it skidded on, creating a shower of sparks that to the men inside looked alarmingly like tracer fire. It came to a halt within fifty yards of the bridge, and even sliced through the first barbed-wire defences around its perimeter. It had been a bumpy landing, but Wallwork's positioning could not have been more perfect. He had just accomplished what was probably the greatest piece of airmanship of World War II.

There was no time for congratulations. The paratroopers were sure that the German garrison would have been alerted by their cacophonous arrival, and were fully expecting to be fired upon at any moment. The men scrambled out of the tangled, splintered wreck as quickly as they could. Some of them kicked their way through the plywood walls of the aircraft – they were that flimsy. Unbelievably, the Germans on the bridge had ignored all the racket made by the crashing gliders. There was an air raid going on over Caen, and they had assumed the clatter was the sound of bits of English bomber falling harmlessly in the fields, having been brought down by German flak. No patrol came to investigate

The Germans soon realized their mistake. As the British raiders ran silently and breathlessly towards the bridge, they were spotted by a lone sentry, who shouted *'Fallschirmjäger!'* – 'Paratroopers!' He succeeded in firing a warning flare before he was cut down by Sten-gun fire. It was now about a quarter past twelve on 6 June, and that German soldier – his name was Helmut Romer, and he was seventeen years old – was the first man to be killed on D-Day.

The bridge was protected by a series of pillboxes. Small detachments of paratroopers rushed up to these emplacements and deftly deposited high-explosive grenades through the slits as if they were posting letters into a pillar box. There was a dull thud from each of them, a puff of sulphurous yellow smoke, and the pillboxes were out of action. More Germans were dug in around the bridge, and they now began to shoot back. Bands of paratroopers went off looking for them, and vicious little skirmishes took place in the darkness all around.

But the bridge itself was already in British hands. In the course of the fighting, Major Howard had been hit by a bullet that penetrated his helmet, skittered across the top of his scalp and came out the back. He was dazed, but not badly hurt. Once the Germans in the dugouts had been killed or taken prisoner, the paratroopers took up defensive positions and waited. The capture of the bridge across the Orne, the vital preamble to the seaborne assault, was over. It had been accomplished in about the time it takes to smoke a leisurely cigarette.

A little later in the night, Charles Thornton of the Oxford and Buckinghamshire Light Infantry moved up to the bridge. He had been lobbing mortars at it from a distance.

I was still at the River Orne when an ominous rumbling of tanks was heard at the T-junction near Pegasus Bridge. Major Howard sent for our platoon. We marched in regimental order to the bridge, where I was given a Piat anti-tank gun and told to go up to the junction. I passed the Gondrée café and crawled along a hedge on my stomach to get within 30 yards of the junction. My hands were shaking so much I could barely control them. I could hear two tanks moving about. Their commanders got out and exchanged words and then got back inside. I knew that I would have to act immediately.

The lads behind me were only lightly armed with Bren guns and grenades. They wouldn't stand a chance if I missed. I was so nervous I was talking to myself: 'This is it! You mustn't miss.'

The first tank, a Mark IV, had begun moving slowly down the road. I pulled the trigger. It was a direct hit. Machine-gun clips inside the tank set off grenades, which set off shells. There was the most enormous explosion, with bits and pieces flying everywhere and lighting up the darkness. To my delight, the other tank fled.

We now had a breathing space and I suggested to Lieutenant Fox that we went along the canal banks to see if we could find any Germans. Sure enough, we discovered a bunker. We were amazed to see that five Germans were still asleep inside, oblivious to all the noise. Fox went to rouse the first one while I covered him with my Sten gun. He shook him and declared: 'You are a prisoner.' But the German seemed to think it was just one of his mates having a joke and turned around and went back to sleep.

I started laughing and Fox said: 'Blow this for a lark! You take over.' I suppose I could have shot them all, but I don't believe in murdering people in cold blood so I put my Sten gun on to automatic and fired it along the bottom of the bunks. They moved like greyhounds!

Meanwhile, some of the other lads had knocked on the door of George Gondrée's café. It became the first house in France to be liberated. He led them to the cellar where his wife Theresa and her children were sheltering, and she hugged and kissed everyone so much her face became black with camouflage paint. George dug up 98 bottles of champagne he had buried in 1940, but unfortunately I missed out on the celebration!

Most of the gliders had come down hard, and many of the pilots were killed or injured. Lieutenant CT Cross had a typically hairy landing, and wrote to his parents about it three weeks later, 'having just changed my underclothes and washed my feet for the first time since I left England.'

The glider flight was bloody! said Lieutenant Cross. It was of course longer than most I've done before because of the business of getting into formation, collecting fighter escort and so on. After about quarter of an hour I began to be sick, and continued until we were over the Channel where the air was much calmer. The Channel was a wonderful sight – especially the traffic at this end – Piccadilly Circus wasn't in it. We were not over the coast this side long enough for me to be sick again, and we were pretty busy thinking about landing. The landing was ghastly. Mine was the first glider down, though. We were not quite in the right place, and the damn thing bucketed along a very upsy-downsy field for a bit and then broke across the middle – we just chopped through those anti-landing poles as we went along. However, the two halves of the glider fetched up very close together, and we quickly got out ourselves and our equipment and lay down under the thing, because other gliders were coming in all round and Jerries were shooting things at them and at us,

so it wasn't very healthy to wander about. Our immediate
opposition – a machine gun in a little trench – was very
effectively silenced by another glider which fetched up plumb
in the trench, and a couple of Huns – quite terrified – came out
with their hands up! Having bound up a few scratches, we set off
to the scene of the battle.

At about this moment the parachutists were forming up in the dark. They
were not scattered far and wide like the American troopers behind Utah
Beach, but finding one's travelling companions in the dark was a nerve-
wracking and time-consuming business all the same.

At about 00.40 hours I thumped on to a cornfield in Normandy,
said Richard Todd. Once in the wood I heard voices and froze
momentarily, only to realise that they were speaking English. In a
little clearing, there stood Colonel Pine-Coffin and about a dozen
others. The CO said there was no way of knowing if the glider-
borne attack on the bridges had been successful, and that we
must get to the rendezvous as quickly as possible. We broke out
from the woodland and set off at the double. Scurrying figures
were everywhere.

By about 01.00 our group, numbering by then some fifty, was at
the rendezvous. A bugler repeatedly blew our rallying signal, and
men came stumbling towards us, shadowy, bulky figures. But
still no mortars, no machine guns and no wireless. At about
01.30 hours the CO gave the order to move off to the bridges
even though we still numbered only 150 men, a quarter of our
strength.

All seemed quiet as we reached the bridge and trotted over it. I
got my first sight of a D-Day casualty: a legless German lay at the
roadside, a groaning sound coming weirdly from him. Internal
gas, I supposed. Normally the sight of blood turns my stomach,
yet I felt only mild curiosity.

We doubled along the causeway towards the canal bridge, a
large iron structure that could be opened to allow the passage of
sea-going craft. Suddenly all hell erupted on the road ahead.
Heavy explosions, flashes and tracer bullets rent the night like a
spectacular firework display. 'Christ!' I thought. 'This is it. Here

we go.' We speeded up our jog-trot. Then, as quickly as it had started, the tumult died down. An old tank that was probing the bridgehead had been hit by a PIAT bomb and this was its ammunition exploding.

We reached the little café-bar at the west end of the bridge and the CO directed me to set up Battalion HQ 300 yards away below the hamlet of Le Port, whose church could be seen on the crest. Here, in the darkness, the remnants of our headquarters party began furiously to dig in. We used explosive charges to blow our foxholes.

So far, so good. Phase one of our task had been accomplished. The bridges had been captured intact and the western bridgehead established. Now we had to hang on until later that day.

It was a long wait. Lord Lovat's commandos were still at sea, and D-Day had still not officially begun. The paratroopers were surrounded and under-strength. So the start of the naval bombardment was like music – very noisy music.

Minutes before first light, a shattering cacophony erupted, with a glare that made full daylight seem pale, continued Todd. For about half-an-hour the din, the vibration of air and ground, the magnitude of that assault, was far beyond anything I could have imagined.

From our grandstand position at Le Port, I felt sorry for the poor sods cowering in those German bunkers. How could they possibly emerge and fight back? But they did, and with impressive vigour.

Quite a lot, on a smaller but no less deadly scale, was going on in the 7th Para area. There was no cessation in the Germans' probing with patrols and counter-attacks, some led by tanks. The regimental aid post was overrun in the early hours. The wounded being tended there were all killed where they lay.

So too was Padre Parry, who had evidently fought like a tiger to defend them. Our position had developed into a classic airborne situation. There was no front line as such and the battalion had evolved into four pockets of resistance: the three rifle companies and the Battalion Headquarters group, largely out of touch with each other, but each in positions of their own choosing.

From our site on the slope we had a good view of the open ground between us and the canal bridge, and more than once we were able to drive off the enemy, infiltrating groups with enthusiastic bursts of small-arms fire. I had primed my plastic Gammon bomb and kept it handy just in case a tank might break through. There was sporadic enemy mortar and artillery fire we could do nothing about. One shell landed in a hedge near me, killing a couple of our men. I dearly wished we had recovered some of our own three-inch mortars, especially now that a handful of mortar men had got through to us.

In Bénouville, A Company was reduced to a strength of less than twenty. From time to time, we could hear its commanding officer, Nigel Taylor, shouting encouragement. He was lying by the window of a house, one leg shattered. His second in command, Jim Webber – himself shot through his chest – got through to us to report.

Things might have been worse for A Company but for the actions of one man, nineteen-year-old Private McGee. Fed up with being shot at by a tank as he ducked down in his foxhole, he leaped up and charged down the street firing his Sten gun from the hip. The tank crew closed up the shutters and were temporarily blinded, whereupon McGee threw a plastic Gammon bomb from a few yards and crippled the vehicle, which slewed across the road blocking any further tank movement. McGee was awarded the DCM posthumously: he was killed a few hours later.

B Company in and around Le Port repelled repeated attacks. One of the worst problems was the many snipers, who were making movement difficult as they picked off men from cottage windows, rooftops and the church tower. That stout little Norman tower was right in the centre of B Company's area, and very difficult to deal with. The church was surrounded by open ground and virtually impossible to attack.

Finally, Corporal Killeen of the anti-tank platoon found a solution. With his PIAT hand-held bazooka he crept from cottage to cottage until he found a position that had cover and was within his bombs' range. His first blew a hole in the tower, and succeeding ones practically shattered it. He then rushed the church, determined to finish off any snipers, but he had no need. His bombs had killed all the occupants. 'When I got to the church door, I looked up and och! I was sorry to see what I had done to a wee house of God – but I did take off my tin hat when I went inside.'

As day came up and the invasion got under way, more waves of gliders set off for Pegasus Bridge to provide reinforcement. Flight Lieutenant Cullingford was a Dakota pilot, tugging along a glider like an airborne dog on a leash. He was at the very front of the formation, and so had a uniquely panoramic view of the air and sea armadas as they went into battle.

We were very vulnerable to fighters and had been promised a strong protective screen of fighter aircraft. When I looked up through the astro-dome, what I saw was very reassuring – the sky full of fighters at all heights above us.

I looked behind us. It was an amazing sight. There in a loose, broad formation were dozens and dozens of tugs and gliders, including Halifaxes towing the enormous Hamilcar gliders which were carrying light tanks. No one had ever seen anything like it, and I believe that I am the only person to have seen it from the very front of the formation.

As we approached the coast, I went up front to have a look. There lay the invasion beaches, an awe-inspiring and rather frightening sight. Off the beaches lay the navy, including one huge battleship, *Warspite* I believe, with an umbrella of protective balloons. Between the navy and the beach the sea was alive with landing craft. On the beach and inland there was lots of smoke, movement and activity. As a backdrop to the whole scene – it was just as though we were in the dress circle looking down at it all happening on stage – there was a great pall of smoke. The whole scene was unforgettable.

At this point I made an important decision. It seemed unlikely that we would be attacked by fighters and I reasoned that any gunfire would be coming up at us rather than from either side. I therefore detached the lower part of my flak suit and sat on it

We were now descending. I had the return course ready for when we turned after our Horsa had cast off. It was easy to know when this occurred as our aircraft suddenly felt very different.

Our instructions were to fly on for a short distance before releasing the tow rope. It was long, thick and very heavy, and we hoped it would clout some Germans.

LORD LOVAT'S PRIVATE ARMY

As the Dakotas headed back out to sea, Lord Lovat's commandos were coming ashore on the far left of the invasion force. Their plan was to bypass the fighting on the beach and head straight for Pegasus Bridge.

The commandos were quite a distinctive and arresting sight. Their commander was himself an imposing figure: tall, moustachioed, dressed in a white sweater and carrying a walking stick. Lovat's men were easily identified by their green berets – they felt no need to wear tin hats. They were an exotic outfit consisting of handpicked and hard-trained British regulars – many of whom had taken part in the disastrous Dieppe raid in 1942 – along with a number of foreign units made up of Frenchmen, Norwegians, anti-Hitler Germans and other nationalities. They all wore their hatred for the Nazis like a campaign medal. 'I remember holding the head of a man who lay dying in the bottom of a landing craft as we withdrew from Dieppe,' said ADC Smith. 'He had had his face kicked in by the Germans as he lay wounded on the ground.'

Smith was with Lovat on the crossing.

> I remember his address to the Brigade. He never gave it a moment's preparation, but he spoke naturally and confidently and with great inspiration, like Henry before Agincourt. There was drama enough in the occasion to justify his words, without any sense of sentiment. The strange and startling beauty of his words was strengthened by the stirring simplicity of his delivery. Phrases like 'your children and your children's children will count you as giants among men' are too rare to be forgotten, but so far as I know no record was ever kept of them and posterity will be the poorer for the lack of it.

Lovat, like Winston Churchill, used his eloquence as a kind of secret weapon. But he had one other morale booster in his repertoire, something that guaranteed him a place in the mythology of the invasion before any of his men had fired a shot. It was Bill Millin, his personal piper.

One day in May 1944, Lord Lovat told me he was forming his own commando brigade, and would like me to join and play the pipes, said Millin. At that time the War Office had banned pipers in action. Lovat told me he was not bothered about the War Office and that I would be the only piper playing at Normandy. I took it as an honour.

Everyone liked Lord Lovat, although we all thought that, at 32, he was a bit too old for the kind of daredevilry he enjoyed. He was a typical aristocrat who would walk calmly with his head held high while all the rest of us would be ducking and diving to avoid shells. Everyone regarded him as crazy and, in retrospect, I suppose they thought that I was pretty crazy too. I had a special relationship with him. He always called me Bill, although it would have been form to use surnames.

We were the first out of our troop to reach the shore. The ramps on the boat went down and as we stepped off Lovat ordered me to play *Highland Laddie*. I started playing as soon as I touched the water. Whenever I hear that song I remember walking through the surf.

Playing the bagpipes in the middle of a war was no easy job. Millin was constantly exposed to fire – so much so that some nearby soldiers begged him to stop drawing attention to them with his music. Others grunted 'Well done, Jock' as they ran past, and still others told him he was a mad bastard. He didn't care: his job was to give heart to the British fighting men, and strike fear and wonder into the hearts of the Germans.

I was not really frightened because we had practised landings so many times before, but this time we were being fired on. I remember the shells bursting in the water. There were bodies floating in the water and lying across the beach, and two tanks were burning fiercely. It was pure noise and confusion.

Wounded men were shocked to see me. They had been hoping to see a doctor or some kind of medical help. Instead they saw me in my kilt and playing the bagpipes. It was horrifying, as I felt so helpless.

There was a small road leading off the beach and ten or twelve soldiers were lying wounded at its entrance. Some of them said:

'Are the medics here, Jock?' I told them not to worry; the doctors would be coming. I took shelter behind a low wall and watched as a flail tank made its way towards the road and the wounded men. I quickly got up and started waving my arms frantically above my head, hoping to get the attention of the commander whose steel hat was just visible out of the top of the tank. He seemed not to notice and went straight ahead over the top of the wounded soldiers. It was very traumatic watching those men die.

I dashed back to Lord Lovat and he asked me to play *Road to the Isles* up and down the beach. There was no time to feel any real emotion. Normandy was a most upsetting campaign because there were so many casualties. It was a killing ground.

Later, when we had fought our way off the beach and were heading inland, I was able to talk to French people. I will never forget a little French girl who came up to me. She had red hair and a white freckly face. She looked dirty and was barefooted. She was jumping around saying 'Music, music.' I asked Lord Lovat for his permission to play a tune, and he agreed. I played *Nut Brown Maiden* for her. She ran after me but I had to tell her to go back. As I did, the local people clapped in appreciation.

It is not clear what the foreign commandos made of it, except that they were pleased to be there. One of Lovat's European fighters was a twenty-year-old named Harry Drew – a German Jew from Berlin.

I was born Harry Nomburg. At the age of fifteen, I was sent by my Jewish parents to England to escape Nazi persecution. I left on May 21, 1939. It happened to be Mother's Day. I never saw my parents again.

I was eighteen years old when I joined the British Army. In 1943, I volunteered for the commandos. Together with a green beret, I was also given a brand new name – Harry Drew.

My unit was 3 Troop, 10 Commando, in which I was given extensive intelligence training. As I was fluent in German, I was loaned to No 6 Commando shortly before D-Day.

My own personal feelings were those of most twenty-year-olds: adventure and glory. But the boat was small and crowded, and the sea choppy, and even though I stayed on deck throughout the night, I was on the verge of seasickness at the time our LCI finally ground to a halt, and I could run down the ramp and jump into the water.

Wearing the green beret and holding my Thompson sub-machine gun high above my head, I waded on to a beach in Normandy. It was 7.30am on June 6 1944.

My tommy gun had up to this point always been equipped for the twenty-round magazine. But shortly before the invasion, I was issued the first thirty-round magazine I had ever seen. Alas, no one had informed me that when filled with a full thirty rounds of .45-calibre bullets, the magazine would get so heavy that it would come loose and drop off. It should never be loaded with more than twenty-eight rounds. Of course, I filled it all the way, with the result that the magazine got lost in the water and I hit the beaches of France and stormed the fortress of Europe without a single bullet in my gun.

Looking around me, I saw an armada stretching along the entire length of the horizon as far as the eye could see. Overhead, the Allied aircraft filled the sky with not a single German plane in sight. I also noticed three bodies in the surf. Yet, opposition turned out to be far lighter than I had expected.

As I dashed across the beach to the sound of the bagpipes, I noticed a tall figure stalking just ahead of me. At once I recognized the brigadier, and getting close to him, I shyly touched his belt from behind while thinking to myself 'Should anything happen to me now, let it at least be said that Private Drew fell by Lord Lovat's side.'

Lovat's commandos pushed on towards the Orne bridges. The French commandos, meanwhile, were preoccupied with their own mission, which was to take the German strongpoint called 'the Casino' in Ouistreham. They were designated 10 Commando, and were commanded by Phillipe Kieffer, a charismatic French officer in the swashbuckling Lovat mould.

It was clear that the Franco-Britannique Commando had landed at a critical moment, said Lieutenant Commander Rupert Curtis, who put them ashore. They crossed the beach with utmost dash and determination to force a path through the defence and start the attack by swinging left on to Ouistreham. In the beach crossing they suffered some forty casualties and would have suffered more if they had not moved with speed. Some men were killed and wounded in the assault craft. Colonel Robert Dawson was wounded on the beach so that his second-in-command Major RP Monday, together with Commandant Kieffer, led the gallant drive into Ouistreham to silence the German batteries and over run the Casino strong-point – a task which they carried out successfully after heavy fighting and many losses.

The chaos on the beach and determined German opposition held up Lord Lovat's force. By mid-morning it was looking as if he would not be able to keep his luncheon appointment with John Howard. But somewhere between noon and one o'clock, Richard Todd and his fellow paratroopers heard an unexpected sound even more pleasing than the raucous music of the morning's naval guns. This time it really was music.

The bridge over the Orne was coming under sniper fire as we approached it, said Bill Millin. **Lovat made a wave of his hand, telling us to go on and for me to continue playing. Some of our commandos were shot while crossing the bridge but I piped my way. A tall man appeared and said to Lovat: 'Very pleased to see you, old boy.' As they shook hands, Lovat replied: 'And we are very pleased to see you, old boy. Sorry we are a few minutes late.'**

The officer greeting Lovat was Henry Sweeney, who escorted him to Major Howard. 'John, we have made history today,' said Lovat as the men under his command marched on to the bridge. They embraced the airborne troops like long-lost relatives. Many men were in tears.

It was a fine sight, said Richard Todd. **And there was great jubilation as red and green berets mingled on the road.**

The airborne troops and the commandos knew that they had accomplished one of the great feats of arms in British military history. As for the young actor-turned-paratrooper Richard Todd, he had an opportunity to relive his experiences twenty years later, when he played Major Howard in the film *The Longest Day.*

British soldiers hitch a lift across Pegasus Bridge on a Bren carrier. These little vehicles, a cross between a tank and a troop transport, were a reassuring presence for frontline infantrymen. Some of the vehicles carried a Bren gun, others had a three-inch mortar or a flamethrower.

SWIFTLY INLAND

By mid-morning, Sword was securely in British hands, and men were trooping away from the sea or scouring the villages for Germans. By now it was clear that the plan for the easternmost beach had gone pretty well. The initial traffic jam was slowly untangling and a steady stream of tanks and men was moving inland.

Casualties, though not negligible, were lighter than expected. Resistance on the beaches had been quelled. Back-up waves of infantry were surprised to find that they had nothing more irksome to deal with than the odd bomb or sniper. 'I am a devout coward, but I wasn't scared then . . .' said Bill Colyer, the jazz-mad truck driver who had brought three long-playing records with him to the invasion.

. . . I had too much to do getting the truck ashore and getting ready to go. I had to slash the ropes to get the canvas covers off the front, take the waterproof plugs off the battery. I had the beachmaster shouting at me to get a move on, and there were German mortars coming in. I thought the whole thing was a marvellous madhouse. Our sergeant major said it was 'hutter choase, hutter choase,' by which he meant 'utter chaos.'

The mood was good as the infantry and their tanks queued to go through the beach exits and on towards Caen. And it was not just the soldiers who were pleased with their morning's work. Many French civilians in the towns and villages behind the British landing grounds seemed to think the invasion was some kind of carnival or circus parade. Too overjoyed to pay attention to the sporadic German gunfire, they cheered and clapped and provided a commentary on the battle to those indoors. Above all, they gave their liberators a warm welcome. 'They came out with bacon-and-egg rolls and wine,' said Private Frank Rosier. 'Then the order came down the line: leave the booze alone.'

Major Baxter, who minutes before had been pinned down by machine-gun fire at strongpoint COD, was now one of the first to receive an official salutation.

Over the top of the low dunes came a gleaming brass fireman's helmet, surmounting the figure of the mayor of Colleville. He was accompanied by a young French girl, who quickly made her way to render help in the first-aid post. These were the first French people to greet us.

On the way inland, the Funnies proved their worth yet again. GD Jones was a tankman on one of Hobart's 'Flying Dustbins', a Churchill tank adapted to hurl a cylindrical 40-pound mortar called a petard at concrete strongpoints.

We had news of resistance down at the mouth of the Orne. We made our way there and blew a pillbox to pieces with our petard. We then got to the Orne river and about 100 Germans were hidden in a large boathouse. We got them out after difficulty and marched them back to the beachhead for penning up by the

Military Police. From there we were off to Lion-sur-Mer where one of our Assault Squadrons, 77th, was in trouble, but we were stopped halfway as the naval guns sorted it all out.

British infantrymen were now roaming like packs of wolves down the roads and through the fields. Everywhere they encountered bands of Wehrmacht soldiers – some of them up for a fight, some of them more than ready to throw down their weapons.

The road down which we moved away from the beach would, under any normal circumstances, have been labelled pleasant, said Lieutenant-Colonel E Jones. It was an avenue, with a broad grass verge lined with trees.

It was there I learned one of my first lessons of practical man-management. One of my section-leaders, whom I had regarded highly, was a bright lad, a policeman in civilian life. I explained to him what I wanted his section to do, but got no reaction. I had just realised that he was too upset by the situation to comprehend what I was telling him, when another of my section commanders came over. He was a regular soldier whom I had previously believed to be rather slow as he always asked for a detailed repeat of orders. I realise now that he was only making quite certain what my instructions were. He said 'What are you asking him to do, sir?' I explained that I wanted him to take his section into this house, whilst the others gave covering-fire.

He turned to his section, said 'Follow me!' and took them into the house. There was no opposition and the rest of the platoon followed. They found Polish or Russian conscripts still in the cellars, waiting for the barrage to lift. This presented us with another problem. We had received no instructions on how to deal with prisoners at this early stage. Finally, we disarmed them and locked them in the cellar, and moved on down the road leading from the beach.

I was pressing inland when a shout from one of my NCOs checked me. He had found that the grass verge contained skilfully camouflaged dug-outs filled with German soldiers. We cleared these out and added the prisoners to our original captives.

A hundred yards or so ahead, our avenue was crossed at right angles by a lateral road heading towards Lion-sur-Mer half a mile away. There we linked up with Bob Pearce and 7 Platoon. He had moved through the gardens of the houses on our right, clearing up in the process a German mortar detachment who were so pre-occupied firing on to the beach that he was able to take them by surprise. We were also joined by the remnants from 9 Platoon and Company HQ and started to move towards Lion. The Germans had not had time to remove their minefield notices, so these were all neatly labelled.

German resistance grew stiffer as the invaders of Sword fanned out. There were many enemy positions in and around the seaside villages of Lion-sur-Mer, Hermanville and Riva-Bella. Snipers were a constant hazard, and there were mortar companies hidden invisibly in the fields behind the tall hedgerows. Lieutenant-Colonel Jones and his men soon found themselves under attack from an unseen enemy.

A shell exploded on the road close by and a fragment of shrapnel ploughed through the torch clipped on my webbing belt. I doubled up with pain and Bob Pearce rushed across and tore open my battledress blouse to reveal the piece of shrapnel which had only just broken the surface of the skin. It had been slowed down by the torch, but was hot enough to burn my stomach.

We now moved rapidly down the road towards Lion-sur-Mer. There were no German soldiers here, but a number of French civilians, most of whom seemed too stunned to comprehend what was happening. Despite the bombardment, some were still tilling the fields on the south of the road.

Lion had been cleared of civilians and occupied by German troops. Buildings had been converted into blockhouses and some streets had been completely blocked with coil upon coil of barbed wire practically to roof level and 20 to 30 feet in depth. The reason for this was soon made plain. As I reconnoitred cautiously with two men down one of the streets, these two men, on either side of me, were expertly picked off by hidden riflemen.

We moved round to the south of the village and entered farm buildings which gave us a view across open country to the east.

We now began to move further inland to engage the group of buildings from which the Germans had launched their attack. We lost one or two more men in this attempt, but we reached the safety of a sunken lane with a stone wall on one side and a bank and hedge on the other.

Completely without warning, a cluster of mortar-bombs landed in the middle of us, killing and wounding many of our men. Amongst the wounded was Lieutenant Pearce, who already held the Military Cross, and gained a bar to it for his D-Day actions. We extricated the wounded to the shelter of the stone wall and dressed their wounds. We were here joined, apparently from nowhere, by a young French girl aged ten or eleven, who kept repeating 'J'ai peur' – 'I'm scared.'

We made our way back along the lateral road, which the Germans were now shelling consistently. One of my platoon, a tall, thin young lad with sandy hair, was badly wounded in the neck by a piece of shrapnel, and was bleeding profusely. An artillery captain emerged from a foxhole alongside the road, expertly applied pressure to the wound and said, 'You go on! I'll look after him.' We heard the officer calling for stretcher-bearers as we left. I was delighted some weeks later when one of my platoon showed me a photograph in a local newspaper that he'd been sent depicting this lad, accompanied by a brief account of how he had been wounded on D-Day and saying he was well on the way to recovery.

As the chilly morning turned to sunny afternoon, 'the endless stream of vehicles kept moving slowly from the beach.' Major FJ Hoadley was watching the procession when he spotted one of his own company's three-ton trucks, 'loaded to the gunwales of course . . .'

. . . I shouted to the driver Corporal Dickman, 'You'll have to load this gear on to your truck.' 'But we're full up, sir,' he shouted back, to which I replied 'That's what you think.' We flung all our equipment and what we could of my HQ gear onto the roof and the bonnet of this three-tonner and away we went.

White tape, gapping signs, wrecked vehicles, marching troops, no civilians, clouds of dust and ruined houses – that was the immediate picture. Some of the familiar 3rd Division unit signs could already be seen stuck up on buildings, where detachments had found a temporary headquarters. The 9th Field Ambulance, I remember, had set up shop in the last big house on the right as one left Lion for Hermanville.

The road to Hermanville (Mexico, I believe they called it on the bogus briefing maps) was seething with vehicles, all taking jolly good care to keep off the verges: wounded were being carried back on stretchers towards Lion. On our right I remember a cornfield waving in the breeze and dotted with red poppies.

Our rendezvous was in the village of Hermanville, in a field between the church and the chateau. Our CO, John Asher, was already there when we arrived. There was just time to say 'Hello, thank God you've arrived,' before we found it necessary to disperse around the field under the trees: the Boche had started a bit of ground-strafing from low-flying aircraft.

Right in the middle of the field, a civvy shelter had been dug in an enormous rabbit hole and half the village seemed to be in it. Every so often a boy crawled out and wriggled through the long grass until his mother uttered a howl and dragged him back below.

Very soon I heard the crack of a rifle from the direction of the church and the surrounding farm buildings: a curt reminder that we were not entirely surrounded by friends. Sniping was a familiar feature in those early days – a small party went off to investigate this but there was no one to be found but French peasants. Soon after the sniping incident I was standing talking to Sapper Jack Holt, a cockney of the best type and a first-class soldier, when like lightning another air attack came in over the trees and, before we could get our Brens on to it, Holt caught a packet in the arm – a clean shot, but he was for Blighty.

Our job was to open the route forward to Caen, but the Boche were dug in. Of particular trouble to us was the strongpoint known by us as HILLMAN. It was built into the hill at the back of Colleville-sur-Orne on the side of the road which led to Biéville and Caen and it commanded a magnificent view of the low-lying land between it and the beaches.

Montgomery had promised that his men would take the city of Caen on the first day. This was hopelessly ambitious. The spearhead of the troops was slowed down and depleted by German resistance at the stubborn Hillman blockhouse. It was eventually taken, at heavy cost, by men of the Suffolk Regiment. Meanwhile, the King's Shropshire Light Infantry marched purposefully inland towards Caen without tank support, but had to stop short of the suburbs. The momentum of the Allied advance had dissipated, and it became obvious that Caen would not be taken on D-Day. In the end, Caen had to be bombed to rubble from the air and, to the bitter disappointment of the High Command, did not fall into Allied hands for some weeks.

Nevertheless, by evening the regular infantry had caught up with the commandos and the airborne on the bridge over the Orne Canal. Already, someone had rechristened the little crossing, taking their inspiration from the badge worn by the 6th Airborne. Now it was Pegasus Bridge, and a crudely painted sign announced the new name. It has gone down as such both in the annals of D-Day and in the present-day toponymy of Normandy.

As night fell, AJ Lane, the soldier who had found the insect life on the sand so troublesome, found himself on guard duty on the far side of Pegasus Bridge. Here he had yet more unwelcome company.

> I settled in to my lonely foxhole position. It was getting to be late evening, with light failing fast, and I cannot say that at that moment I was looking forward to passing my first night on foreign and hostile soil.
>
> I was not particularly charmed by the three corpses I found close to me. I could almost reach out and touch the most gruesome of the three, who was a German who had his brains blown out through a great jagged hole in his steel helmet. There were two Germans and one of our airborne. I pondered long and hard about the position of one of the corpses: it seemed almost impossible, the way it was lying on the steep river bank without rolling down. I concluded it could only be a very dead body indeed – rigid muscles, rigor mortis – that could cling on in such a way.
>
> I was, in truth, cold, frightened, confused, terribly tired and hungry: not a very brave young soldier. Before being swallowed up by the night I reflected on the long, long day, and consoled

myself with the thought that if D-Day plus one was perhaps just a tenth as bad, I should have only have to survive a mere ten possibilities of getting killed.

Somewhere nearby, Private Harold Lee, who had been so upset by the immolation of a tank crew, was also bedding down for the night. The last thing he noticed before falling asleep was the peculiar odour of the land he had conquered.

It was an amalgam of the reek of cordite, the sickly-sweet smell of corpses both human and animal, and of the beautiful Normandy roses which, amid all that misery, continued to bloom and scent the air.

8
HOME FIRES BURNING

On the afternoon of 6 June, prime minister Winston Churchill went to the House of Commons to make a statement. He teased the honourable members for a full ten minutes by wittering on about the campaign in Italy – but then he came to the news they had crammed into the Palace of Westminster to hear.

> I have to announce to the House that during the night and the early hours of the morning the first of the series of landings in force upon the European continent has taken place. In this case, the liberating assault fell upon the coast of France. An immense armada of upwards of 4,000 ships, together with several thousand smaller craft, crossed the Channel. Massed airborne landings have been successfully effected behind enemy lines.
>
> So far the commanders who are engaged report that everything is proceeding according to plan. And what a plan! This vast operation is undoubtedly the most complicated and difficult that has ever taken place. The ardour and spirit of the troops, as I saw myself, embarking in the last few days was splendid to witness. Nothing that equipment, science or forethought could do has been neglected, and the whole process of opening this great new front will be pursued with the utmost resolution – both by the commanders and by the United States and British governments whom they serve.

The phrase 'the first of a series of landings' kept the Germans guessing. They took it to mean that Normandy might yet turn out to be a diversion, and that the main landing could still come in the Pas de Calais, or even in Norway. This is a sign of how desperately short of reliable intelligence they were: they hoped that the British government might give them a clue as to what was going on.

Conversely, the mass of British people learned of the invasion only from German reports quoted by the BBC.

> At 8am the news said that Germans reported dealing with landings on the coast of France – this must be it! wrote Mrs N Carver in her diary for 6 June. Reports were unconfirmed. However, at 9.45 an announcement was made that the Allies had landed at dawn this morning. It was rather awful to hear the actual statement but terrifically exciting too! I went into St Paul's for a few minutes before 11am. I don't think anyone in there had heard – all was quiet until I reached the office which was seething with excitement. I wonder whether we shall have any heavy raids now? Some people seem to fear so.

Joan Carr-Jones was a Wren in Southampton, and already knew that today was the day. 'The town, skeletal through bombing, had for weeks been filling up with men and weapons. On that day – a beautiful one – it was suddenly empty and dead, as if all life had been sucked out of it.' Now she went for a walk through the ravaged streets, trying to kill time until there was definite news from the brand-new battle front.

> A local cinema was showing *Gone With the Wind* (a poignant title indeed). We watched half of it and saw nothing. Across the floor of a department store a mouse ran suddenly, heightening the weird unreality of the day. In a local cafe, a snippet of news was followed by 'The King'. This brought us all to our feet, a soldier rising in the swiftest movement I have ever seen, standing rigidly and proudly to attention. In WRNS quarters, nearing news-time, the radio was surrounded by a sea of girls.
>
> We had anticipated being heavily bombed, but there was nothing. Only an empty town and a sunny day, our thoughts and prayers elsewhere. A sense of living with destiny, and a fierce and joyful pride. There never was a day like it.
>
> My fiancé came back that evening from his naval duty of getting the troops safely across the Channel. At a local bar the barmaid looked at his uniform and said, 'Back from the other side, sir?' He nodded, and she reached below the counter for something special.

In workplaces and on the streets, the first person to hear the news would rush round like a latter-day Paul Revere, announcing to everyone the sensational turn of events. Doreen Mee, nineteen years old, was at work in Leicester on the Wolsey factory, where she and 200 other women were engaged in making underwear for the troops.

> During the early hours of June 6th, the noise of heavy aircraft thundering through the skies had kept most people awake. So nobody was surprised when the early morning news flash told us what we'd been waiting for: it was D-Day. An announcement relayed to us over the 'Music while you work' system confirmed it, the invasion was under way.
>
> Most of the women in that room had a husband, son, brother or boyfriend in uniform and we all felt helpless. Suddenly with one accord, we started to sing. We sang every stirring song and every patriotic song, funny songs, you name it, we sang all morning. Imagine 200 women willing their menfolk to rid the world of a tyrant with a song!

Margaret Clark was in school, feeling deeply bored by a lesson on English grammar, when she heard.

> A quiet morning session was interrupted by the sound of running footsteps in the corridor outside ('Walk, don't run' was the rule). The door was flung open and a young woman teacher stood in the doorway beaming from ear to ear. Without waiting for a suitable pause in our lecture, she breathlessly announced: 'The allies have landed in France' before closing the door and running on to the next classroom. Discipline was forgotten as excited chatter broke out and for once our teacher appeared human; then after a few moments she said 'I think we should get back to our lesson.'

The wonderful news even seeped through heavy oaken doors and into the dark interiors of churches.

> I was attending a service held in the parish church of Minfield St Mary when the service was interrupted by the verger giving the

News of the invasion was greeted with jubilation. Reports from the front exaggerated Allied successes, claiming that British soldiers were on the streets of Caen, but for today no one cared. In Moscow, state radio broadcast a chorus of Yankee Doodle *after the evening news.*

news to the vicar, said Irene Jackson. There was a stunned silence as it was passed on to the congregation. The form of service was scrapped in favour of a short homily. Before closing, we knelt to sing Hymn No 595 from the Ancient and Modern –

Holy Father in thy mercy, hear our anxious prayer,
Keep our loved ones, now far distant, neath thy care

Choked with emotion we somehow managed the six verses – tears in most eyes. Never was the Amen sung more fervently.

Most of America was still asleep when the first reports were heard in Britain. Peggy Kauffmann, a young hospital supervisor, was one of the first to hear it because she was working the late shift. She had not seen her husband since 1942, when he left the US Army base at Fort Bragg, North Carolina, to go and fight in North Africa.

I got off duty at midnight, changed out of my uniform and took the street car to our apartment – my apartment, Mike had never seen it. The first thing I always did was to take my dog out for a walk. Then I came in and turned on the radio. This was my nightly ritual. I was sitting there writing a letter to Mike when they interrupted the program with General Eisenhower's little talk: 'Ladies and gentlemen, our troops have now invaded France and have established a beachhead in Normandy.'

I dropped the paper and pen, and my dog jumped up in my lap and began to lick my face. So here it was. I called my parents who lived about forty miles away and I told my father that the invasion was on and he said 'Thanks for calling, I'll listen.' Then I woke up the neighbors that lived next door to us – we were very close friends – and I said 'Katherine, please come over, the invasion has started and all I can see is Mike's body sprawled on the sands of Normandy.' So she spent the night with me.

Mike Kauffman was not sprawled dead on a French beach. He survived the war and came home unscathed. He was one of the luckiest ones.

THE RETURN OF THE WOUNDED

The first people to hear about the invasion first-hand were the nurses working in the southern ports of England. The wounded began arriving on the evening of D-Day – and by the end of the week they were being shipped home in their thousands. Mary Burke was a nurse in Southampton.

Casualties came to us still in uniform as they had fallen in battle. There was just a field dressing in position. Any emergency treatment carried out on board was duly noted, on the medical card which was either around the neck or in the breast pocket of the battledress. If morphia had been administered a red M was marked on their forehead.

All over England medical staff stood by. LF Taylor was a nurse at the Queen Elizabeth Hospital in Birmingham.

A number of wards were cleared to receive the wounded. As student nurses, we were given the task of scrubbing walls and disinfecting beds and lockers. When the wounded soldiers, sailors and airmen arrived they seemed to fill the hospital. Most of them were army casualties. One room which was actually just big enough for five beds was crammed full of beds all over the floor-space and there was hardly room for one's feet.

I recall one French soldier – older than most – who had the croix de guerre. He asked me for a drink of water with charm such as one seldom encountered in the British soldier! One very badly wounded airman had terrible burns on his back and had to lie prone all the time. He would only allow a very pretty nurse to dress his wounds, and she seemed the only person who could console him. His cries were quite shattering and really brought home the horrors of war-inflicted wounds.

My uncle-in-law was admitted from the battlegrounds of Normandy; he had shrapnel wounds in his leg and arm. To see him I had to search a big area covered in makeshift beds on the floor – all crowded and occupied by soldiers who between them had sustained every type of injury. I recall it being rather an ordeal facing a sea of faces as I tried to find my uncle. I also recall a wounded officer affectionately known as Sasha who would visit his men on the ward. He had a large black moustache and he hobbled about on two sticks wearing a hospital dressing-gown.

C Lowry was a Wren in Portsmouth. She was off duty during the invasion week, and had watched the soldiers depart on 5 June. Now she rushed down to the port to see the first of them come back.

Magdalen Court, our block of flats, had a flat roof, and I used to sunbathe there. As the weather was very warm, I used my week off to acquire a tan. While I was on the roof, every day an endless stream of army vehicles rolled past the flat on their way to the harbour. They were practising for the big day, and I waved to them from the rooftop, and they smiled and waved back.

On June 5th, they began to roll through London Road again, but this time it was different. The soldiers' faces were blacked up, and they sat upright in their vehicles – grave-faced. There seemed to be no noise, except for the rumble of the machines. It suddenly dawned on me, that this was the real thing – they were actually going to invade that very day. My heart went out to them, and there was no one I could tell because everyone was at work, so I just watched them go rolling by. I was excited, yet scared at the same time. Aircraft flew overhead, and still the endless wave of men and machines rolled down to the harbour to embark for Normandy. D-Day had arrived, and all free countries would rejoice, and all occupied countries would be overjoyed to hear of our advancing armies.

As I was still on leave, the next day I hurried down to the Southsea seafront. What a fantastic sight met my eyes. The sea was full of ships, from the harbour to far, far out to sea – all the way to France. As I watched, a destroyer coming into the harbour sounded its siren and the crew lined the decks as is customary when entering harbour. This destroyer had sustained an enormous gash in its side, and the few people watching waved and cheered as the ship limped home.

The newspapers screamed D-DAY! in the headlines, and were giving some details. So at last I knew why the strange-looking long-boats had been moored in all the creeks, harbours and backwaters along the coast. These boats took hundreds and hundreds of soldiers to France. Another secret that had been well-kept were the man-made harbours that were towed to France, which enabled equipment, food and vehicles to be unloaded safely on the beaches, then driven inland. What a nation, to keep those plans so secret that no details escaped to the enemy. No information was let loose, and my father said proudly: 'Now I can tell you, we have been working hard to assemble those harbours on time.'

Eileen's mother was a Red Cross nurse, and she was attached to a front-line hospital. This hospital was the Milton Teaching College, and taken over for the duration. Mrs Brading asked if we could help at all, and the Matron said, 'Yes, we would be grateful if they could help with the washing-up.' So, we hurried up to the hospital, as soon as duties permitted, but we didn't wash up. Instead, we helped dispense the drinks trolleys, and helped the injured to drink.

Most of the men had gangrene, owing to the long wait on the beaches. All had a leg or arm amputated, some had pneumonia, and others had burns. On the trolley was milk, fruit juices, beer, coffee and tea. We went to each patient, asked what he wanted to drink, and talked to them softly and gently.

On the third night, I had a late duty, and could not go to the hospital, but the next night I went. The Matron came out to see me and said, 'I'm glad you've come. One of the young men has been asking for you, and he is being moved inland tomorrow.' I knew which young man it was. He had been in the sea, and burned by the burning oil, and had both legs amputated. He was an absolute sweetie, and we got on well together. I gave him his drink, and held his hand, while we talked. He told me that a German seaman had been picked up, badly wounded, and was in a bed further along the ward. I saw the German, and I was startled by his appearance, with his dark beard, he looked like a picture of Christ – quite startling to behold.

We followed the news on the radio and on the cinema screen, and thrilled to the successes of our invading forces, and worried over any setbacks. The Russians were advancing steadily, and it really was developing into a race to get to Berlin first. Meanwhile, another terrifying weapon was launched by the Germans – a desperate attempt to stem the Allied advance. We called the weapon 'the flying-bomb'.

I discovered this menace when I was walking along the London Road near North-End. Hearing a noise overhead, I glanced up at the sky, the plane flashed by, then suddenly the engine stopped dead, and the plane lost height. A loud explosion soon told me that the plane was really a bomb. Another flying-bomb came over, then another, all on their way to London.

The flying bombs, the Führer's angry response to the attack on his Atlantic Wall, were a terrifying new experience for British civilians. The 'vengeance weapons' were deployed against London in order to get the best use out of them before the launch sites in France were overrun. Mrs V Rayner saw the first doodlebugs pass through the skies above Dover on their way.

What fearsome things they looked as they came in across the Channel, making a most unpleasant humming sound and smoke belching out of their rear. My first sight of one was when Dancy and I were dispensing tea at a site below the East cliff. Seven or eight came in across the harbour at great speed and were over before a single gun could fire. Nobody knew what they were until later, when the explosions came.

It was a fiendish instrument. It gave one a very unpleasant feeling when we got to know more about its devilish mechanism. When the engine cut out you knew it was coming down to complete the destruction of whatever lay in its path. I stood on my veranda during one noisy night, when some were coming in over the western heights and the anti-aircraft batteries were opening up with all they'd got. They were by no means easy targets to hit owing to the speed, but the sight of one caught with a direct hit was an awesome thing.

By night that smoking tail was like a sheet of flame, and any one of them hit went up with a deafening roar as it disintegrated. I saw many of the devilish instruments of destruction brought down. Once, when we were loading up the tea car at headquarters, one of them came buzzing overhead, the engine cut out and we all held our breath until we heard the explosion.

But the 'second blitz' of the flying bombs was, from a military perspective, a wasteful and pointless exercise. A less petulant commander than Hitler might have launched the doodlebugs to devastating effect against the Normandy beaches and the advancing Allied troops. British civilians didn't much like them, but most of them had seen worse in 1940 and 1941.

THE FRENCH REJOICE

No one was happier about the beginning of the liberation of Europe than the French. True, some of the more dour people of Normandy, who had had a very quiet war up until the morning of 6 June, were distinctly disgruntled to find that their farms and fields had been selected as the cockpit of this decisive battle. There were even a few instances of French civilians sniping at Allied troops. But the vast majority of French people were delighted that their liberation had begun. They were intoxicated with elation and patriotism, and in some cases with calvados and cider. And they were not feeling kindly disposed towards the Germans, as US Army Sergeant Charles Rost discovered when he took the surrender of some Waffen SS men.

These prisoners that came out of the bomb shelter were wearing dark blue or black uniforms with lightning streaks on the right lapel. It was the first time I had seen uniforms like this. I called the company commander via radio and said 'We have seventeen prisoners, where do you want them?' He gave us map coordinates to a location not far ahead, where we were to turn the prisoners over to a French underground group. We left the POWS with the French, as instructed.

Later I received a radio message from some military police, inquiring where I had dropped off prisoners. I gave them the map coordinates. The MPs asked 'Can you identify the prisoners?' I said 'All I know is that they were wearing dark uniforms with lightning streaks on their collars.' He came back, 'Well, we have seventeen people laying here on the ground and their throats are cut from ear to ear.'

It was not just the French resistance who now hit back at the Germans, and not just the SS who were on the receiving end. Newly liberated Claude Guillotin, fifteen years old at the time, led a spontaneous hunt for Germans a couple of days after the invasion.

On the morning of June 8th there were quite a number of customers in our café. Everyone was talking about what they had seen and what they thought would happen. Suddenly the roar of aircraft engines and the crackle of automatic cannons and machine guns rent the air. Everyone ran outside. A twin-engined German plane was on fire, and would crash near Cully. The Spitfire which had accounted for it climbed high into the blue sky. A single German parachute was floating down in the direction of Secqueville.

I yelled: 'He must not be allowed to reach their lines. We must go and get him!' I ran off at full speed and went through the little wood opposite our house. I had correctly judged the feelings of those I had asked to follow me. Spirits were high after the night of June 6th, and the calm and resolute behaviour of the Canadians had given us a feeling of strength and invulnerability. We no longer feared the Boches. I had no doubt the group were going to follow me, I just had to give the lead.

I got through the barbed-wire fence of Mr André Lefevre's pasture and continued on my way with my eyes fixed on the parachute which was coming down in a corner of the pasture. The Germans had dug out a machine-gun nest there, and they might have been able to re-occupy it again in the night. With my arms crossed in front of my face, I forced my way through the narrow gap in the thorn hedge. I was held up briefly, and when I raised my eyes again there was no sign of the parachute. The German had landed, rapidly gathered it up, and disappeared.

Undiscouraged, I quickly resumed my run to the point of the airman's descent, which I worked out was about a kilometre away along a line between the clock towers of Cully and Secqueville. I looked back for a moment and saw Claude Ducet 200 metres behind me. I let him catch up with me a little later, without stopping running. Meanwhile another group of five or six lads had appeared, coming through the hedges. We reached the road from Camilly to Cainet, and we took care to jump over the high tension wire which was lying on the ground.

We thought there were now only 300 or 400 metres to the spot where the airman had landed. Soon, being more cautious, we went in a zig-zag manner, our nerves tense and our eyes anxiously searching the surroundings. It was essential to see before being seen. At this point we were in a field of oats, which was over knee-high and where the dew wet our legs through our trousers. The sky was azure blue, but no skylarks were singing. All the birds seemed to have fled after the terrific bombardment.

Our friends were spread out like hunters after game. We saw them stop. Two of them made signs to others. Something had happened. Our friends had closed up in a semi-circle around one spot, and we saw Desiré Marie, the oldest and the toughest amongst us, dive to the ground as the others rushed up. When Desiré Marie got up, he was holding a German by the collar. It wasn't the pilot we had been following, but a Wehrmacht soldier put there as a lookout.

By now the German soldier was half undressed, had been searched carefully, and was shaking with fear as we circled around him with knives in our hands. For myself, I didn't want to hit him, being fully satisfied with our little victory. I would have been very uneasy if my friends had decided to kill him. They were all older than me, and some had good reasons to want revenge. The tension relaxed, and the German's life was saved. We even gave him back his haversack which contained some food.

Charles Brisset put the belt and ammunition on himself. Raoul Saint-Jean held the Mauser, and with the bayonet pointing at the German's back the procession returned to the village. In all the youthful excitement, nobody suggested continuing the search for the German pilot. He had gone from our minds as if he had disappeared from life.

That German soldier, captured by enthusiastic French boys, was handed over to the Canadians. Many others like him were led down to the beaches and shipped across to England where, if they were not badly wounded, they were kept in large cages constructed on Southsea Common.

Many of those German POWs grinned with relief all the way to England, and congratulated each other on their good fortune as they languished in their open-air prisons. They knew the war could not be won the moment they saw the massed ships off the beaches. So how much better was it to be safe in an English cage than to be hiding out in a French field, waiting to die a futile death in a lost cause?

9
THE BEACH AND THE BOCAGE

We found a huge and beautiful draught horse behind a hedgerow . . .

. . . said RR Hughart of the US Airborne. He had by now been fighting in France for some days.

One day there was this real strange noise coming from the other side of the hedgerow and there was a wheezing, gurgling, like an air-hissing noise. Nobody could figure out what it was. None of us had ever heard this wheezing, whizzing noise . . . very peculiar. Somebody says 'Well, it's one of them. It's a trick. The Germans have got some kind of a thing there and they want us to go on the other side and then all hell will break loose.'

Those hedgerows in Normandy were pretty thick and they were pretty tall. And they had a bunch of young trees and bushes and rocks on top of them. Finally, somebody got up enough nerve to investigate and crawled up and over the hedgerow.

Well, he came back and said: 'There's a horse standing there with its head down and he's making this funny noise.' So we all went over to take a look and there was this beautiful, brown draught horse that had been shot in the side a couple of times. And the poor thing was in awful shape: air and pink bubbles of blood were coming out of it.

So I said, 'Well, one of you guys shoot it and put it out of its misery.' But, ohhh no, we can't shoot a horse. So I asked 'Why not, gosh, you guys shoot Germans, why can't you shoot a horse?' Well, nobody would shoot that poor horse. So I shot him in the head with an armour-piercing bullet and he dropped like a log and that was the end of him. It was a terrible thing to do, but he was too far gone.

'I can see again the earth banks, the green hedgerows, the white dust of Normandy. And I can feel the grim and threatening quiet that hangs over a frontline position. The men speak in low, tired voices, almost fearful of breaking a spell.' Major Cooke, Royal Scots Guards

The Allies were unnerved by the countryside in which they found themselves fighting. The French word *bocage* describes a very particular feature of the Norman landscape. The fields of Calvados are divided by high banks, almost like Dutch dykes. On top of the banks are ancient, tangled rows of trees or hedges. So in battle conditions, every country road becomes like a dry moat, and every field can be defended as if it were a kind of walled fortress. The fields themselves are often planted with apple orchards, which provide cover, and there are hundreds of thick little copses where a man can keep lookout but cannot be seen. It was perfect defensive territory, and the Germans made very good use of it.

For the Americans and British, the Norman topography meant that progress was much slower than had been hoped. They advanced field by field, planning each assault with meticulous thoroughness. Tanks and artillery were less effective than had been expected. Gun-aimers could not see further than a few hundred yards, and tanks could simply not get down the narrow roads. It fell to the infantry to clear the way, often by means of close-quarters fighting. Every claustrophobic lane became a potential valley of death, because there was always the chance that a machine-gunner or a mortarman was hunched and ready a few yards away in the next field.

It was in these first days that the advancing troops began to get to know their enemy. The learning experience began for US Army Sergeant Ralph Steinway on the first night.

> On guard duty on D+1 you would hear somebody fire down the line and it would seem that all of a sudden there was a domino effect. The firing would go on for a little while and then stop because somebody realized that they really weren't seeing anything, and if they saw anything then it was a cat or a dog or at best, a cow.
>
> The 352nd German Division, which was an experienced fighting division, had of course re-stocked its casualties with younger soldiers. And these guys loved to play cowboys and Indians. They just loved to get in those hedgerows and pop up and take a shot at you. And by the time you got to where they were, they might be behind you. They had tunnels, they had all sorts of things to drive one nuts. It was effective, because it kept slowing the progress of everything. You were constantly walking on the balls of your feet, all the time. Always looking and always trying to figure out where the next shot was going to come from. And if it didn't, it just made it harder on your nervous system.

In the daytime as well as at night, men would open fire blindly at any little movement or noise, which was why so many animals were killed. The sight and stench of dead cows, their piebald bodies puffed up like balloons and their legs sticking comically up in the air, became one of the universal memories of the Normandy campaign.

The difficulty of the terrain was one of the reasons it took the British so long to reach Caen. Monty's promise to get there on D-Day itself soon began to look like an embarrassing joke.

> It took four weeks, said Private Bill Colyer of the Hampshires. And all the while we were living in a slit trench. That was when a kind of First World War mentality set in – pissing and shitting in the

same place because you were afraid to move. You learned fast that there were snipers out there. We lost a lot of guys – British and Canadian – while we were dug in outside Caen. But all the while there were shells coming over from the ships. They came over so low you could almost have reached up and touched them.

My job was to bring up supplies from Arromanches in a three-tonne truck: ammo, grub, blankets, whatever was needed. We put up hessian blinds so the Germans couldn't see the trucks moving and target them. The military police had signs saying 'five miles per hour – dust means death.' (The MPs were always out in front – they were under-rated guys.) So we crawled back and forth at a snail's pace. Much later on there was sign saying: 'Let your wing flaps down.' Now we could motor – meaning we could go up to 20 mph – and that felt great.

The slow progress of the Brits was a cause of tension between American and British commanders, in particular between Montgomery and Bradley. The American general declared himself bitterly disappointed with the failure to get into Caen, even though his troops were experiencing exactly the same problems with the terrain.

It was an ideal place to defend, said Earl Harness, who had landed with the 4th Division at Utah. If you were on the attack you would expose yourself. They lay in the defense area, real quiet, and you didn't even see them until they began to fire at you. So we lost several men going across an open field on the offensive because they were already protected. They would kill more of us than we would kill of them, to begin with.

Harness found that one way to even up the odds was to use country boys for night patrols.

Maybe I'm prejudiced because I'm from the south, but if it was a very difficult task I would send somebody from hill country like the Ozark mountains. They seemed to be able to maintain their directions, get out there and get the wounded soldier and get him back home. Them Yankees from the cities didn't have the same bird sense as the fellas who were hunters at night.

There was another ever-present danger in addition to snipers, mortars, concealed artillery and German patrols. Mines were everywhere – and they came in a frightening variety of shapes and sizes. The dreaded S-mine looked like a tin of soup with a fuse on top. It launched ball-bearings into the air before detonating; Americans called it a 'Bouncing Betty,' while the British knew it by the rather more graphic term 'the de-bollocker'. Then there were the Teller mines, which looked like a big drum of film and which had been used to such devastating effect against landing craft on the beaches. They were designed as anti-tank weapons, and could easily blow the tracks off a Sherman or a Churchill. A man who stepped on one would simply be atomized in a puff of smoke.

The Allies had crude metal-detectors, but these could seek out only one mine at a time. There were more than five million of them in the immediate vicinity of the Atlantic Wall. They were scattered across the countryside wherever the enemy was likely to set foot – in neat rows in fields, haphazardly in ditches, across the width of roads and in the doorways of houses. Some mines were made of non-magnetic materials such as Bakelite to make them undetectable. There were glass mines like vicious little jam jars. There was even the cardboard 'shoe-mine', barely bigger than a cigarette packet, but capable of taking off a man's leg at the knee.

The Germans had a particular fondness for booby traps, as mine-clearer Captain DG Tugwell of the British 6th Beach Group found:

> In clearing our new location, a small paddock with high walls, we found no mines, but one booby trap, an incredibly complicated affair consisting of layers of tin and wood, all buried. The key of the whole affair was a toy cannon, cocked but not loaded, with no fuse or charge to be found.

Non-specialists such as Ralph Steinway were also gaining insights into the German way with minefields – and were figuring out quick, safe ways to get across them.

> The Germans are great ones for putting up 'Achtung Minen' signs. Some big, some small, and you had to really believe all of them. After a while we learned that in a lot of cases there were no mines. But it slowed you up because then you'd want to have somebody come along with a sweeper and see.

Occasionally we'd run across lanes where they had these little yellow and black pennants. They had a black skull-and-crossbones, and they measured about three inches across and four inches long. They were in a triangular shape, and they would have them ten-feet apart on both sides of a path. We learned quickly that you could bank on anything you saw like that, and stay in that path. Because that's what it was for. If you stepped out of the path marked by those pennants, you were in deep trouble, because there were plenty of mines around. All kinds. The big 'Achtung Minen' things didn't mean as much as this grand little pennant.

Some unfortunate soldiers learned about mines the hard way. Company commander John Ahearn had taken a tank into Utah Beach. He got out of it to help three injured paratroopers that he had spotted in a field:

I immediately returned to the tank and got the first-aid kit. When I saw a break in the hedgerow, I proceeded to cross it. While I was standing there contemplating my next move, a personnel mine went off under me. The mine explosion threw me into the bank of the hedgerows, and I was unconscious for a while.

Subsequently I awakened and began yelling. Two of my crew, Sergeant St Zampiello and Corporal Beard, came out to take a look. It was hard to find me, because I had rolled up against the embankment. But when they did, I cautioned them not to come over because of the mines. I subsequently learned from our battalion maintenance officer that they had discovered some 15,000 mines in that vicinity, so the odds were not very good.

During that night, it was decided that I would need surgery. As it turned out, I had heavy paratroop boots on. Both feet, I guess, were still on at this point, but terribly mangled, and they decided that they would have to operate on me. I was given about six bottles of plasma, and was visited by the chaplain. Then, in the early evening, I was operated on in a makeshift tent with white sheets for walls.

Subsequently I found that the decision was made that they would just amputate the one foot because they felt that I would not be able to withstand both operations. So during the night, the one foot was amputated, and I was then prepared for a transport the next day to England.

There were many hospital wards and operating theatres hastily erected more or less in the open air, and this too presented dangers both to doctors and patients. Robert Bogart, a medic, was caring for American wounded quite close to the beaches.

> We had set up our ward tent on top of this cliff. I don't think we really had any direct fire, but there were stray bullets going through the tents, probably from shooting a mile away. I was talking to one friend of mine. I'd bent over and I heard a 'zzzzip'. He put his hands up to his chest. Just by accident, one had come through the ward tent and hit him in the left side in the ribs and went out the other side. We got him down to the ship to go back to England. Never saw that chap again.

In those first days particularly, surgeons found themselves working in conditions that Florence Nightingale would have recognized.

> The thing that I remember most was this, said Doctor David Thomas. A soldier had his leg blown off right by the knee. Only his patellar tendon was left attached. And I had him down there in this ditch and I said 'Son, I'm gonna have to cut the rest of your leg off and you're back to bullet-biting time because I don't have anything to use for an anesthetic.' And he said 'Go ahead, Doc.' I cut the patellar tendon and he didn't even whimper.
>
> So then we were able to take him into this cottage with a thatched roof which was being used as an aid station. Actually what we could do was minimal because the only thing we had was what we carried in our packs. All the medical bundles that were dropped from the planes were somewhere. We didn't have one. All we could do was give them some morphine as long as it lasted, bandage their wounds, and hope something happened.

Something did happen. Medical supplies of all sorts began to come in by air and sea – including countless gallons of much-needed English blood.

I was in charge of the Shock and Wounded tent of the clearing company, said Captain Richard Fahey. I was despairing because there were no blood transfusions available. All I could do was to run from one man to the other, stopping the bleeding.

When I was complaining, one of the sergeants came up to me and said, 'Don't worry Captain, take a look out here. Here is all the blood you could ever use which the British have collected off their people and shipped over here by plane. The planes are landing on the airstrip over there, and they are coming in from England, bumper to bumper. They are pushing it out of the planes on to the ground and there is a pile of supplies one-half mile long and six-feet high piled all along that runway. They are unloading their cargo at one end of the airstrip and loading up with wounded before they take off at the other end of the strip. They are heading back off the runway going to England to return with another load of cargo. No worry, Captain, all we have to do is find it in that pile back there and bring it to you.' No one had ever prepared me for this unbelievable service. The devotion to the cause was enough to bring a tear to anybody's eye.

As soon as possible, wounded soldiers of both sides were ferried to hospital ships and taken to England. Aboard one of these ships, moored off Omaha Beach, was the American war reporter Martha Gellhorn. She had bluffed her away aboard a ship in England on the morning of 7 June and in classic stowaway style had locked herself in a toilet until the ship set sail. Now she found herself sailing into what she called 'the greatest traffic jam in history.'

Battleships, destroyers, transports were strewn haphazardly across the water, a seascape solidly filled with ships. It was so enormous, so awesome, that it felt more like an act of nature than anything man-made.

Naval guns were firing over the beach to unseen land beyond. On shore, bulldozers scooped up and detonated mines. Tanks, looking toy-size at this distance, moved slowly up the four dirt roads that scarred the bluff. Before us now was a weird forest of tall iron rods, like pieces of railroad track, with shreds of barbed wire trailing from them. Far below, bodies floated face down, swollen greyish sacks, drowned infantrymen.

We had six water ambulances that could be lowered and raised to the boat deck. Each held six litter cases and as many walking wounded as could crowd aboard. A very young man with a colourless, drawn face and open unblinking eyes lay on a table in the middle of the ward. Whoever picked him up sent his story, by word of mouth, with him. He had been blown out of the turret of his tank and lay watching and hearing his comrades burn to death inside it. He was unwounded and could not move or speak. A nurse shot him full of pentathol. He was put on a bunk, covered with blankets, and left to sleep. Twenty-four hours later he was all right, at least in his body.

A soldier with a smashed shoulder and a soldier with a smashed knee were worried. 'That ranger over there, Miss, he's in a bad way, can you do something?' Quickly find a nurse. 'Miss, this man here needs water.' A soldier with two bloodied bandaged legs talking for a man next to him whose head was shrouded in bandages. Nobody complained except for one deeply unpopular German. And no American soldier asked a service for himself; they watched out for each other. It was very moving to see this gentleness of hurt men.

IN CONTROL OF THE BEACHES

A couple of days after the invasion, Ralph Steinway had the opportunity to go back to the sea. On the way he took a moment to inspect the pillbox at the Vierville draw, one of the strongpoints that had apportioned death so generously to his buddies on Omaha Beach.

It was a marvel of German efficiency. The bunker not only had gun slits that faced the beach; they had all of the various areas of the beach marked in meters as to the range needed to fire at a particular spot. And they had these marked right above the gun slits. So they didn't have to consult a form or anything, they just looked up above and set the gun and fired away when you got there. The other thing was that on the other side, the concrete bunker also covered part of the road that ran from Vierville down towards Grandcamps, and again they had various parts of the road there. I'm sure they either measured or they might have even practised firing a round, to make sure that they had the right settings so that they could shoot at any troops or vehicles coming up or down the road.

Steinway and a fellow non-com were on a private mission to get a better gun, and to do 'a little bit of government re-issue for ourselves.'

As sergeants, we were given 30-caliber carbines – which might be good in fighting inside a house somewhere, but that's about as far as I ever thought they were worth anything. Supposedly you could fire them with one hand: stick your arm around a wall and fire like they do on TV. But we traded our 30-caliber carbines for the good, reliable M-1 Garand rifle. And we exchanged our ammo belts with those that had no longer a need for them.

Arnold Benthien also went to inspect the vast military cash-and-carry on the sand. But the main item on his shopping list was food.

It was the second day, and we weren't very far away from the bluff by then. One of the line sergeants, Frank Pitchler, and I decided we could use some more rations and ammo. We were pretty sure there'd be some down on the beach.

Nobody told us to go, and nobody told us not to go. Frank and I just decided we'd go down there. I was a little amused when we headed down the road a little ways and came across an MP. He was a 2nd Division MP, and the 2nd Division had landed the day after we did, on D+1. He was wanting to stop us, and he says 'There's snipers down that way.' And Frank said, 'What do you think we've got up where we come from?' And he said no more. We walked on past him. We never got shot at, although we had been shot at by snipers before, they never seemed to connect.

I was glad I went back for one reason, just to see that beach absolutely covered with everything you could think of. Vehicles; I suppose some of them ran, but most of them didn't. Most of them were knocked out. There was debris everyplace you looked, and then there were the rows of dead. The graves registration people had apparently laid them out in rows. I still remember the translucent look of their faces laid out there. I'm sure they were getting everything in order to check dog tags and all that. There were just long rows of those dead bodies, all with a sort of clean, waxen look to the skin.

But we loaded ourselves with K-rations and a few bandoliers of ammo. We didn't know when we'd get any more supplies, and we liked to be a little prepared. We loaded up there. Nobody asked us where we'd been, and we distributed all the goodies we'd brought up to a few guys around us. But it was worthwhile to have seen that beach in that condition.

All sorts of interesting things were happening on the American beaches now that the fighting there was more or less over. The medico Robert Bogart bumped into a fellow countryman who had been an ambulance driver during World War I – but they did not hit it off:

On D+2, I noticed a man in a correspondent's suit – an overbearing, big man with a beard and kind of a foul mouth. I said to somebody, 'Who in the hell is that fellow?' And they said 'That's Ernest Hemingway.' Well, I changed my mind about him. Just before I went into the service I had been to the movies and saw his story *For Whom the Bell Tolls*. I had a different impression of him after seeing what a foul-mouthed guy he was.

The great writer might have been even more vituperative if he had known that his estranged wife, Martha Gellhorn, was less than a mile away on a hospital ship. They were probably the only married couple to take a trip to Omaha Beach that week.

Strangenesses abound in war. Something very curious happened to Arden Benthien of the American 1st Division the same day that Robert Bogart met Papa Hemingway. He saw someone get shot with a toy bullet.

The German unit, the 352nd Infantry I think, were carrying on anti-invasion maneuvers. We came in right among them. For the purposes of maneuvers, they were apparently issued with wooden bullets for both rifles and machine guns. The rounds did fire. One of our guys took a hit in the upper arm with one of these things. It didn't make a deep wound, didn't penetrate at all. Sort of exploded right there, made a sort of a nasty flesh wound. They had to bandage it up. I've never seen this noted anywhere, but it is real. I've still got one of the rounds.

On Sword Beach the shells were still real enough, but few and far between. For a week after D-Day the 6th Beach Group worked hard to turn the narrow strip of sand into a serviceable dockside. This involved a good deal of Robinson Crusoe-style salvage work, and a large amount of rather hazardous tidying up. Here are some extracts from Captain DG Tugwell's diary for the week after the invasion.

> June 7th. In the evening I had settled down to make a brew, when wild cries greeted the arrival of a corporal towing a handcart loaded with two boxes of compo, and a petrol cooker which we had selected from the mass of salvageable equipment at the high-water mark. Soon I had the happiest platoon in the sector. Earlier in the day we found our two handcarts full of tools and explosives. These had been jettisoned from the LCI, as there was no way of getting them to shore. They had been washed up, and thanks to the careful waterproofing on the outside, the contents were in good condition.
>
> Some time that afternoon I was in the platoon area when a terrific sheet of flame shot up from the petrol dump about a quarter of a mile up the road. I saw a plane making off inland. The whole dump of petrol and ammunition seemed to have gone off at once, and it was not possible to approach this place for many hours, owing to the exploding ammunition.
>
> June 8th. After a good night's sleep we carried on with the routine beach maintenance, which we knew so well from our many exercises. The work consisted of clearing wire and debris to open up new beach exits and maintaining the existing exits and laterals. Life was getting simpler now as we knew where everybody else was and organisation was returning.
>
> There was spasmodic shelling quite close to us, but always in the same place and just offshore, so that everybody avoided it. By this time we had realised that in this area, at any rate, all the minefields were marked with various signs, though many of these were dummies.

At about 23.00 hours I was just getting into my hole (we were all in slits) when at the far end of our field sprouted vast numbers of small flashes, seeming to approach our area. This was followed immediately by many small explosions. It was a canister of SDI bombs, small anti-personnel bombs rather like three-inch mortar bombs. Happily, they landed in the middle of a large and uncleared minefield, so no damage was done.

June 9th. We continued with our beach work, which was easier now owing to better organisation, and we were rewarded in the evening by the arrival of our transport – 48 hours late. We had just started to offload this transport in order to get the cooking equipment, when a signal came ordering us to move to the other end of the beach about a mile away, and to start clearing beach obstacles first thing next morning. We packed up and arrived at our new location after dark. Happily, I recognised a young Frenchman whom I had met on D-Day, and he guided me to the best billets, large houses previously occupied by the German garrison. The weather being good, we slept in the gardens for that night, disturbed only by the vast array of AA guns and two incendiaries which had the bad taste to fall in the road.

June 10th. We started on the removal of beach obstacles from the west end of the beach. The main frontage of the beach had been cleared on D-Day and we were now doing a deliberate clearance westward to widen the effective size of the beach.

With the working members on the job, I sorted the platoon. Five large cellars for the section, a basement garage for the cookhouse and an upstairs window for the wireless operators. As it happened, my platoon had no casualties from shelling but we always made the most of available cover.

While we were in this location our fitters started refitting drowned vehicles. The beach REME were fully engaged on other tasks. At our peak we had six Jeeps, one Weasel, two motorcycles and sundry trailers, as well as an armoured bulldozer which we could not start.

The beach obstacles were mainly nine-inch timber uprights about ten-feet high with one raker, and a mine or shell mounted on top with a press igniter. We dealt with these by removing the mine or shell and detonating it at the base of the upright. This was then chopped free, the raker pulled out and the whole dumped above high water mark. We also opened up some more beach exits, which were blocked by mines, wire, and concrete obstacles. At this stage we had no interference by shelling, although German aircraft usually came over once a night.

When a plane did come over, it was the custom for the entire fleet to open up on it. It was spectacular, but usually pointless. Many men speak of seeing the night filled with tracers, like bright doodles on the sky, as hundreds of anti-aircraft guns shot a quarter of a mile behind a lone Focke-Wulf or Messerschmitt.

The occasional German plane was brave enough to overfly the invasion fleet in the daytime too. To protect the fleet from these determined remnants of the Luftwaffe it was usual to place 'smokepots' in the sea. These created a choking cloak of fog around the ships. Lawrence Orr of the US Navy came across a gruesome sight and a rather dim-witted British officer while on 'smokepot detail'.

> I put out smokepots for about a week, every afternoon while the Germans would come over and drop bombs and try to blast us out. We had this big aircraft motor that was mounted on a barge, and it was the British who took care of it. One afternoon I was putting the smokepots out. We were under attack and I'd come back to the ship and was going to tie up alongside, but the officer of the deck hollered down to me 'Ahoy, down there in boat three, would you mind going over to that barge and finding out why the airplane motor is not blowing the smoke over here?'
>
> I said 'Well, fine. Aye aye.' I took off, went over, saw what was the problem, came back. I said 'Ahoy on deck! Officer of the deck! The operator, evidently because of the roughness of the sea, has fallen into the propeller and it's cut his head off.'
>
> Now get this, the officer of the deck hollers down to me and says 'Did it kill him?' 'Yeah,' I said, 'it sure did.'

The landings did not, of course, cease on D-Day. Men continued to wade on to the beaches in vast numbers. The sheer weight of manpower, the massive preponderance of Allied forces, was bound to tell on the enemy sooner or later. Many of these new arrivals had experiences no less hair-raising than those who arrived on the first day. Larry Micka drove in an amphibious DUKW on 7 June.

Some units of our brigade landed at H+6, but I did not receive clearance to debark until 09.30 or 10.30 the next day, which didn't make me a bit mad.

We were offloaded a few miles out. We were given a compass bearing toward shore and each duck was on its own to hit the beach under its own power. As that forbidding coast of France came into view I wondered what destiny awaited me there. I didn't wonder too long before I started to pray. I had heard that the instinct of self-preservation is the strongest instinct known to man. I don't know who coined that phrase, but truer words were never spoken.

Ducks don't move too fast in the water, and with a top speed of 5 knots it seemed forever before my front wheels hit the beach. I always thought that I came in on Sugar Red Beach, but our company history lists it as Uncle Red Beach. I didn't care what they called it as long as everyone I saw was on my side.

My duck was loaded with pontoons to make infantry foot-bridges and I reported to navy control point on the beach and was directed to where my cargo would be unloaded. After unloading it at an engineers' dump, I drove back to the beachmaster's station. A couple of the older hands in my company had the strong urge to drive up toward the front to see how things were going. They chose my duck to do their sightseeing in. I thought they were crazy, but I was stuck with them. This was my first taste of combat, but these guys, along with most of the company, had already seen action in North Africa, Sicily and Italy.

We drove up toward the front and I was quite ill at ease to see dead Germans lying along both sides of the road, and having French people peeking out from behind curtain windows to see if it was friend or foe out there. When these older hands decided we had gone far enough, which was to my everlasting relief, we turned around and headed back toward the beach.

We had no sooner pulled up to the beachmaster's station when I heard fighter plane engines behind me. I turned toward the water and saw three Messerschmitt 109s bearing down on us. They had side-slipped down the beach with their engines cut and when they got over us they started their engines and opened up with their guns at the same time in a strafing maneuver. I went off of that duck head-first, with my rifle going one direction, my helmet in another. I ate sand trying to get out of the line of fire. But, I got out of the line of fire, and our anti-aircraft guns made short work of those planes.

We established a bivouac area a short way inland behind the beach, and the next day, June 8th, I along with several other drivers were dispatched up toward the front to seek out however many glider pilots we could find and transport them back to the beach and on out to a ship going back to England. For all practical purposes, for those guys the war was over.

They were still hiding out from the wee hours of June 6th. It gave me a kind of eerie feeling to see them come crawling out from their hiding places still wearing their black faces and camouflage, bewhiskered, and muddy and dirty. They smiled when they saw me and treated me like a long-lost cousin. I got them down to the beach and on out to a ship that was also transporting wounded back to England.

THE MULBERRIES ARRIVE

Offshore, the long-planned construction of the Mulberry harbours was under way. There was to be one at St Laurent off Omaha and another off Gold at Arromanches. The first caissons – great concrete cubes like floating office blocks – were towed slowly out of England on D+1. With them came the block ships that were due to be secured nose-to-tail to create a five-mile-long breakwater. The caissons were carefully positioned inside this sunken embrace and submerged by opening their sea cocks. Together they made up the outer shell of the harbour.

The American Mulberry progressed more slowly than the British, partly because the engineers working on it had had less training than their British counterparts, and partly because they were more consistently bombed and shot at as they worked. But by 17 June, less than two weeks after D-Day, both harbours were in use. It was like having two Dovers side-by-side on

The Mulberry harbour at Arromanches became known as Port Winston, despite the fact that Churchill had expressly forbidden the use of this name. The Mulberry was designed to last for 90 days, but parts of it are still there – an immovable concrete atoll off the coast of France.

the French coast, and it greatly increased the volume of supplies that could be landed in France and transported inland.

Arthur Bradford was an American merchant seaman bringing *matériel* into the Omaha Mulberry.

> They were still making the breakwater while we were there. We would watch them bring in old damaged ships and detonate them, sink them down, to make a stillwater harbor for the ships.
>
> We stayed there for five weeks unloading the ammunition and trucks. They would take about three slings of shells in crates and lower them down to ducks – that was a mobile boat with four wheels and a propeller. They would drive them ashore, up the beach, unload it, come back and get another one.
>
> The fighting had moved inland, so the captain let Jim and me go ashore as long as one of us stayed aboard at a time. He would

go in the morning and I'd go in the afternoon or vice versa. Every night at dusk there would be a great fireworks display. There would seem to be a German observation plane that would dive down over the beachhead, keeping track of what was going on, and everybody was shooting at him. But by the time the fireworks were over, the decks were loaded with shrapnel. It came down like rain.

One night I remember standing on the starboard wing of the bridge with an army officer and watching the show, keeping our heads underneath the overhang, when there was a fantastic explosion quite close to us. I banged into him and he fell on to the ladder. Seems that the German bombers were dropping mines and one of them landed right on an English trawler which literally blew it all apart.

The final stage in the construction of the Mulberries was the installation of long floating roadways from the pierheads to the shore. Once these were in place – and there were due to be six miles' worth of them – men and machines would be able to come ashore without getting their feet or their tyres wet. But on the day that the individual sections, called 'bombardons', were towed across to France, a violent gale blew up. It was the worst summer storm in fifty years, and it burst through the Mulberries like a ball through skittles. Donald Irwin, the American captain of an LCT, found this entirely uncharacteristic storm almost as terrifying as the ferocious whirlwind of Omaha. He was at sea when the bad weather struck.

It lasted three days and three nights. The only chance we had of keeping our landing craft from being beaten to bits was to anchor a long way off the beach out in the Channel and hope we could ride the storm out. This we did, with orders to let out all the anchor cable we could to give the anchor a better holding action. The strong winds and huge waves buffeted us day and night, and although our anchor did drag bit by bit, we rode the storm out successfully. I was so fearful that the anchor cable might snap I recall sleeping on the floor of the chart house during the night, so that if it did give way, I would have a better chance of not drowning, as I was up considerably higher than if I was in my bunk.

We were fortunate that the storm ended when it did because our anchor had dragged so much we were very close to a line of sunken ships that had been put out as a breakwater. If we had smashed into them, our ship would have been pounded to pieces.

I made a promise to myself then and there that if I was ever on solid land and I was confronted with a storm, I would never be afraid of it.

Brigadier Bruce White, director of ports and inland war transport at the British War Office, was sent out to France personally by Churchill to inspect the damage to the Mulberries.

I visited the devastation at Omaha Beach, where I saw bombardons whirling about in the water. There were numerous vessels drifting ashore, and three small landing craft piled on top of each other on the beach. It was a tragic sight, and I felt it could have been avoided if certain key personnel had been prepared to follow our instructions. The American harbour was destroyed, possibly because the breakwaters had been founded without sufficient freeboard, with the result that the violent seas gained entry into the units.

The British Mulberry suffered damage too, but in the form that the bombardons broke loose. Floating freely, they crashed into the caissons, causing havoc to the breakwaters.

Two days after it had been completed, the American Mulberry harbour was so badly damaged that it had to be abandoned. The storm that had raged solidly for three days had destroyed five times more shipping than the Germans had been able to sink in the preceding fortnight. But the British Mulberry was repaired, partly with recycled sections from the American one, and by the end of 1944, 39,000 vehicles and 220,000 troops had passed through it.

They landed dryshod in France, said Brigadier White. General Eisenhower stated that 'Mulberry exceeded our best hopes.' The invasion of Europe, impossible without the artificial harbours, had been accomplished by British engineering skill.

PUSHING THROUGH CALVADOS

Within a few days of the invasion, the tens of thousands of Allied soldiers in France were settling into the humdrum routine of war. There were the dull, workaday tasks such as moving equipment, organizing work parties, digging in, tidying up. There were the mildly diverting personal victories of a day at the front: finding a safe place to wash; liberating a bottle of cider from a farmhouse; or getting a letter or a newspaper from home. And then there would be moments of high excitement (more frequent than one would like) when someone was trying his hardest to kill you.

Larry Micka found that some improvization and a little rule-bending helped make the life of a GI in Europe more bearable.

> We had some very enterprising cooks in our company. We were only on the beach a couple of days when a strange-looking, metallic two-wheel cart with an enormous pot situated between the wheels and a smoke stack on it turned up in the company area. It turned out to be a German field kitchen that no other outfit could use because they were always on the move. Since our mission was to stay right where we were and work ship to shore, our cooks figured out how to work that contraption and we were eating soup, stew, and hotcakes as early as June 8th or 9th. I felt very fortunate to be member of the 479th.
>
> Those guys had learned from their experience in Sicily and Italy. While the old man didn't encourage us to steal, he suggested that since we were hauling cargo from ship to shore it would pay us to always know what we were hauling, and if we thought it was useful, to detour by the company area on our way to the ration dump. I think we were attached to the 1st Army for the purposes of drawing rations, but that was totally unnecessary. This outfit took care of itself.
>
> Our motorpool sergeant was no slouch either. Due to our round-the-clock operation, our ducks were taking a beating, breaking a lot of rudder cables. He told the old man that if there were no objection, he thought the flap cables on all those wrecked gliders laying around in the fields could be put to our use. They just happened to be so close to the size we needed, we never bothered our ordinance department to requisition any. I always admired these guys for their ingenuity. If we didn't have it

and it wasn't available from any source, we made it. I know we weren't the only company to operate in this fashion. I think the American servicemen were known for being very enterprising.

The units working the beach considered themselves lucky that the war was moving slowly away from them. The frontline American and British units were still primarily concerned with staying alive, not salvaging booty. Lieutenant Colonel E Jones and his unit moved up to the Orne Canal on 8 June, D+2, to reinforce the 6th Airborne Division. The Germans were still trying hard to drive the paratroopers off Pegasus Bridge.

Aircraft bombed and strafed our positions during the day, intermittently and in small numbers. I was amazed at the speed with which the strafing took place. There was certainly no time to dive for cover as one sees happen in war films. The pattern of bullets streaked across the ground, and you were either already in cover or out of the line of shots. Otherwise, it was too late.

A short distance to our left was the chateau of Le Londel, surrounded by a solid stone wall, with its accompanying farm house, out-buildings and barns. This was reported to be held by the enemy, but on the 10th we were able to walk in, occupy the position and begin to dig in. We could detect signs that the enemy were similarly occupied at the Chateau de la Londe, some 600 yards from us across a field of growing corn.

The enemy position was much more heavily wooded than our own, so that it was impossible to discover any details except by actual penetration of these trees by patrols. To the right of the enemy position, we could see two or three British three-tonners on the road from La Deliverande to Caen. They must have driven straight into the enemy lines.

The enemy were obviously recovering from the shock of the D-Day assault. Shelling and mortaring were increasing, and we could hear the sound of the movement of tracked vehicles in the rear of La Londe from time to time. At first light one morning they brought up a troop of SP guns and shelled my platoon position for several minutes, and then withdrew before a response could be organised. Several of the platoon were killed; the farm buildings, though built of solid stone several feet thick, were reduced to rubble. The area was littered with large pieces of shell-casing, some fragments over an inch thick.

Though the Germans had the advantage of a strong defensive position, the British had the solid support of the Royal Navy. The English Channel was still bristling with big guns, itching for something to shoot at. Lieutenant Colonel Jones describes the naval bombardment known as a Victory Salvo, and the strange effects produced by the fact that the boom of the guns, the flash of light from their muzzles, and the shells themselves, all travelled through the ether at different speeds.

> Brigade HQ was in direct radio contact with HMS *Rodney*. They could call on the ship to engage targets such as enemy artillery positions. Having been harassed by persistent enemy shell-fire, it was a great solace to be told to expect a Victory Salvo. These normally took place at night.
> The sequence of events was somewhat surprising. Over the Channel a great flash, like lightning, would suddenly light up the sky, followed shortly afterwards by a rumble overhead like a tube train emerging from its tunnel. Then would come the sound of explosions from the Channel, and a long pause – long enough for you to say to yourself 'They must be firing rubber shells.' Then, from the direction of Caen, would come a series of loud clumps as the shells landed.

ADC Smith, an intelligence officer with No 1 Commando, happened upon a more refined and playful method of shelling the Germans into a frenzy.

> I remember enjoying a game which I called 'Cookhouse Chasing' or 'Stonk the Sauerkraut'. It started in the summer, when No 1 Commando was holding a part of the line east of the Caen Canal. It was the very brute of a position, with the enemy facing us ensconced in a thick wood called Le Bois de Bavent. This wood provided excellent cover from which to shower upon us a heavy and unpleasant volume of mortar bombs. But further south the battles were going against the Germans. Even in the comparative comfort of their wooded covert their morale was beginning to show signs of deterioration, evidenced by a fairly steady trickle of

deserters through our lines during the hours of darkness.

It was while I was interrogating one of these that the rules of the game came into my mind, not without a certain amount of gleeful satisfaction. It appeared that the German forces opposite us had no regular cookhouses, but relied on a mobile canteen which visited each platoon position in turn at set times each day. My excellent deserter cast all his security training aside in his enthusiasm to boast of the excellence of the cookhouse, and gave me full details of the times and places of its appearances. A short conference with some friendly gunners and the game started. At set times every day certain points in the wood were treated to a liberal dose of high explosives.

A couple of days later another deserter was brought before me with a sorry tale to tell. It appeared that the troops had been without hot food for the last two days and their temper was suffering badly as a result. He painted a most satisfactory picture of the irate Germans arriving hungrily and hopefully at the rendezvous only to find themselves in the middle of an artillery barrage, and to see their beloved cookhouse disappearing at top speed. However, they had altered the times and the rendezvous and the issue of rations was back to normal. Fortunately this second deserter was equally gourmand, and was able to give me details of the new timetable.

And the fun went on – though the prisoners always looked at me as if I was a bit mad when I asked for news of their cookhouse almost before I had asked the usual military questions.

Smith's role led him to feel little more than contempt for the Germans. But some of the fighting infantry developed a good deal of respect for their adversaries as they fought their way through the bocage country.

They also had a cute trick, said US paratrooper RR Hughart, the man who found the draught horse. They'd dig a good-sized hole and drive the tank in it and then cover it all up except just let that turret stick up, which they could swing around 360 degrees with a machine gun and an eighty-eight, or some other good-sized weapon. And they could really make things hot for anybody trying to take that thing out of there.

There was an old saying. I don't know how true it was, but, it went like this: 'When one soldier dug in, it took three to get him out.' And I sure agree, because those Germans, they could really dig themselves in. And they were good professional soldiers.

We were told, over in England, that a German non-com had to know about as much as our company commanders to come up the ranks. Now that was for straight army. I would say the parachute officers were a cut above the rest.

One thing I can say about our officers is they were always up front leading. None of this: a couple of blocks behind, telling some sergeant 'Take your squad and go this way.' Our officers were up front all the time. We lost a lot of good men that way because they were up front and saying 'Follow me.' They led the way and we followed. We'd follow them into hell and back.

At the same time, many officers developed great respect for the men that they led into battle. Major CK King – 'Banger' King as he was known – had cast himself as King Hal and recited Shakespeare to his troops on the way into Sword Beach. A month after D-Day, writing a letter to the mother of his batman, he adopts a more thoughtful tone:

Dear Mrs Blenkhorn,
This is a short note to let you know that your son is fit and well, although very tired like all of us. I keep an eye on him and try and keep him out of trouble if I can. Many of his comrades have not been so fortunate and perhaps this may depress him a little, but we shall get relieved in due course and then a week or so behind the line will set him right. We have been fighting the toughest troops in the German Army – Panzers – and a few days ago they beat it. They had had enough. But it has been a long and bitter fight.

I cannot express too deeply my admiration for the men I have been commanding. When we landed at H-Hour on D-Day they went straight in over the beaches in spite of murderous fire and in half an hour had cleared a gap about 200 yards wide in the German defences through which poured the reserve company's commandos – and about half the British Army. We were the first to land – and there can't be many men in the Allied armies who got there before your son, as he followed me out of the boat and we were the first to touch down on our beach. After making the gap, we swung to the right and mopped up various machine-gun nests and a 50mm gun. Afterwards we went inland and attacked a strongly held German position which we captured with the aid of two other companies – plus three cases of champagne which, alas, were drunk by another company.

We have been fighting ever since – at least we have been in the line since D-Day, and recently the battalion attacked and captured a strong German position after two other attacks had failed. The war seems to be going pretty well according to plan as far as I can see – if it continues to do so we shall be home for Christmas if not sooner. I think myself that the Huns will suddenly crack – and the harder the fighting now, the quicker the end will be. Many of the prisoners we have taken are only too pleased to be out of it and have no confidence in the future. The Germans now have only very limited reserves. When they use these up there are no more. It is better that they should use them up now.

In a later letter to Mrs Blenkhorn, after her son is wounded, Major King goes further. No longer does he see himself as a commander leading his troops into battle; he is a father taking the best care that he can of his adopted children.

> Dear Mrs Blenkhorn,
> I hope you are not worrying too much about your son. As a bachelor, I haven't any family worries, but I feel that it's up to me to get as many of my company through this business as I can. The men take the place of a family in my estimation. I have never cared very much what the higher authorities think (which is probably why I'm only a major!) and you can be sure that I won't lead your son or any of my company into any damn suicide act. We are a very happy company – and quite efficient too, which is the best protection your son could have.

Major King's expectation that German resistance would collapse was, of course, wishful thinking. Once the second-rate foreign and elderly troops

Artillerymen lob shells from a 155mm howitzer towards the German lines near Caen. These guns could cause immense carnage. Reconnaissance vehicles sent out to observe their effect had to be washed down with disinfectant to remove the human and animal remains.

on the Atlantic Wall had been mopped up, the British came up against keener, younger opposition. Frank Rosier of the Gloucester Regiment was on patrol when his unit saw some Germans marching towards them:

> They looked like helmets on matchstick legs – they were boys. The officer said 'Open fire.' Someone said 'Sir, they are children.' 'Never mind that,' he said, 'their bullets will still kill you.' So we opened fire, and afterwards we went up to them. Some of the wounded lay there and spat at us. They were fourteen years old at most.

Lieutenant-Colonel Jones also found that the going got harder after D-Day. 'The battalion now entered upon what was to prove for them the grimmest phase of all the fighting in north-west Europe,' he said, speaking of the last weeks of June and the first weeks of July 1944.

In a sense the landing on D-Day had been easier than anticipated and the casualties lighter. It had not been expected that the battalion would emerge from D-Day still a viable fighting unit, and it had! Some of the subsequent fighting, in the flooded areas of Holland with their multitude of anti-personnel mines, or as we first set foot on German soil, was nastier. But the La Londe battles were the most harrowing. Most of the original battalion officers still with their companies, and many of the longer-serving men, were lost there. The battalion was never really the same again.

We had been trained in the tactics of right and left flanking movements, but here there were no flanks and the enemy had to be reached by direct approach across open cornfields – some of the older officers prophesied a stalemate and a repeat of the trench warfare of World War I.

It is surprising how isolated the infantryman in the forefront of the close-contact battle can become. The listeners to the BBC News at home probably knew more of the overall strategic picture than we did.

Shelling and mortaring of the Le Londel area intensified, with little respite. The enemy, too, were subjected to heavy shelling by our own artillery, but when these ended they would reply with long bursts of automatic fire, as if to show their indifference and invulnerability.

THE BATTLE OF THE TANKS

It wasn't just the fighting spirit of the Germans that was good. In many respects they had the better equipment. German tanks in particular were better protected and more heavily armed than British or American ones (something which was a source of bitter resentment to British tank commanders). Shermans would explode or catch fire after a single hit – the Germans called them 'frying kettles', and the British, with their usual gallows humour, dubbed them 'Ronsons' after the cigarette lighter.

The Tiger tank was especially feared. Anti-tank rounds would bounce off Tigers like tennis balls. Later in the campaign there was worried talk in high military circles of Allied troops developing 'Tiger psychosis'. But the fears were well-founded: at 60 tons the Tiger was almost twice as weighty as a Sherman; it could travel much faster, and it packed a bigger gun: the hated 88mm that had rained such terror on the beaches. One day early on in the campaign, US paratrooper RR Hughart got a chance to take a close look at an intact Tiger tank and its interesting contents.

> We saw these huge tank tracks alongside of a field. We followed them and they were the biggest, widest tank tracks we'd ever seen. They went into a woods to a little pathway and came out into another field – and there the thing sat.
>
> The top turret was open and the other two turrets, for the driver and the assistant driver, were open. And we couldn't see where the tank was damaged at all. There was no sign of the crew. There was about four or five real small suitcases opened up on the ground and somebody had pulled out women's undergarments, brassieres, silk panties. There was a bunch of letters written in German and in French, and a whole bunch of dirty French postcards with naked women and things like that.
>
> We inspected that tank pretty good and couldn't see what the heck happened to it. We didn't know how to check the fuel on it, so we figured that it had probably ran out of fuel and the crew abandoned it. Why they didn't take their personal effects, I don't know. But I'm telling you that when we first saw them tracks, it put a little fear into us because paratroopers can't do too much against great big German tanks like that.

Austin Baker, by contrast, saw at first hand the kind of mess that German firepower was capable of making of a British tank.

> A brewed-up tank is always a grim sight – the outside is usually a dull, dirty rust colour, and the inside is a blackened shambles. There is a queer, indescribable smell. The bottom of Jonah's tank had been blown right out, and we could peer inside from underneath. There was no trace of anybody in the turret, but there was some stuff in the driving seat that must have been Walker. There was a body on the ground by the left-hand track. Somebody had thrown a groundsheet over it, but we lifted it off. It was probably Brigham Young, but it was impossible to recognise him. He was burnt quite black all over, and only parts

of his webbing anklets remained of his clothes. Nobody ever found any sign of Wally. Nick Wide's tank, also burnt out, was standing on its nose on the station platform. Jock Burn and Tubby Edwards were buried beside it.

In this situation, tank regiments began to experiment with ways of reinforcing their armour. The ARV (Armoured Recovery Vehicle) was sent out to cannibalize knocked-out tanks and bring their tracks back to base. Baker noted in his diary . . .

> . . . The reason for this was that in A Squadron's last battle, one of the tanks had been hit by an SP and, amazingly enough, had not been knocked out. Some lengths of track had been welded to the front as an experiment, and the shot had shattered them but failed to penetrate the armour underneath. After this it was decided to weld track plates all over the front of every tank in the regiment, and we never went into action without this additional protection, but it wasn't nearly as effective as had been hoped.

A more successful piece of tank customization was dreamed up by an American sergeant named Cullin. A man after Percy Hobart's own heart, he had the idea of cutting up the mass of German 'hedgehog' girders on the beach and welding them on the front of tanks in rows of sharp metal 'shears'. These shark's-tooth accessories made it possible for tanks to cut through hedgerows quickly – with the result that the tanks were less likely to become stationary targets for German bazookas, and also that there were more gaps through which infantry could advance. 'I remember that little staff sergeant,' said Alfred Allred. 'His idea worked. It pulled that tank down instead of it rearing up. General Bradley really loved that.'

Both sides learned that the key to tank warfare in the bocage was close cooperation with the infantry. 'Tanks against infantry will lose,' said Private Frank Rosier. 'Or at least if you kept cavey, they couldn't find you. But if you encountered tanks with infantry it was a different ball game, because you can't hide from them.' Sergeant Mackenzie came up against this deadly combination, and was saved by a visitation from the air.

> It was learnt that a couple of Tiger tanks along with about one hundred infantrymen had been bypassed by our forward troops,

and were dug in a wood a few hundred yards up the road. The three tanks attached to headquarters had got up, but two of them were 'brewed up'.

Apart from our own personal arms, we had nothing. We expected them to attack us that night, so every man slept with his weapon and ammo, ready for a do! I didn't mind the infantry, but tanks! You can't knock them out with personal-arms fire. Went to bed resigned to the fact that we would be for it. An hour later, twelve rocket-firing Typhoons came over, the first time we had seen them in action. What a sight, what a terror. They got those tanks all right.

The Typhoons were by far the most effective weapon against German tanks. Faced with a prowling Tiger, forward infantry would summon a 'Tiffer' on the radio, and greeted its arrival with awestruck gratitude, as if it were an angel from above.

We could see three Panzers and a Tiger coming our way, said Frank Rosier. As the Typhoons came in the Germans jumped out and ran for it.

MEETING THE ENEMY

Most Allied soldiers could not find much to say to their prisoners. They left the talking to their intelligence officers. But the endlessly curious paratrooper RR Hughart seems to be one of the few Allied soldiers who was willing to chat to Germans as well as shoot at them. On one occasion he became embroiled in a discussion with a prisoner about New York. The conversation told him a great deal about the Nazi propaganda machine.

I would say this prisoner was probably in his late forties or fifties. Being twenty-three, I thought he was an old, old man. He had lived in New York City for a long time. He spoke real good English. He asked me about where I'd left the States from. And I told him I'd been in Camp Shanks and then went down to the New York port. 'Oh,' he says, 'there isn't much left of New York any more, is there?' I say 'What do you mean?'

'Well,' he says, 'you know its been bombed by the Luftwaffe bombers.' I say 'Really?'

He says, 'Why sure – are you sure that's where you left from?' I say, 'Why yeah, now how do you know it was bombed?'

'Well,' he says, 'they showed us pictures.' I say, 'Come on off that. Now you know that it's a long way from Germany to New York, right?'

He says, 'Oh yeah, I remember.' So I asked, 'Well how far do you think it is?'

He says, 'Well, it's probably about three thousand miles.' 'So,' I say, 'now figure this out. For a bomber to leave Germany and go over to New York is three thousand miles, right? Then it's got to turn around and go back to Germany. That's six thousand miles. Now you know that your guys, our guys and the English and nobody else has got a bomber that's gonna go six thousand miles round trip without refuelling.'

Well, that kind of stumped him for a while. 'Well,' he says, 'Hitler's got a secret way of refuelling the bombers mid-flight.'

I said, 'You believe that?'

'Oh yeah,' he says, 'Hitler's got a lot of secret weapons and we're gonna win the war.' I said, 'Well, maybe you're gonna win it, but you sure haven't been doing much to convince me and my buddies about it.'

Well, I couldn't convince him that it was an impossibility. Goes to show you that if you tell somebody a big enough lie, and show them some fake pictures and keep showing it to them, then no matter how smart he is, he's going to really believe it. I guess seeing is believing.

I don't know how they fake those pictures. Maybe they took some pictures of some seaport in Europe that the Luftwaffe flattened and told the poor people 'This is New York.'

In the early days of the campaign, prisoners were seen as exotic, and treacherous as cobras. Army doctor Captain Richard Fahey had an edgy encounter with German POWs on D+1 as he was carrying a wounded man back to the field hospital near the beach.

The shooting had quieted down by this time, and we suddenly found ourselves carrying the stretcher bravely right into the midst of hundreds of Germans who had come out in the open to surrender. We felt very uneasy as they parted to let us walk through, but of course we gave them no indication of our fear.

Nicholas Butrico of the 5th Ranger Battalion was also given a fright by a shiftless gaggle of prisoners.

> We were taking a group down at night. There must have been about a hundred. We were walking on the sand. A couple of them were pretty old, but not old where they couldn't still fight or shoot at me, that's the way I look at it.
>
> They couldn't keep up, so the sergeant says to me, 'Nick, stay behind. We'll wait for you near the stockade.' So, I stood behind with these three prisoners. It was dark, and as I was walking I fell in one of these big shell holes. And before you know it, these three Germans jump into the same hole with me. 'Jesus, they're going to kill me now!' But the funny thing is, they picked me up, they cleaned the sand off of me, they cleaned the gun, and they handed it back to me.

As the Allied troops became more used to fighting, they became less afraid of the men who had given up the fight. In the first week, Germans were shot trying to surrender, or even after they had been disarmed. The rules of war reasserted themselves – and sometimes a little human kindness crept in – as the campaign progressed.

> On one occasion the arrival of a deserter was reported to me at Brigade Headquarters, said ADC Smith of No 1 Commando. I instructed the unit to send him back to me as soon as possible, but after waiting nearly half an hour there was still no sign of the prisoner and I phoned for an explanation of the delay, imagining that he must have escaped on the way. I was told, rather severely I thought, that 'he seemed rather nervous so he was being given a cup of tea.'

For some soldiers, especially American airborne troops it seems, any kind of close encounter with Germans was seen as an opportunity to pick up a memento of their time in France. Some men took the business of souvenir hunting too far.

I had a good friend by the name of Travis Ramsey, said RR Hughart. He was from Texas and he was a cut-up. He could think of some of the most screwball things to do. Well, I remember we were in this building in Sainte Mère Eglise. Some German officers had been living in this building, and we were going from room to room and going through all the stuff that they had left. And Ramsey says, 'I'm going to check that last room way down at the end.' I say, 'OK.'

I could hear him fussing around down there. Then things got kind of quiet. And, maybe ten minutes later I came out of this room and I heard a noise at the end of the hallway. And there stood a German officer in a class A uniform: boots, ribbons and everything. I raised my rifle to shoot and I heard the voice of Ramsey. He fell on the floor and called, 'Don't shoot, don't shoot, it's me, it's me.'

I said to him 'You damn fool, you don't know how close you come to getting killed.' 'Well,' he said, 'I looked in the mirror and I thought I was a pretty handsome fellow.' I said 'Get that damn uniform off quick before somebody else sees you and puts some bullets in you!'

It was good advice. Some soldiers were so utterly incensed by their experiences on the beaches that the rules of war no longer applied. For them, the Geneva Convention had expired with their buddies on Omaha Beach, and they were now ready to kill any Germans – wounded ones, surrendered ones, captured ones. Anything in a German uniform was a legitimate target.

I could see the soldiers coming over the hill down the beach at twilight, said Ray Voight. I said 'What? The troops are coming back!' And someone said 'No, they're all German prisoners.' So I took the gun I had on the beach there and opened up. It was a carbine. I opened up with it. I must have shot about four shots and the guy hollered to me to stop, because they had guards walking with them, and it was dark. I could have shot the guards too. But I was out of control. I just couldn't understand anybody taking prisoners when we had so much to do, and all the room we had was for our wounded. We couldn't be taking prisoners on the ships until we got our own wounded back and taken care of. That was our primary purpose, not to fool around taking prisoners. Not after that slaughter.

Ted Billnitzer of the US Navy spent the first five days of the invasion ferrying prisoners out to the fleet. He was himself born of German parents – his father was a Lutheran preacher – and perhaps this made it easier for him to see the man inside the Nazi uniform.

> I was patching here, giving shots, relieving pain, bandaging, splinting, and helping with minor surgery. Being able to speak German, I interviewed prisoners. I really felt sorry for Hitler's older troops – 45 years and beyond – who wanted no part of the war. We went on the beach to bring back some of the German officers, who were always saluting us.
>
> The upper crust of Hitler's army never gave out and admitted anything, in contrast to the older wounded captives who were usually conscripted into the German army. When captured, they would say '*Lass mich gehen, lass mich gehen, ich habe keine Amerikaner geschossen*' – 'Let me go, let me go, I have never shot an American.'

10
OUT OF NORMANDY

Churchill once remarked of General Montgomery's earlier encounter with Rommel that 'before Alamein we never had a victory, after Alamein we never had a defeat.' This implies that Monty's campaign in Normandy was a straightforward triumphal progress: victory following on victory as the Germans fell back. In fact, Montgomery's conduct of the campaign damaged his reputation as a commander, and strained relations with the Americans to breaking point.

The crux of the bad feeling between the Allies was Caen. Montgomery had promised to take it on D-Day itself, but six weeks later the British and Canadians were still dug in outside the town. To the Americans, pushing hard towards the seaport of Cherbourg, the stand-off at Caen looked like unforgivable timidity on Montgomery's part.

To end the stalemate, it was decreed that the city where William the Conqueror was born, and where his bones rested in the ancient cathedral, would have to be bombed to rubble. Colette Pilot, a young girl whose family ran a hotel in Caen, witnessed the first phase of the operation.

> The bombs are dropping closer and closer. My grandfather gets hold of a huge beam which has lain on the floor for years and props it up to the ceiling for extra support.
>
> The noise is deafening, I bury my head in my lap, closing my eyes tightly. The earth is trembling, my teeth chattering. Things fly in the air. I keep telling myself that as long as we can hear the whistle followed by the explosion of the bombs, we are safe. You wouldn't hear the one that hit you. Eventually the noise diminishes and then stops. There's dust everywhere, in my mouth, in my eyes. How could it be when they were so tightly shut?
>
> It's time to see the damage. We climb up to the ground floor. At least the walls are still around us but all the windows are

broken. Debris, glass and dust cover the floor and the furniture. My tropical fish are all right in their aquarium but the two cats have disappeared – they must be hiding, poor things. We don't give a second thought to the chickens and the rabbits in the courtyard. There's no time to think of animals. My grandmother, who is terribly houseproud, is almost in tears. 'It will take weeks to clean up this mess!' she says.

Grandfather takes hold of a yard broom and starts sweeping the pavement. I go on collecting more shell splinters, but there are so many, soon my bag is full. It's no fun anymore. My mother is almost frantic. 'You must all be mad, cleaning and sweeping,' she cries out. 'Can't you see that if we stay here any longer we will all be killed? We must go quickly while there's a lull. Come on, I beg you.'

'You go with Colette if that makes you happy,' replies grandfather, 'but I will stay with your mother. We can't leave, who would look after the hotel?'

Mummy and I go back in the cellar, this time to collect our bicycles which are stored there, we take them up and lean them against the wall in the hall. If we have to leave on our own we will ride to Fleury. Mummy is still not happy about it and once more she asks my grandparents to come. The argument does not last very long as a third attack forces us back to the shelter. The noise is unbearable, everything is vibrating, we hear masonry falling. We fear the hotel is hit, but how badly? We seem to be in the cellar for an eternity and when at last we go upstairs we know we can't stay any longer.

The house across the road is no more, the one next door but one is just a pile of rubble. We have been lucky; the hotel did not get a direct hit, but there are many gaping holes, doors blown off their hinges. Our bedroom is unrecognisable. The window is just a gaping hole with torn net curtains. My toys have been thrown all over the floor. The wardrobe is badly damaged, the mirror shattered; it does not look like the same piece of furniture, and I stand there for a while looking at it. This wardrobe containing so many treasures, where my mother keeps the lovely trousseau she embroidered herself. All my communion presents are safely put away on one shelf.

The assault on Caen was preceded by a 500-bomber air-raid. British and Canadian infantry then advanced through the rubble. The Allies had arranged civilian 'refuges' in the city, areas which were not to be bombed. But hundreds of French people were killed in the battle.

Fleury is a village on the outskirts of Caen, by the River Orne. It is well known for its huge caves in which mushrooms are cultivated. My mother and I walked this distance many times in the summer. It has always been a most pleasant outing.

Today, however, it is different. When we reach the top of our road and cross the rue Saint Jean we realise how lucky we have been until now. So many houses are destroyed. The house where my school friend lives is no more, nor is the newsagent's where we bought our daily papers. What happened to the people living there, are they dead? Are they buried alive?

The noise of the bombing goes on and on and the darkness never comes. The sky is lighted up by the burning fire. The colours around us are unbelievable: red, orange and gold. No fireworks could equal such brightness. No one can survive this hell . . .

Hundreds of civilians were indeed killed in the bombing of Caen, but so were many German combatants. On the morning of 18 July, 5,650 tons of bombs were dropped on German forward positions in the space of forty-five minutes. The survivors were in no state to fight, choked as they were with dust, dizzy with concussion, thoroughly deafened and defeated. The Canadians and the British took possession of a ghost town.

Meanwhile, the Americans pushed south through the Cotentin peninsula, trying to get out of the bocage and into easier fighting country. To do this they had to take the town of St Lô. The battle for the town lasted for a week, and as at Caen, was accompanied by heavy aerial bombardment.

> **I've never seen so many planes in all my life**, said Alfred Allred. **They had B-17s, B-24s, British Lancasters, Mustang 51s, P-38s. They were intended to strafe the Germans if they ever hit the road. They got hit pretty hard.**
>
> The Germans were on the run. When we tore up that 7th Army down there at St Lô, they didn't have any resistance. I've seen a lot of gruesome things that I don't even like to talk about. We just killed so many of them and wounded them. You could walk for a quarter of a mile without setting your foot on the ground for the dead Germans and horses. Absolutely, that's the God's truth. Especially horses. I've seen horses and Germans lying and bleeding to death and dying.

THE UNEQUAL STRUGGLE

On 15 July, Field Marshall Rommel had remarked that 'the unequal struggle is drawing to a close.' Two days later, Rommel was making his way back from a visit to the front when his staff car was strafed on the road by two Allied aircraft. The car skidded off the highway and crashed into a tree. Rommel was thrown clear on to the roadway, and was found some yards behind the wreckage of his car. He was badly wounded. He had been struck by shrapnel in his cheek and temple and he was bleeding profusely from the mouth. He was taken unconscious to the nearest village – which by a peculiar irony of war was called Sainte Foy de Montgomery.

By the end of July the Allies were in possession of the entire Cotentin peninsula, a vast equilateral triangle bounded by the Bay of the Seine in the north and the Gulf of St Malo to the east. The Allied front, the third side of the triangle, ran between these two seas – from Avranches to Ouistreham.

Now the Americans broke out to the left and right. One army sped towards the westerly port of Brest; another worked its way around the back of the German armies defending the Normandy front and moved little by little towards Paris.

The German 7th Army, situated in the space between Vire and Falaise, was now almost surrounded. The British and Canadians were in front of them, and the Americans were at their rear. They could withdraw, or they could make a stand. They decided to make a stand, and so hold up the British advance as long as possible. This was the battle for the 'Falaise pocket', and it was a bitter struggle. The Germans fought like men with nothing left to lose.

What a slaughter, noted Sergeant Mackenzie of the Royal Engineers. Nothing but Jerries and tanks and vehicles and guns all smashed up. Graves of Canadians all the way up. Horrible stench of death. We had just entered a leaguer when, whoosh, we are being shelled, nothing we can do about it as we haven't had time to dig in. Only about a dozen shells come over, but one unluckily falls among a group of Royal Engineers, killing five. Later on some small-arms firing, bullets whizzing just over our heads. Probably a small pocket still to be mopped up.

Investigate cause of smell, find ten horses dead in wood and German gun crew dead at their gun. German prisoners are brought in to bury their dead. Have an uneasy feeling at night, so has George. I doze off, but George lays on his bed fully dressed. Then it happened. Jerry comes over and drops flares right over our heads. This is it: George runs to the wood where he knows of a dug out. I had to put my boots on, and am well behind him and lose sight of him. I run into wood with another chap and crouch by a wall, while Jerry just circles round and drops more flares and sprays the place with machine-gun fire.

I have got the wind up. The place is like daylight and you feel so naked and helpless. Then Jerry drops a green flare, which is his OK for the bombers to come in. The next twenty minutes I am digging my nose nearer. There are terrific explosions in the distance. Jerry goes away. He has hit some petrol and ammo dumps quite a distance away from us and the flares and explosions go on all night. Next day I dig a deep slit trench.

We are moved back to the central sector again and are not
sorry. The Falaise gap is practically finished now and we are in
front of it. We are given a brief talk by our colonel. Our next job
is to cross the Seine, and flog on into Belgium and Holland.

The gap was finally closed on 21 August. Two days before, a full-scale
uprising had broken out in Paris. The people had decided not to wait for
the Allied armies to liberate them, but to take back their freedom
themselves. Hitler gave orders for the revolt to be suppressed, and added
that Paris must not be allowed to fall into Allied hands 'except as a field of
ruins.' The commander of the German garrison in Paris, Lieutenant-
General Dietrich von Choltitz, chose to ignore this order – and covered up
his insubordination by telling his superior officer that Notre Dame, the
Arc de Triomphe and the Eiffel Tower were mined and ready to blow.

Von Choltitz told his little lie in the knowledge the war was lost. And in
any case, he had enough trouble on his hands. In a venerable Parisian
tradition, stretching back through the Commune of 1871 to the
revolutions of 1848 and 1789, the people of the French capital had thrown
up barricades and fought. Now they were attacking the German garrison
with any weapons they could lay their hands on.

The street war continued until the Allies arrived on 25 August – and for
a while afterwards. A French armoured column rolled triumphantly into
the city that morning, and met up with the US 12th Infantry Regiment
coming from a different direction. General de Gaulle paraded down the
Champs Elysées the next day, while the last Germans and collaborators
sniped at him from the Bois de Boulogne.

Hitler, on hearing the news that the garrison had withdrawn, asked
laconically 'Brennt Paris?' – 'Is Paris burning?' – and was disappointed to
be told that it wasn't. Everyone else was very pleased that the city had come
through the war undamaged, not least the American soldiers who now had
the chance to spend some happy time there.

We got into Paris, went by the Eiffel Tower and the Arc de
Triomphe, said US artilleryman Alfred Allred. The French girls,
beautiful girls, some of them – those girls were climbing all
over us, and giving us flowers. Some of those girls had the
most beautiful teeth. They must have been getting good food
somewhere. Some of them were even wearing make-up.

The war rumbled on after Paris and for almost eleven months more. The fighting and destruction persisted, and people continued to die – bravely, tragically, sometimes needlessly. Jeffrey Ashton was a British army medic. Here are some extracts from his diary for the week after the liberation of the French capital.

Sept 1st – Friday. Fine sunny periods – strong breeze.
Young soldier brought in this a.m. Accidentally shot by rifle which went off as his friend was 'easing springs'. Bullet penetrated chest and man died short time after admission, in spite of blood transfusion, etc. He had been married only six weeks, had spent five days only with his wife, and had been in France just eight days.

Sept 2nd – Saturday. Full moon. Cold high wind.
Had party of French people brought in, victims of bad road accident. One girl aged twenty-two dead, two men various injuries not serious – but created great fuss with their constant cries of 'Mon Dieu, Mon Dieu,' etc – also young boy and elderly lady shocked. This old lady asked me to help her off with her stays which by signs she indicated were pretty tight – when I saw the massive strips of metal in the stays I realized why she had escaped serious injury – a medieval knight would have coveted them.

Sept 3rd – Sunday. Fine sunny – breezy.
Had busy day – two more civilian accident cases treated and despatched to civilian hospital in Caen. Loaded Sapper Bracken on ambulance and saw him off to Bayeux. Major Davies – surgeon who operated on him – doubts if he will survive journey. His kidneys refuse to excrete urine. Will no doubt die of uraemia. Everybody busy on striking canvas and packing up ready for another move. Took canvas and linen back to their site at Falaise. Saw the remains of the town destroyed by bombers and artillery. Terrible sight, worse than Caen.

Sept 4th – Monday. Fine sunny, breezy.
Up 06.15 hrs. Breakfast 07.00. Personnel tentage struck and stowed aboard lorries by 08.00 hrs. Men paraded and allotted

lorries and ambulances and off we went – this time to Dieppe, just liberated by Canadian 1st Division. Interesting journey. Passed through many wrecked villages surrounded by bomb craters and dead cows.

Saw a few 'killed' tanks (German) and remains of lorries blasted by RAF when Germans were retreating towards Seine. Passed through Lisieux – terribly battered, but famous cathedral intact. As we passed these newly liberated towns and villages people lined streets to cheer the convoy – and beg for cigarettes which were thrown to them by the lads from backs of lorries. Crossed River Seine at Elboef. River seemed wide here about 150 yards – Reseve Bridge wonderful example of Bailey Bridging. Rouen was in a terrible mess – RAF had bombed it.

Doctor Ashton was still hard at work when the year of liberation tick-tocked into the year that (as everyone knew by now) would see the hard-won victory. Celebrating Christmas in liberated France, still in the midst of war, Ashton and his comrades scraped together some good cheer and hope for the future – along with the makings of a pretty decent Yuletide dinner.

December 25th – Christmas Day. Hard frost, bright, sunny. Each patient received 6 cigars, 50 cigarettes, 2 boxes matches and 2 bars chocolate. Dinner consisted of five courses – (1) Soup, (2) Red Salmon (tinned), (3) Turkey, Pork chop, 1-inch thick, and baked potatoes, stuffing, Brussels sprouts, gravy, (4) Sliced peaches with evaporated milk, (5) Xmas pudding with rum flavoured custard, (6) Tea. Where all these 'sick' men found such sudden healthy appetites beat me.

Unit had same fare in men's dining hall. Commanding officer gave speech and was constantly interrupted by Private Rawlings who was very drunk – much to everybody's amusement. The major reviewed briefly our ups and downs since we landed and hoped we would continue to do well, etc, etc. Lance Corporal Duxbury rose to reply amid thunderous cheers from the lads. In evening Corporal Ashton and Private Woods came over to mess and cheered things up. Wilf played piano and Jimmy strummed a guitar – good evening.

December 31st – Sunday. Sleet, hail – cold.
Unit entertained about 240 French children accompanied by
fond mothers. After tea (children served by the men) a show was
put on, much to children's delight. Corporal Stewart dressed as
Father Xmas gave each child 2 bars choc (given by men from
weekly ration). In evening unit gave a dance for local French
people – well attended. Heard a cannon-firing aircraft about
midnight – heard it dive twice and then it flew off.

Jan 1st – Monday. Mild, cloudy.
Last night's aircraft I heard killed two or three men and injured
others in some lorries on the St Omer–Devres road. Injured men
brought into our MI Room and transferred to General Hospital
by ambulance. Much blood on MI Room floor: must have been
bad injuries. Aircraft was a German – road strafing.
   Part 1 orders causing much comment – men are wanted for
Far Eastern service – volunteers to hand in names by 09.00 hrs
tomorrow. If no volunteers are forthcoming CO will choose men
himself.

Jan 2nd – Tuesday. Mild – dull.
CO published the names of the men for Burma – Clegg,
Hempstock, Haywood, Rottenburg, Moreton, Neal, Coppin,
Scopes, Scarlett, Newman. Everybody feels very sorry for these
lads, but mighty relieved at same time that they haven't got to go.

Jan 8th – Monday. Very cold – dull – windy.
Men for Far East left today.

The men who drew the short straw for Burma had eight months of hard
fighting ahead of them. For those who remained in Europe, it all came to
an end sooner: Germany surrendered on 8 May 1945.
   Among the American, British and Canadian soldiers who were still in
Europe when victory came, there were many who had fought all the way
from the beaches of Normandy: from Utah, Omaha, Gold, Juno and
Sword, through the bocage, on into Belgium and the Netherlands, over the
Rhine into Germany itself. And there were the many, many thousands who
fought on the beaches, but did not live to tell their story.

Ernie Snow was one of the men who made it through to the end. He was a USAAF mechanic, and he was working at an airbase at St Dizier, France, when he heard the news that the Germans had surrendered.

The boys were all celebrating. I had a big flare gun. I was going to shoot the thing, but I handed it to a friend and, son of a gun, he fired it – right straight up in the air. And boy, we could hear that executive officer come a-running. But then he said 'Ah, to hell with it. Let them kill themselves. The war is over.' A fine fellow, really.

CHRONOLOGY

3 September 1939 Britain declares war on Germany.

10 May 1940 Germany invades France, Belgium and the Netherlands. Winston Churchill is appointed prime minister of a National Government.

26 May–4 June 1940 The British Expeditionary Force is driven out of France by advancing Germans. 250,000 men are evacuated via Dunkirk, among them General Montgomery.

July 1940 Britain braces itself for invasion.

August 1940 The Luftwaffe fights the RAF for control of the skies as a prelude to the invasion of Britain.

September 1940 The 'Battle of Britain' ends, and the blitz of British cities begins. Hitler postpones the invasion of Britain and orders the construction of the 'Atlantic Wall', a defensive line to stretch along the coast from Norway to the Spanish border.

March 1941 The Lend-Lease Act is passed in America. President Roosevelt pledges material support for Britain's war effort.

21 June 1941 Germany invades the Soviet Union, violating the treaty of non-aggression between the two countries.

7 December 1941 Japan attacks the American naval base at Pearl Harbor, Hawaii. Hitler declares war on the USA.

June 1942 General Eisenhower goes to Britain to orchestrate the build-up of American forces there.

October 1942 General Montgomery launches an offensive against Field Marshal Erwin Rommel at El Alamein. The Germans are slowly pushed back.

8 November 1942 General Eisenhower commands the American landings in North Africa.

January 1943 Russian troops destroy the German army at Stalingrad and begin to advance west. Churchill and Roosevelt meet in Casablanca to discuss the opening of a 'second front' in Europe. The COSSAC group is given the job of formulating a plan.

May 1943 German forces are routed in Africa.

June 1943 Normandy is chosen as the landing ground for the planned invasion.

10 July 1943 Allied forces land in Sicily.

August 1943 The invasion of France is given the codename 'Overlord'.

December 1943 Eisenhower is appointed Supreme Allied Commander for Operation Overlord.

January 1944 General Montgomery is appointed commander of land forces for the invasion. He substantially alters the plan to increase its size and scope. A rapid build-up of *matériel* and intense training of troops takes place over the next three months.

8 May 1944 The countdown begins when 5 June is selected as D-Day.

15 May 1944 Montgomery gives a final presentation of the invasion plan.

23 May 1944 Training of the troops comes to an end, embarkation camps are sealed, and briefings begin.

1 June 1944 Embarkation of the invasion force gets under way.

4 June 1944 With many troops already aboard ship, and some ships already under steam, Eisenhower postpones the invasion because of storms in the English Channel.

5 June 1944 Eisenhower is told there is a chance of a short lull in the bad weather, and gives the order for the invasion to go ahead the following day.

6 June 1944 D-Day. The Allied armies land in Normandy.

7 June 1944 Bayeux falls as the Germans retreat from the town. The first sections of the Mulberry harbour depart for Normandy.

8 June 1944 British troops from Gold Beach link up with Americans from Omaha.

9 June 1944 Troops from Omaha Beach link up with troops of the American 4th Division from Utah.

18 June 1944 A great storm hits the Normandy coast. It rages for three days and wrecks the new Mulberry harbour off Omaha Beach.

27 June 1944 American troops take Cherbourg, but the port has been thoroughly destroyed by the retreating Germans.

10 July 1944 British and Canadian forces take Caen after bitter fighting and aerial bombardment.

17 July 1944 Rommel is badly wounded in an air attack.

30 July 1944 American forces break out of the Cotentin peninsula.

17 August 1944 German forces begin to retreat from the 'Falaise pocket'.

21 August 1944 The Falaise pocket is closed.

25 August 1944 Paris falls to the Allies.

12 September 1944 American 1st Army crosses the German frontier near Eupen.

16–25 December 1944 Germans counter-attack against thinly-held lines in the 'Battle of the Bulge'.

7 March 1945 American forces cross the Rhine.

25 April 1945 American and Soviet forces meet on the Elbe.

8 May 1945 Germany formally capitulates. Victory in Europe is declared.

GLOSSARY

All American Nickname of the US 82nd Airborne Division

ARV Armoured Recovery Vehicle. Sherman tank fitted with rescue and repair equipment

AVRE Army Vehicle Royal Engineers. A more formal term for some of Hobart's 'funnies'

Battalion Infantry unit of between 600 and 1,000 men

BAR Browning Automatic Rifle, the standard squad weapon for the US Army

Berlin Bitch The voice of the Germany's English-language radio broadcasts. Known more politely as 'Axis Sally'

Brigade British Army unit usually consisting of three battalions

C-47 American aircraft used for parachute drops and as a glider tug. Also known as a 'Dakota'

CIGS Chief of the Imperial General Staff

CO Commanding Officer

COSSAC Chief of Staff to Supreme Allied Commander

CSM Colour Sergeant Major

Czech hedgehog German beach obstacle consisting of sections of railway track welded together

CP Command Post

Dakota Alternative name for the C-47 transport aircraft

DD tank Duplex Drive tank, a swimming tank equipped with two boat screws. Also known as a 'Donald Duck'

Division Large army unit consisting of between 12,000 and 18,000 men

DUKW Amphibious truck, known as a 'Duck'

DZ Drop zone (for paratroopers)

E-boat Allied term for German motor torpedo boat

Element C Large, fence-like structures used as beach obstacles. Also known as 'Belgian gates'

Eighty-eight Allied term for a German 88mm anti-aircraft gun. It was used to great effect against tanks as well as planes, and against advancing infantry on the beaches

ENSA Entertainments National Service Association, the organization that arranged morale-boosting concerts for British servicemen

Hamilcar Large glider, capable of carrying a small tank

Horsa British troop-carrying glider

HE High Explosive

Higgins boat The standard American beach landing craft. Officially known as an LCVP

K-ration US compact meal (and cigarettes), issued for battlefield conditions

LCA Landing Craft Assault. It carried about 30 troops

LCG Landing Craft Gun. It was equipped with 120mm and 20mm guns

LCI Landing Craft Infantry. It was 75 metres (300ft) long, and accommodated 200 assault troops

LCT Landing Craft Tank. Flat-bottomed craft capable of holding four to eight tanks

LCT (R) Landing Craft Tank (Rocket). British landing craft armed with 5-inch barrage rockets

LCVP Landing Craft Vehicle and Personnel. The American model for the LCA, also known as a 'Higgins boat'. It carried about 30 troops

Lee-Enfield Standard British rifle

LSI Landing Ship, Infantry. A sea-going troop ship that came in various sizes. The largest carried about 1,400 troops and 24 LCAs, the smallest about 200 troops and 8 LCAs.

LST Landing Ship Tank. An LST was a ship of about a hundred metres in length with opening bow doors. It Could hold about 20 tanks

Luger German service pistol

M-1 American service rifle

MG-42 A German machine gun. Known to the Allies as a 'Spandau'

MP Military Policeman

NAAFI Navy, Army and Air Force Institutes. British army jargon for a canteen

NCO Non-commissioned officer

Nebelwerfer German mortar with six barrels. Known to the Allies as a 'Screaming Mimi'

OP Observation Post

Osttruppen 'East troops'. The German term for captured Soviet and East European soldiers conscripted into the German army

P-38 US fighter-bomber

PIAT Projector Infantry Anti-Tank, a British hand-held anti-tank weapon similar to a bazooka

PIR US Parachute Infantry Regiment

PLUTO 'Pipeline Under The Ocean' – an oil supply line from Britain to Port-en-Bessin in Normandy, which was installed after D-Day

RAP Regimental Aid Post, i.e. a field hospital

RE Royal Engineers

REME Royal Electrical and Mechanical Engineers

Rhino ferry A flat barge used for carrying vehicles and artillery into the invasion beaches

RHQ Regimental Headquarters

Screaming Eagles Nickname of the US 101st Airborne Division

SP gun Self-propelled gun, i.e. a mobile artillery piece or heavy machine-gun mounted on a tank base or a truck chassis

Spandau Allied term for the German MG-42 machine gun

SS German acronym for Schutzstaffel – 'protection squad'. The SS was a paramilitary organization within the Nazi party which provided Hitler's bodyguard and constituted the German security forces. Fighting SS units – the Waffen SS – were a military elite

Sten gun A British sub-machine gun

TCS Troop Carrier Squadron

Teller mine German anti-tank mine

Tobruk German look-out or machine-gun post, sunk into the ground

Typhoon British rocket-firing fighter-bomber, known as the 'tank-buster'

USAAF United States Army Air Force

Weasel A small amphibious truck with caterpillar tracks

Waffen SS Combat divisions of the SS

Wehrmacht Regular German army

Wren Member of the Women's Royal Naval Service

ACKNOWLEDGMENTS

I would like to thank Michael Paterson for the resourcefulness and erudition he showed in researching the voices in this book. Many thanks are due to Ruth Binney, to Andrew Whitmarsh at the D-Day Museum in Portsmouth, to Sarah Paterson at the Imperial War Museum, to Tim Crowe and Wendy Cimicata in Canada, and to Margaret Harris for cheerfully keying in hundreds of smudged photocopies. To Kim Davies I say thank you for being good company in Normandy and for pointing out where the commas go.

A special debt of gratitude is owed to Betsy Plumb at the National D-Day Museum in New Orleans. This project would have been vastly more difficult without her generous help.

I take my hat off to the following Normandy veterans who helped me: the late Canon Mike Crooks, Bill Colyer of the Hampshire Regiment, Frank Rosier of the Gloucester Regiment, Jim Wilkins and Doug Hester of the Queen's Own Rifles of Canada. They did a very fine thing on D-Day – as did all the men and women who took part. I am glad to be telling their stories.

CONTRIBUTORS INDEX

Key

+ Passages courtesy of the Eisenhower Center for American Studies at the University of New Orleans and The National D-Day Museum Foundation, Inc.

* Passages courtesy of the Documents Division, the Imperial War Museum, London

≠ Passages courtesy of the Warren Tute Collection, D-Day Museum, Portsmouth

∞ Passages courtesy of the Frank and Joan Shaw Collection, D-Day Museum, Portsmouth

Passages courtesy of the Rupert Curtis Collection, D-Day Museum, Portsmouth

¥ Interview with the author, reproduced by kind permission

† Kind permission of the Worshipful Company of Armourers & Brasiers in the City of London

Publications

1st Battalion the Highland Light Infantry of Canada,
pub. Highlight Light Infantry of Canada
Association, Ontario 1951 208–9
[Quoted in] *1st Battalion* the Regina Rifle
Regiment 1939–46, ed. Capt Eric Luxton, Pub.
Regina Rifles, Saskatchewan 1946 183–4,
203–5
[Quoted in] *50th Anniversary D-Day Magazine,* Ed.
Barrie Pitt, 1994 52–4
*Artificial Invasion Harbours Called Mulberry: a
Personal Story, The,* Sir Bruce White, pub. Sir
Bruce White 1980 17–18, 282
(middle/bottom)
[Quoted in] *Breakout at Normandy,* Mark Bando,
MBI Publishing 1999 261 (top)
[Quoted in] *Churchill's Secret Weapons,* Patrick
Delaforce, Robert Hale 1998 16
Crusade in Europe, D.D. Eisenhower, Heinemann
1948 29–30, 31
[Quoted in] *D-Day: June 6 1944,* Richard Collier,
Cassell 1992 12
[Quoted in] *D-Day Encyclopedia, The,* Helicon 1994
112 (top)
Daily Mail, 6 June 1994 165 (middle)
Daily Mail, 21 February 1994 176 (middle),
233–4, 240–1, 243 (middle)
[Quoted in] *Daily Telegraph, The,* 3 June 1994
229–31, 235–8, 243 (bottom) 271–2
Eyewitness on Omaha Beach, 1st and 2nd edition,
Harold Baumgarten, Halrit Publishing Co,
1994, 1999 20–1, 48–9, 124–6, 150–1, 153

General's Life, A, Omar Bradley (with Clay Blair
Jnr.), Sidgwick and Jackson 1983 132 (bottom)
Great War Speeches, Winston Churchill, Corgi
1957 10, 11
[Quoted in] *Guardian, The,* 20 May, 1994 (©
Guardian) 28–9, 158–9, 167 (top)
[Quoted in] *Illustrated Hitler Diary,* 1917–1945,
The Ed. Stuart Laing, Marshall Cavendish 1980
19 (top)
*Little Black Devils: A History of the Royal Winnipeg
Rifles,* Bruce Tascona and Eric Wells, Fyre
Publishing for the Royal Winnipeg Rifles 1983
194–5, 198 (top)
Newsweek, June 11 1984 118–19, 124 (middle)
Quoted in Major and Mrs Holt's Battlefield
Guide. *Normandy Landing Beaches,* Major and
Mrs Holt, Pen and Sword Books Ltd. 165–6,
231 (bottom)
Second World War, The, Winston Churchill, Cassell
1949 15, 32–3, 34, 252
Slightly Out of Focus, Robert Capa, Henry Holt, NY
1947 115–16
Spectator, The, 'One Man's D-Day', Iain Mcleod, 5
June 1964 156–7, 170 (bottom),
181 (bottom)
[Quoted in] *Two Sides of the Beach,* Edward
Blandford 123 (bottom) 207–8
Up the Johns! The Story of the Royal Regina Rifles,
Stuart A.G. Mein, pub. by the Senate of the
Royal Regina Rifles 1992 197
[Quoted in] *Yorkshire Post,* 5 June 1984 220
(middle), 251 (bottom)

PICTURE CREDITS

GENERAL INDEX